Cervantes

1 'A world of disorderly notions, picked out of his books, crowded into his imagination; and now his head was full of nothing but enchantments, quarrels, battles, challenges, wounds, complaints, amours, torments and abundance of stuff and impossibilities.' A drawing by Goya of Don Quixote in his study.

Richard L. Predmore

Cervantes

Dodd, Mead & Company · New York

Grateful acknowledgment is made to the following for
permission to reprint the material indicated.
Penguin Books Ltd for excerpts from
THE ADVENTURES OF DON QUIXOTE by Miguel de Cervantes Saavedra,
translated by J. M. Cohen, copyright J. M. Cohen, 1950.
The Viking Press, Inc. and Cassell and Company Limited
for excerpts from THREE EXEMPLARY NOVELS by
Miguel de Cervantes Saavedra, translated by Samuel Putnam,
copyright 1950 by The Viking Press, Inc. and for excerpts
from DON QUIXOTE DE LA MANCHA
by Miguel de Cervantes Saavedra, translated by Samuel Putnam,
copyright 1949 by The Viking Press, Inc.

First published in the United States of America and Canada
1973 by Dodd, Mead & Company, Inc., New York

ISBN 0-396-06797-2

Library of Congress Catalog Card Number 72-13587

Printed in Great Britain

Contents

Preface

In the Prologue to Part Two of *Don Quixote*, Cervantes found occasion to remark that he well knew what the temptations of the Devil were and that one of the greatest was for a man to get it into his head that he could write and print a book that would win him both fame and fortune. How often these words have come to mind since that day, some three and a half years ago, when Dodd, Mead & Co. invited me to write for the general reading public a short biography of Cervantes! If it was in part the Devil who prompted me to accept their flattering but risky invitation, it was also in part my desire to live intimately for a while with a man as admirable for his life and death as for his published works.

A preliminary question to be answered was this: is another biography of Cervantes in English really needed? I believe the proper answer is Yes; and not only because each student of Cervantes' life will hold his own version of it to be closer to the truth than previous ones, but also because no biography in English fully exploits all the relevant facts uncovered in the last quarter of a century.

Somewhere there is a frontier separating popular biographies from scholarly ones. I have tried to walk on the popular side of that uncertain frontier, but it has not been easy. Not wanting to encumber my work with the full apparatus of documentary scholarship I nevertheless wanted to be believed, which made documentation indispensable. My compromise can be described like this: for the most part, I have not documented the fully accepted facts of Cervantes' life, nor have I rehearsed the full bibliography of all the disputed facts; I have merely indicated the sources I have relied on in each instance. Since my notes seldom contain information intended to supplement that of the main text, they are relegated to the end of the book, where they can be safely skipped by readers chiefly interested in getting on with the story.

There are biographies of Cervantes that are marvelously detailed: they describe their hero's thoughts on his tenth birthday or the brightness of the stars when he attempted his first escape from Algiers. I have tried to avoid all such fiction. On occasion I venture what look like reasonable guesses, but I am careful to report them as guesses.

Much is reliably known about certain periods of Cervantes' life: parts of his military service, his five years of captivity in North Africa, his trials and tribulations as commissary and tax-collector in southern Spain. Unfortunately, other periods – particularly his boyhood and adolescence – are lacking in

7

solid facts. And one does not have for Cervantes the kind of personal papers and intimate letters that are so often available for prominent men of more recent times. I have sought to compensate for this deficiency by judicious use of his published writings.

Aware that there are pitfalls in using a man's fiction to illuminate his life, I have nonetheless considered it both possible and desirable to do so. I have quoted liberally from Cervantes' works, because it seemed fitting that his own voice should be heard in the telling of his story; I have, however, tried to guard against the easy assumption that whatever his characters say, feel and do necessarily reflects their creator's personal experience. For example, I have been unwilling to assume, as some scholars have, that Cervantes' own marriage was unhappy, simply because he once wrote a farce about unhappily married couples seeking divorce. Finally, I have included some critical comment on Cervantes' outstanding works, because I cannot imagine trying to re-create the life of a writer without paying some attention to what he wrote.

One of Cervantes' most devoted nineteenth-century readers, James Y. Gibson, expressed in the preface to his translation of Cervantes' *Journey to Parnassus* some eloquent thoughts about the all-pervasive presence of Cervantes in his works:

'Whoever has felt the spell of this Wizard of the South must know how his personality is stamped, like a hall-mark, on everything he wrote; how the romance of his life is interwoven with the romance of his writings, so that a peculiar loving interest in the matchless storyteller is born, and increases with our love for his works. All the world knows that this is eminently the case with his *Don Quixote*. In that tale of tales, and behind the visor of the immortal knight, who seems born for no other reason than to banish "loathéd Melancholy" from the world, and replace it with "heart-easing Mirth" and "Laughter holding both his sides", we are confronted with the face of a man, whose eyes betray no spark of insanity, but a glowing enthusiasm tempered with all sorts of humorous gleamings; whose mobile lips have always a winning smile for his friends, and a slight curl of irony for his foes; whose brow, furrowed with care, and sorrow, and thought, bespeaks the man of vast experience, both of men and of things, which gives him the right and power to speak on all matters that concern humanity; in fact, one of those rare heroic characters, of gentle manners, splendid gifts, and noble thoughts, whom to know and to love is of itself a liberal education.'

Whether or not it is as easy as Gibson suggests to see clearly the great man behind his great creation, it is not difficult to understand the love and admiration with which he writes.

1 The World of Cervantes

Miguel de Cervantes Saavedra was born in 1547, towards the end of an age of great kings. Seldom has history crowded into one half-century four such formidable rivals as Henry VIII of England, Francis I of France, Suleiman the Magnificent of the Ottoman Empire and Charles I of Spain, who was also Charles V of the Holy Roman Empire.[1] These four knew each other well, though less as international colleagues than as powerful opponents. Of the four, Charles was clearly the most powerful. He was also the most cosmopolitan and the most quixotic.

Charles V had become one of the most powerful princes in Western history as a result of several generations of carefully planned marriages. He himself was the son of Joanna the Mad of Castile and Philip the Fair of Burgundy. His maternal grandparents were Ferdinand and Isabella, and through them he was heir to all the kingdoms and possessions of Spain. His paternal grandfather, of the house of Austria, was Maximilian, emperor of the Holy Roman Empire; through him the Habsburg dominions also became part of the empire on which it was said the sun never set, and which included at its peak most of Italy, Germany, Holland, Belgium and Spain, as well as portions of France, nearly all of Central and South America, and islands and other possessions too numerous to name.

2 Fifteenth-century woodcut of an infidel.

Born in Ghent in 1500, Charles was a frail and ill-favored child. His parents did not educate him in Spain, nor did they ever take him there. Instead, they left him in the Flemish town of Mechlin, where he was brought up by his royal aunt Margaret of Austria, who became his regent in the Netherlands, and by the Burgundian noble Guillaume de Croy, who became his grand chamberlain and lifelong adherent. Under them, Charles received the kind of training considered appropriate for a Renaissance prince.

Of the histories and chronicles he was required to read, he preferred those that told of knights active in the defense of the Christian faith. He was particularly interested in the deeds of some of his own forefathers, men such as John the Fearless, for example, who had fought against the Turks and whose ambition it was to restore Constantinople to Christian rule. Charles' favorite exercises were hunting, riding and jousting. In them he developed exceptional skill despite his delicate health. Both his Christian zeal and his mastery of military horsemanship were to be conspicuous features of his imperial career.

3-7 Three generations of the Spanish monarchy who brought the nation political unity, imperial power and world-wide dominance. Above, a representation of Charles V enthroned while Francis I of France, Pope Clement VII, Suleiman the Magnificent and the Landgrave of Hesse pay him homage. Left, King Ferdinand of Aragon and Queen Isabella of Castile, Charles' grandparents. Opposite, Philip the Fair of Burgundy, his father, and the tomb of Philip the Fair and Joanna the Mad in the Royal Chapel, Granada.

Charles was unable to converse in Castilian when, in 1517, he arrived in Spain with a train of Flemish courtiers whom he promptly appointed to high office. If the circumstances of his first appearance in Spain did nothing to promote his popularity with his Spanish subjects neither did his efforts to raise huge sums of money to secure his election to the crown of the Holy Roman Empire nor his departure for Germany in 1520 to claim that crown. Evidence of the unrest that greeted him and his Flemish officials with their foreign interests were the uprisings in Castile and Valencia that troubled the early years of his reign. But these unhappy events and attitudes contrast with the esteem in which he was finally held by his Spanish subjects, who came in time to regard him as one of their greatest rulers.

Charles was never to develop uniform laws and institutions for his vast realms. Most of his estates were inherited rather than conquered, and so he felt bound to maintain their separate laws, customs and institutions. Although he did create important councils to help him administer his great empire, his rule was more personal than institutional. Indeed, despite the brilliant Renaissance culture that flourished in his day, one may think of him as the last of the medieval emperors. The last of the Holy Roman emperors to be crowned by the Pope, he cherished as a constant policy of his rule the medieval ideal of Christian unity. Unlike his bureaucratic son Philip, he sometimes assumed the role of the Christian knight and took the field in person to defend his Christian faith. Perhaps it was this crusading spirit which, when added to the possibility of adventure and plunder, converted the initial hostility of the Spanish nobility into enthusiastic support.

8   Europe in the sixteenth century.

The dominant concerns of Charles' reign were two: to maintain the estates of his dynasty, which involved him for most of his rule in war with Francis I of France; and to defend the integrity of Christendom, which drew him into war with the Ottoman Empire and the Protestant princes of Germany.

The lifelong rivalry between Charles and Francis began as early as 1519, when both became vigorous contenders (along with Henry VIII of England) for the crown of the Holy Roman Empire. The immediate causes of their numerous wars thereafter varied, but among them two territorial claims were usually present: Charles' claim to several pieces of French-speaking territory – notably the Duchy of Burgundy, a part of his patrimony which he was loath to renounce – and his claim to most of Italy, especially the Duchy of Milan, which he needed in order to maintain communications between the northern and southern halves of his empire. Intermittent war with France was Spain's fate until the death of Francis I in 1547, and nothing ever remained settled as a result of Spanish victories. Not even the capture of Francis himself in the battle of Pavia in 1525, nor his incarceration in Madrid, nor the holding of his children as hostages was effective in securing his permanent acceptance of Charles' territorial claims.

9 Contemporary painting of the battle of Pavia. Francis is shown surrendering on a white horse in the foreground.

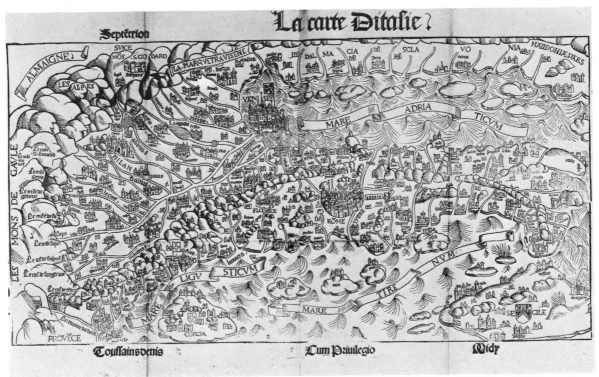

10 Early sixteenth-century map of Italy, showing the passes over the Alps from France and Germany.

As one who held that offensive war was justified only against the infidel, Charles was particularly indignant at Francis' ability constantly to divert him from his crusading campaigns against the Moslems. Eloquent expression of how he felt can be found in his famous speech delivered in Spanish on Easter Monday, 1536, before the Pope, the cardinals and the ambassadors of Europe. The occasion for the speech was yet another invasion of northern Italy by the French. In it Charles gave an account of his relations with Francis I, stressing his own desire for peace and friendship and the French king's recurrent perfidy. He had been about to collect forces for an attack on Algiers, he declared, when Francis once more frustrated his plans by invading Italy; and Charles' peroration concluded with a challenge worthy of Don Quixote himself:

'Therefore I promise Your Holiness, in the presence of this sacred college and of all these knights here present, if the king of France wishes to meet me in arms, man to man, I promise to meet him armed or unarmed, in my shirt, with sword and dagger, on land or sea, on a bridge or on an island, in a closed field, or in front of our armies or wherever and however he may wish and it be fair.'[2]

Less than a year before this speech in Rome, Charles had proclaimed himself 'God's standard-bearer' when he set sail from Barcelona with a hundred

11 Khair-ed-Din Barbarossa, the chief admiral of the Ottoman Empire and Charles' opponent at Tunis

12 The emperor's review of the Tunisian expeditionary force at Barcelona, 1535.

13 Landing of the imperial fleet near Goleta on the Tunisian coast.

warships and three hundred transports to take Tunis from the Turks and Moors. The attempt was successful, and Charles set a valiant example of personal bravery in the fighting. At no time in his career was he more justified in thinking of himself as one of Christendom's crusading knights.

Charles' troubles with the Ottoman sultan, Suleiman the Magnificent, and his chief admiral Barbarossa were as constant as his problems with the king of France. The Ottoman Empire threatened Spanish possessions in the Mediterranean both from home bases in the eastern Mediterranean and from North Africa. The capture of Tunis left Algiers intact, while Barbarossa had escaped from Tunis to pursue his harassment of Spanish lands and communications more energetically than ever. At last Charles decided to try to finish in Algiers what he had started so auspiciously in Tunis. Arriving off the Algerian coast on 21 October 1541, the Spanish forces disembarked with minimum provisions and encountered little trouble in capturing the heights commanding the city; but on the night of 24-25 October there arose a terrible storm, which scattered the fleet and left the stranded soldiers without supplies. The Algerian campaign turned into one of the emperor's bitterest defeats, costing him dear in men and supplies and leaving Algiers free to enslave Christians, as Cervantes was to learn at first hand more than thirty years later. One wonders what the result might have been had the emperor accepted the offer of Hernán Cortés to remain ashore with a small portion of the army to conclude the conquest. Cortés had certainly overcome heavier odds in Mexico.

In the early years of Charles' reign, Spain was open to all the spiritual and intellectual currents of Europe. Much credit for the beginnings of this period of intellectual and spiritual vitality belongs to an extraordinary Franciscan, whose long service to Church and State brought him more high offices and honors than he ever desired. He was Cardinal Jiménez de Cisneros, archbishop

16

14   Courtyard in the University of Alcalá.

15, 16   Cardinal Jiménez de Cisneros (1436-1517), founder of the University of Alcalá; right, the last page of the New Testament from the Polyglot Bible, commissioned by Cisneros and printed in Alcalá in 1514.

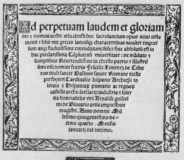

of Toledo, confessor to Queen Isabella, inquisitor general and twice regent of Castile. Imbued with the hostility towards Islam that is so marked a characteristic of the early centuries of Spanish history, he financed and personally led a successful expedition to capture the Algerian port of Oran. Throughout his long career he vigorously fostered religious and moral reform, but without the excessive concern for narrow orthodoxy that was to mark the times of Philip II. His encouragement of humanism took many forms, including the founding of the University of Alcalá de Henares in 1508, where an epoch-making Polyglot Bible was compiled and edited at his expense. In his day and for a few short years thereafter, the works of Erasmus of Rotterdam were widely known in Spain and he counted many friends and followers there, not the least of whom was the emperor's secretary, Alfonso de Valdés. Soon after his death in 1536, the writings of Erasmus came under sharp attack from the Inquisition. But in the meantime Spanish intellectuals had enjoyed an ample measure of tolerance and of communication with the outside world.

In his twenty-first year, the young emperor proclaimed to the world of his day where he stood on the question of Christian unity. The day after Martin Luther took his stand for conscience before the Diet of Worms, Charles declared himself in these words:

'For it is certain that a single monk must err if he stands against the opinion of all Christendom. Otherwise Christendom itself would have erred for more than a thousand years. Therefore I am determined to set my kingdoms and dominions, my friends, my body, my blood, my life, my soul upon it.' [3]

But it was still Charles' enduring wish to reconcile the differences that arose within the Christian world. In summoning the German princes to the Diet of Augsburg in 1530 he indicated that they were 'to settle disputes, to commit previous errors to the mercy of our Saviour, to hear, understand and weigh the opinion of each man with love and charity, and thus come to live again in one Church and one State'.[4] As early as 1524, he had encouraged the Pope to call an ecumenical council. The Council of Trent (1545-63) was finally held, but its purpose was to repudiate the Protestant Reformation rather than to repair the schism within Christendom. And so Charles finally resorted to force to put down the Protestant princes of Germany. This he succeeded in doing at the great victory of Mühlberg in 1547, a victory in which he himself took part and which seemed for a while to have lifted him to a new pinnacle of power and prestige. In the end, however, military victories proved as vain as councils in restoring Christian unity, and so Charles' supreme ideal failed to reach fulfillment as totally as did Don Quixote's attempt to revive the noble order of chivalry.

At the time of the victory of Mühlberg, Charles was only forty-seven. To commemorate the victory, Titian painted for the emperor a magnificent portrait (see p. 41). In it the vigorous and triumphant Christian knight betrays no weariness or signs of incipient age. In fact, however, his health was failing. His gout was so bad that he could hardly get his foot into a stirrup. The disease had first struck him as early as 1528 and it now recurred with

18 Symbolic representation of the unexpected abdication of Charles V in 1555. With his
right hand the emperor gives the empire to Ferdinand, and with his left Spain (represented by
the provincial banners and various political figures) and the Netherlands to Philip. The allegorical scene in the foreground symbolizes Spain's supremacy at sea and her empire in America.

increasing frequency and severity. For years his doctors had urged him to
moderate his eating and drinking but to no avail. Charles indulged himself
most in what suited him least: great quantities of meat at his meals and huge
tankards of iced beer at any hour of the day or night. His health would never
be sound again. And he was growing weary of war and the burdens of
empire. Within a year, Titian painted him again; in this new portrait we can
already see the sedentary man who in less than a decade would put down his
heavy burdens and withdraw from active life. The portrait shows him sitting
in a loggia overlooking a pleasant rural landscape which fades into mystery in
the distance. With his jutting Habsburg jaw rendered doubly prominent by
his spade-shaped beard, Charles was not a handsome man; but Titian saw
him as solid and masterful and dignified, the somberness of his black Spanish
clothes relieved only by the small jewel of the Golden Fleece on his chest.
Undefeated but tired, his mind often turned now from affairs of state to
thoughts of death and the life beyond.

In 1556 Charles retired to a remote monastery in the Spanish province of
Extremadura. He abdicated all his Spanish dominions to his son Philip, and
the Holy Roman Empire to his brother Ferdinand, who was confirmed by the
electors in 1558.

It eventually became common for intellectuals to regard Charles' rule as having been a disaster for Spain. The nineteenth-century diplomat Ángel Ganivet believed that under Charles Spain had exhausted its resources in the vain quest for glory beyond its natural borders.[5] A more recent and better prepared historian has rendered just as harsh an opinion:

'Charles V provoked a tremendous contortion in the historical trajectory of Spain. He hindered the process of peninsular unification, because the Spanish kingdoms were incorporated into an exceedingly complex plurality of dominions, and he, as the ruler of this strange community of peoples, was unable to understand the urgency of fusing the differences among the peninsular monarchies and of articulating a state that would accommodate them all. He involved Spain in the tangle of Central European affairs, he embroiled it in the craggy problem of the expansion of Protestantism, and he bound Hispanic destinies to such business for centuries. He converted Castile into the foundation of imperial strength. He made of her a rich nursery of soldiers and a flowing fountain of wealth. He initiated the cruel exploitation of the economic power of the Castilian people after seducing them with the fleeting luster of military glory in the service of faith. And, with his warlike projects in all the theaters of battle in Europe and the Mediterranean, he opened for Spaniards a limitless arena to satisfy their thirst for adventure, their martial impulses, and their militant Christianity.'[6]

There is some truth in these views of Cervantes' world, but Miguel himself would not have been exposed to them. The age in which he grew up still believed in Spain's destiny as the leader of the Christian world, and the light of her military glory had not yet begun to flicker. Cervantes would live to see it fade, but not before he himself had played a notable part in one of the most celebrated victories of the century.

Despite the abdication of Charles V, the middle of the sixteenth century saw Spanish power and prestige still on the rise. Further, it constituted the seedtime of that sustained flowering of literature known as the Spanish Golden Age. All the necessary conditions for its flowering were firmly established: the Renaissance innovations of Italian poetry had been assimilated in Spain and had found exquisite expression in the Castilian poet Garcilaso de la Vega, who was to be followed by a procession of great poets not even remotely rivalled until the twentieth century. The dramatic writers of the fifteenth and sixteenth centuries had gradually assembled the elements that would make possible the national theater, both popular and poetic, on which Lope de Vega was to impose his prolific genius. The romances of chivalry that Don Quixote loved to read had flourished for half a century before Cervantes was born. The narrative forms called pastoral, picaresque and Moorish were about to make their appearance. Cervantes would one day exploit them all to create the first modern novel.

19 Garcilaso de la Vega (1503-36), who lived for several years in Naples where he immersed himself in the culture of the Italian Renaissance.

2 The Early Years

The family names of Cervantes and Saavedra – probably originating in the Galician province of Lugo – were well-known in the sixteenth century in such major Andalusian cities as Granada, Córdoba and Seville. It is not clear how many families bearing these names were directly related to the author of *Don Quixote*, but it is established that his paternal ancestors had lived in Córdoba for at least three generations.[1]

Like all families, the Cervantes had their ups and downs. Traditionally Cervantes' biographers have stressed the downs, and it is perhaps only fair to ensure that in this account the ups are represented too.

Miguel's grandfather, Juan de Cervantes, was born into a respected middle-class Cordovan family. Being a prosperous merchant, his father was able to send Juan to the most famous Spanish university of the day, that of Salamanca, where he studied law. As early as 1502, he became a lawyer for the royal treasury of the Inquisition in Córdoba. Soon after this he married. By about the beginning of 1509 we find him living in Alcalá de Henares, where Miguel's father, Rodrigo, was born. For the next thirty-five years he lived intermittently away from Córdoba, holding a variety of legal positions of importance and trust in various Castilian and Andalusian cities.

For most of this period Juan prospered, associating with the prominent people of the communities where he lived. Then, in 1527, Don Diego Hurtado de Mendoza named Juan de Cervantes deputy magistrate of the court of appeals in Guadalajara. Don Diego was a scion of one of the most powerful noble families in Spain, possessor of almost as many titles as estates, and famous in the literary, military and ambassadorial annals of his country. Some idea of the prominence of his family may be inferred from the fact that Philip II married Elizabeth de Valois in the chapel of the Mendoza Palace in Guadalajara.

As established by numerous royal decrees, the government and administration of justice in the city of Guadalajara and its surrounding lands came under the power of the Duke of the Infantado, which was the title most often used by the head of the Mendoza family. So, although Juan de Cervantes exercised what must be called a public office, he owed his appointment to the duke, whose palace was open to him and whose confidence he enjoyed until the duke's death in 1531.

In his day the duke was regarded as a man of many noble qualities, amongst which no one found cause to quibble about his appetite for extra-

20 Mid-sixteenth-century map of the provinces of Spain.

marital amours. One of these affairs, of eventual interest to the Cervantes family, began on the festival of Corpus Christi in 1488. On that occasion a wandering troupe of gypsy dancers and singers put on a special performance in the palace of the youthful duke. Everyone was enchanted by the grace and fire of a gypsy girl named María de Cabrera. Later, when the gentlemen were jousting with cane spears, María asked Don Diego to borrow a horse so she could participate. Once more she became the center of admiring attention. No one was more captivated than the duke by her skill and her sensuous beauty, and, to no one's surprise, he took her to bed and left her with child. Mindful of his responsibilities, he gave her an inn for her support and educated their son Martín to be a priest. In time Martín came to hold many rich ecclesiastical benefices. With his father's active help, he even dared to aspire to the highest office the Church could offer in Spain, the archbishopric of Toledo. If this aspiration was never satisfied, many others were.

24

21　Courtyard of the Mendoza
Palace in Guadalajara, where
Philip II married Elizabeth de Valois.

22　The University of Salamanca,
founded in the thirteenth century
and the academic home of many of
the great scholars of sixteenth-
century Spain.

23　Aerial view of the Great
Mosque of Córdoba, begun in the
eighth century by Abd-el-Rahman,
who launched Córdoba on its long
and glorious career as the leading
city of Moslem Spain.

In the days when Juan de Cervantes was a familiar figure in the ducal palace, the young priest Martín seduced the deputy magistrate's beautiful daughter María, who in due time bore him a daughter, appropriately named Martina. This affair led to a lawsuit by María which, while ultimately successful, led to the dismissal, harassment and temporary incarceration of Juan de Cervantes in Valladolid at the instigation of Martín's half-brother, the new Duke of the Infantado.[2] In this unfortunate way the family of Miguel de Cervantes became related to the family of one of the grandees of Spain. This episode may represent the beginnings of two unhappy tendencies in the life of the Cervantes family: a tendency for the men to pay involuntary visits to various jails, particularly that of Valladolid; and a tendency for the women to love men who promise but fail to marry them.

Lawyer Cervantes and his family probably spent their most comfortable and prosperous years in Alcalá de Henares from 1532 to 1538. It is not clear what official position, if any, Juan held during five of those years. Legal documents exist, however, that make it abundantly clear that the family enjoyed a high standard of living and the society of some of the best people in town.[3] Such society would not have been open to them had they not belonged at least to the gentry known in Spain as 'hidalgos', and the records of a lawsuit in which Rodrigo was involved in the early 1550s also contain testimony to the effect that this was their social rank.

The statements made in support of the gentle birth of Juan de Cervantes and his family reveal something of their standard of living in the 1530s and of certain standards of social conduct. One witness declared that he had always seen Lawyer Cervantes and his sons 'well treated and well dressed, and with much silk and finery, and with good horses, pages, grooms, and other services and vanities such as hidalgos and caballeros are wont to have and wear in the aforesaid town of Alcalá'.[4] Another witness, asked why he

24 Certificate of hidalgo status, granted to one Diego de la Guardia Espiro by Philip II on 23 September 1589.

considered the Cervantes to be of good birth, responded that at no time during his acquaintance with them had he known them to pay taxes. Furthermore, he had sometimes seen the sons jousting on good and powerful horses.[5] Apparently the avoidance of taxes and the ability to joust constituted convincing signs of gentility.

Since Alcalá was a university town and the family seems to have been prosperous, it is something of a mystery why none of Juan's sons attended the university. Perhaps they were already rather old to begin a university career: the eldest was twenty-eight in 1532. Miguel's father Rodrigo was about twenty-three at this time. He was interested in medicine, but he suffered from deafness and this may have proved a serious obstacle to a university career.

Towards the end of this period the Cervantes family suffered some reversals of fortune. For one thing, they were living beyond their means; for another, Juan and his wife were not getting on well together. In 1538 Juan accepted a royal judicial appointment in Plasencia and took up separate residence there, accompanied by his youngest son Andrés; the separation thus instituted was to become permanent, involving a life of increasing poverty and hardship for the fatherless family.

Except for María de Cervantes, who had won a sizable settlement from her priestly seducer, the Cervantes family in Alcalá de Henares had very little to live on. It is logical to suppose that this was the circumstance that compelled Rodrigo, then approximately twenty-nine years old, to seek a livelihood. Having excellent friends among the medical faculty at the University of Alcalá, it was not difficult for him quickly to learn what was needed to become a kind of practical surgeon. Three books comprised the required reading: a Latin grammar by Antonio de Nebrija, a volume called *The Practice of Surgery* by Juan de Vigo, and a treatise *On the Four Diseases* by

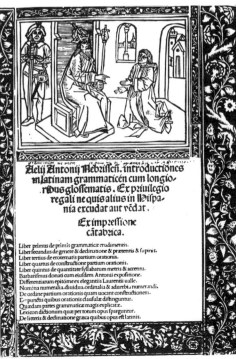

25, 26 The *Institutiones Latinae* of Elio Antonio de Nebrija (1442-1522), the first modern scholar of international stature that Spain produced, endured as a standard textbook for generations. Left, Nebrija lecturing in the house of his patron, who sits on the left. Right, title page of an edition of 1510.

Lobera de Ávila. But Rodrigo was soon to discover that the money he could expect to earn as a practical surgeon was about equal to the science it took to become one. Years later, his son found occasion to mention surgeons in some of his writings, calling them hernia-fixers and otherwise treating them with little respect.

Not too long after acquiring a profession, Rodrigo married, possibly early in 1543. His bride was Leonor de Cortinas.[6] For at least two centuries, the Cortinas had been a prominent and thriving family belonging to the gentry of Arganda, a Castilian town about seventeen miles south-east of Madrid. Leonor herself, however, does not seem to have been born in Arganda but in some nearby town, perhaps Barajas.

Rodrigo and Leonor were more prosperous in offspring than in worldly goods. Of their seven children – Andrés, Andrea, Luisa, Miguel, Rodrigo, Magdalena and Juan – all but the last two were born in Alcalá de Henares between 1543 and 1550. The son who was to become Spain's foremost writer was baptized in the Church of Santa María la Mayor on Sunday, 9 October 1547. It seems most reasonable to suppose that he had been born on 29 September, since his parents christened him Miguel and the anniversary of Saint Michael fell on that day. Both the firm date of his baptism and the probable date of his birth are generally given according to the pre-Gregorian calendar. By the present calendar, therefore, Miguel's birth date would be recorded as 9 October 1547.[7]

Nothing is known about the first years of Miguel's life except what can be inferred from the vicissitudes of his family, the places in which they lived, and the tenor of the times. The year 1547 was also the approximate date of El Greco's birth; of the great (but ephemeral) victory of Mühlberg; of the deaths of Hernán Cortés, Henry VIII of England and Francis I of France; and of the birth of Philip's bastard half-brother, Don Juan of Austria, under whose banner Miguel would one day fight against the Turk.

27   The font in which Cervantes was baptized in 1547.

The city of Miguel's birth lies beside the pleasant river Henares on a Castilian plain rimmed with a row of buttes. It dates back to Roman times, when it was called Complutum, and owes the name of Alcalá to the Arabs, from whom it was wrested by Christian forces under Alfonso VI (famous in the annals of the Cid) early in the twelfth century. While Alcalá possessed an ancient and honorable history, it was not until the early sixteenth century that its heyday began. Numerous kings and queens, including Ferdinand and Isabella, had favored the city in the past, but it was the decision of Archbishop Cardinal Jiménez de Cisneros to found there the University of Alcalá that spurred the growth of population and the construction of notable buildings. In 1500 the cardinal himself laid the corner-stone of the principal college of San Ildefonso. By 1508, when his original design was completed and his university was ready to receive students, it included nine other colleges and a hospital. Others were added from time to time. Stimulated by the founding of the university, the community undertook extensive reforms: old buildings were torn down, new avenues were opened, most of the central streets were paved, drainage was improved, housing for students and book-sellers was increased. Alcalá no longer had the picturesque but crowded look of a medieval town; it was spacious and airy; its new façades wore the air of the Renaissance.

Cardinal Cisneros was, of course, more interested in what went on in his new buildings than in the buildings themselves. He made provision for forty-two chairs, which he filled with the best scholars that could be recruited, whether from Spain or from abroad. Their quality and that of the students they attracted soon won recognition for Alcalá as a great center of learning, especially in the humanities and in medicine.

In his story *The Colloquy of the Dogs*, Cervantes wrote that 'of the five thousand students studying in the University two thousand heard medicine...'. This quotation and others show that the mature Cervantes must have been familiar with Alcalá de Henares and its celebrated university. Yet Miguel was only three and a half years old when his family moved away from the city.

Things were going badly with Rodrigo. It may be assumed that his sister María had long since dissipated most of the settlement received from Don Martín. Rodrigo, then, was responsible for her keep as well as for that of his mother, his wife and their four children (Andrés had died and Magdalena and Juan were not yet born). With eight mouths to feed and little or no income, the family decided to sell María's house in Alcalá and to move to Valladolid, one of the rich and populous cities of the time which was, in 1551, also the seat of the royal court.

By the spring of that year the family was already established in a two-storey house in the quarter of the Sancti Spiritus: Rodrigo and his brood on the first floor, his mother and sister on the second. A clue to Rodrigo's optimism, or to his folly, is that he lost no time in hiring a servant. By November it was easy to see how unwarranted that optimism had been, since he had already been driven to borrow money. It had evidently not proved easy for a practical surgeon and a stranger to find patients in a city even better supplied than Alcalá with famous doctors. On 24 June 1552 Rodrigo's debt fell due and he was unable to pay it. His creditors succeeded in having his goods attached and their owner incarcerated. Rodrigo thus became the second member of his family to spend time in the public jail of Valladolid. While he was still there, his sixth child, Magdalena, was born.

Some idea of the poverty of Rodrigo's household may be gleaned from the list of household goods seized by his creditors.[8] There were a table, three benches and three chairs (two of them broken), eight sheets and six blankets; the only books in the house were Nebrija's Latin grammar, *The Practice of Surgery* and *On the Four Diseases*, which Rodrigo had used to qualify for his profession. Considering the size of the family library it is understandable that Miguel may well have had to indulge his appetite for reading, as he was later to remark, by perusing even scraps of printed paper found in the street.

It is hard to imagine how Doña Leonor was able to feed four children and bear another during the almost six months of her husband's imprisonment. Rodrigo's creditors succeeded in keeping him in jail for most of the period from June 1552 to February 1553. To the student of Miguel de Cervantes, the interesting thing about this sad affair is the information that comes to light through Rodrigo's legal maneuvers to get out of jail. In the initial lawsuit he claimed that he was a hidalgo and was therefore entitled to bail. By convincing the court of the truth of his claim, through the sworn testimony of competent witnesses, he managed finally to win his release. Back in Alcalá, where he still had a little property, he was able to muster enough money to pay his creditors. So ended his efforts to make a new and profitable start in Valladolid.

The family struggled through the summer of 1553 in Alcalá, supporting itself in one way or another. Rodrigo must have written to his estranged father, who had been living comfortably in Córdoba since 1530, earning his living by the practice of law. Juan de Cervantes probably gave his son some reason to believe that he would help him, for Rodrigo and his family set out for Córdoba in September. For eight days they travelled in a cart across La Mancha, over the Sierra Morena and into the heart of Andalusia. Miguel had no way of knowing, of course, how many times he would travel these same roads as a man, nor what these travels would contribute to the tales he would eventually write; he was about six years old when he arrived in the city of the caliphs. He and his family must have needed some new clothes quite urgently, for on 30 October 1553 his father signed a note to a merchant to pay for about thirty yards of linen.[9]

So the family came back in dire poverty to a city still rich but once so fabulously wealthy as to be called the Bagdad of the West. On none of the cities that Miguel had seen up to 1553 had history left so impressive a stamp. Few cities in Europe have been continuously inhabited for as long as Córdoba. Of Iberian origin, it prospered both materially and culturally under the Romans (the two Senecas and Lucan were born there); then it passed in turn to the Visigoths (572) and to the Moors (711). Under the Omayyad dynasty

28 Sixteenth-century view of Córdoba.

(756-1031) Córdoba became the seat of an independent caliphate which finally included most of Moslem Spain. Its age of supreme eminence was the tenth century, when it was said to have 200,000 houses, 600 mosques, 900 bath houses and at least 500,000 inhabitants. With the possible exception of Constantinople, Córdoba was the greatest center of learning in the known world, conserving and adding to the knowledge of antiquity, then largely lost to the rest of Europe. Its library of 400,000 volumes is perhaps the best single reminder of the esteem in which learning was held.

In 1553, when Miguel arrived in the city, it showed but a shadow of its former size and opulence. Yet it still occupied its splendid site in the fertile valley of the Guadalquivir, protected to the north by the wild Sierra de Córdoba; the Roman bridge still carried the traffic of the day; most of the Roman walls were still standing; one could still wander among the thousand columns of the monumental mosque begun in the eighth century and progressively expanded until it became, after that of Mecca, the largest mosque in all Islam. Thus Córdoba still displayed to the observing eye much of the fascination of its colorful past. In addition, many of the old Moorish crafts had been revived, including the world-famous Cordovan leather industry. Nowhere else could such works of art in embossed leather be found. There were also extraordinary silversmiths, weavers of silk and makers of saddles. And to speak of saddles is to be reminded that the author of *Don Quixote* paid repeated tribute to Córdoba for the quality of its horses and the skill of its horsemen.

31

29 Córdoba, the Plaza del Potro today.

Rodrigo settled his family in the quarter of San Nicolás de la Ajerquia, not far from the famous Plaza del Potro, so called because horses had once been sold there. For centuries the Plaza del Potro and its immediate surroundings had been the city's center of commerce and of inter-urban communications. The keeper of the first inn in which Don Quixote and Sancho Panza spent the night labeled it another kind of center: a well-known meeting place for every kind of rogue, ruffian and shady character imaginable. And it was three needle-peddlers from the Plaza del Potro who once helped to toss Sancho in a blanket. Living in the heart of Córdoba from the ages of six to perhaps ten, Miguel was old enough to absorb and retain strong impressions of its pulsing and picturesque life. These first four Andalusian years were to be added to; for southern Spain was to claim about seventeen years of Cervantes' life, something like a quarter of its total span.

Whereas there is little doubt that Rodrigo settled his family in Córdoba for a while, there is no evidence to show how he earned his living. He later claimed to have been a 'familiar of the Inquisition', but this phrase, while indicating some kind of employment or affiliation with the Inquisition, provides no clear indication of what that affiliation was. Rodrigo's father was employed as a judge of property confiscated by the Inquisition, and it is possible that he found his son a job with the Inquisition, perhaps in its hospital. At any rate, Lawyer Cervantes, being prosperous and occupying a respected place in the community, could scarcely have allowed his son to live in abject poverty in that same community. These few years in Córdoba must have afforded Rodrigo some respite from his everlasting struggle with privation.

30 Sixteenth-century woodcut of a bandit.

32

31 Moorish leather shield embossed with the arms of Fernández de Córdoba, a fine early sixteenth-century example of the ancient crafts which were revived in the city during this period.

3 The Education of a Genius

In 1554 Miguel was seven. Of average height and weight, he was an attractive boy with a fair complexion, auburn hair, an aquiline nose, a small mouth and merry eyes. Despite a tendency to stutter, he expressed himself well.[1] He was obviously bright, and he was now of a proper age to begin his formal schooling. There is no certain evidence that he did in fact begin it in 1554, but it seems plausible. There was in Córdoba at that time an elementary school conducted by a certain Father Alonso de Vieras, who belonged to a family friendly towards the Cervantes family and quite possibly related to it. Two young nephews of Father Alonso (Gonzalo de Cervantes Saavedra and Alonso de Cervantes Sotomayor) are definitely known to have been friends of Miguel. The most likely occasion for them to have met was while learning to read and write in their uncle's primary school.

Among friends praised by Cervantes in his mature years are several who later became famous for one reason or another and who were living in Córdoba in 1554 and were the same age as Miguel. One was Tomás Gutiérrez, who learned the hosier's trade from his father but found it too dull for his taste. As a young man he fought in the war against the Moriscos of Granada, after which he lived for many years the life of a successful itinerant actor. When he finally retired from the theater, he established an inn on Bayona Street in Seville where Cervantes often stayed. Another was Juan Rufo Gutiérrez. Son of a Cordovan dyer, he yet managed to study at the University of Salamanca and became a municipal officer in his native city. He was also a soldier, writer, gambler and lady's man whose amorous escapades earned him more than one stay in jail. As a soldier, he fought in that same naval battle of Lepanto in which Miguel lost the use of his left hand. As a writer, he celebrated in his epic poem the *Austriad* (1584) the exploits of Don Juan of Austria, who had led the Christian forces in the battle of Lepanto. Miguel later praised the *Austriad* and its author both in a sonnet and in *Don Quixote.*

However good Father Alonso's school may have been, it provided only the rudiments of learning. For a number of years, the city fathers of Córdoba had been considering the desirability of founding a more advanced school. The chief proponent of such an institution was the well-known mystic, Friar Juan de Ávila, through whose efforts the Company of Jesus was persuaded to found in Córdoba in 1553 the first Jesuit College in Andalusia. Initially it was poorly housed, but in June 1555 it moved into a splendid palace donated by the wealthy dean of the cathedral. It was not long in establishing itself as the leading secondary educational institution of the city and region.

34

There is good reason to conjecture that Miguel began the study of Latin on 18 October 1555, when the Jesuit College of Santa Catarina inaugurated the school year in its sumptuous new quarters. No certain particulars of Miguel's life in this school are known, but from what he later wrote about another Jesuit school one may infer that he remembered with pleasure the kindly and effective teaching of the Jesuit fathers. The observant and loquacious canine protagonists of Cervantes' *The Colloquy of the Dogs*, Cipión and Berganza, had some sympathetic opinions to express about Jesuit pedagogy. For example, Berganza:

'There is something about virtue that affects even one that possesses as little of it as I do, and I could not but take pleasure in beholding the loving care and industry with which the pious fathers taught those children, bending the tender young twigs so they would not grow into crooked branches and training them in the direction of virtuous conduct, which was taught them along with the instruction in letters. I saw how gently they reproved them, how mercifully they punished them, how they inspired them with good examples, incited them with prizes, and prudently indulged them. I saw, too, how they painted for them the horrible ugliness of vice and the beauty of virtue, in order that the young ones might flee the former and love the latter, and thus attain the end for which they were created.'[2]

At least three notable events occurred during Miguel's first year with the Jesuits: the death of his grandfather on 11 March 1556, the accession of Philip II to the Spanish throne on 15 April, and the performance in the same month of two plays at the College of Santa Catalina to celebrate the advent of the new king and to honor the school's patron, Saint Catherine. Probably the least important of these events made the strongest immediate impression on young Miguel. The Jesuits were much given to having their students put on religious plays to mark the opening and close of the academic year and other solemn or festive occasions. And nobody was more disposed to write such edifying plays than the rector of the College, Father Pedro Pablo de Acevedo. His were the two plays acted in April 1556, one being a Latin eclogue called *In Honor of Saint Catherine*, the other a play in both Latin and Spanish called *Metanoea*.[3] In it there appeared allegorical figures such as Avarice, Pride, Penitence, etc. Cervantes later claimed to have been the first to put allegorical figures on the public stage in Spain.

Miguel probably studied another full year with the Jesuits in Córdoba, since there is presumptive evidence that his family continued to live in that city until March 1557.[4] But 1557 was a bad year. The harvests were poor, there was much sickness abroad, and Rodrigo, now that his father was gone, was again having trouble feeding his numerous family. His aged mother had to sell some of her property to help sustain them. Then, shortly after 10 March 1557 (the date of her will), she died. There is no documentary evidence as to the whereabouts of Rodrigo and his family from that date until their trail reappears in Seville in 1564.

One of Cervantes' most learned biographers argues persuasively that Rodrigo took at least part of his family to live for a number of years in the town of Cabra, situated about thirty miles to the south-east of Córdoba.[5] In 1558 Charles V died, and it seemed likely that the year as a whole would be even worse than 1557. Hunger and disease were widespread. Fortunately for Rodrigo, his brother Andrés was well established in Cabra and sufficiently prosperous to help. And the lord of Cabra had already shown himself favorably disposed towards the Cervantes family. He was Don Gonzalo Fernández de Córdoba, third Duke of Sessa, and one of the most prominent noble figures of the day. The duke was to be one of the Christian leaders in the forthcoming war against the Moriscos, and in 1575, while serving as viceroy of Sicily, he wrote letters of recommendation for Miguel (which were meant to be helpful, but which, as we shall see, quite unforeseeably contributed to Cervantes' later misfortunes). In 1558 he may have made it possible for Rodrigo to obtain work in one of Cabra's two hospitals. In any case, it is difficult to imagine a better refuge at the time for Rodrigo and his family than Cabra.

In some ways, Cabra represented quite a comedown from such cities as Alcalá, Valladolid and Córdoba. It was much smaller and possessed neither the commercial, the industrial, nor the cultural advantages of Miguel's former places of residence, though to a boy of twelve these advantages may not have seemed important. But Cabra was attractive, a walled town situated in a beautiful agricultural valley between the Sierra de Montilla to the north-west and the Sierra de Cabra to the south. There were interesting sights to be seen in the environs, one being the mysterious chasm which Miguel surely visited, since he mentions it three times in his later books.

32 Picturesquely disproportionate house in Cabra which dates approximately from Cervantes' lifetime.

33　View of Seville (1593), with the motto 'Who has not seen it has not seen a marvel'. The lively scene in the foreground shows the public mockery of a cuckold and a procuress.

If Miguel spent five or more years of his life in Cabra, they must have been years without formal schooling. He may, however, have continued his studies informally with some local priests, and he surely read whatever books he could lay his hands on. His cousin Juan was about his age, and no doubt they chatted about any interesting items of news that came to their attention. One piece of news that may have caught Miguel's imagination was the marriage in 1559 of Philip II to Elizabeth de Valois, the young and pretty daughter of Henry II of France. One remembers her in relation to Miguel, because about ten years later her premature death inspired three of his early poems.

After five years in Cabra Rodrigo and his family settled in the San Miguel parish of Seville, probably in 1563, although the first certain proof of their residence in that city dates from the early fall of 1564.[6] Miguel, now a handsome youth of seventeen, had lived in other cities of considerable interest but not yet in one to match Seville, which was on the threshold of its most opulent years at the time of the Cervantes family's arrival.

Situated in a fertile plain on the banks of the Guadalquivir some eighty miles south-west of Córdoba, Seville had become the major city of

Andalusia and, because it was the gateway to the treasures of the New World, the leading trading center of Spain. With a permanent population of perhaps 85,000 and a floating population of thousands more from every corner of the known world, Seville was a completely walled city whose buildings and monuments were a visible record of its twenty centuries of history. Beyond the promenade of its ancient walls, one could see in the distance the town of Santiponce, site of the Roman city of Italia where three Roman emperors were born, while within the walls there caught the eye such notable landmarks as the Tower of Gold, the Moorish Alcázar, and the Giralda Tower, which had been the minaret of the great mosque now long since replaced by one of the largest Gothic cathedrals in Christendom and one of the richest in artistic treasures. Among the public buildings of the city, there was one that Miguel would later have particular cause to remember: the royal jail on Sierpe Street.

From the Giralda Tower in Seville one could look northwards on a clear day and see the silver-green olive groves stretching away to the distant Sierra Morena, where Don Quixote experienced some of his fantastic adventures. South-west by the Guadalquivir, Spanish galleons and Spanish imaginations sailed off to lands as remote and exotic as those in Don Quixote's dreams. Was young Miguel's imagination kindled by the frequent reminders in Seville of these new lands to the west? As he watched the silver and gold from Mexico and Peru being unloaded on the river bank, did he think of the

34   Silver mines at Potosí, Bolivia; opened in 1545, Potosí accelerated the influx of wealth from the 'new Spain' into the old, wealth which, instead of increasing the Spanish people's prosperity, largely had the effect of depressing and undermining home resources.

35 Symbolic representation of the 'Virgin of the Navigators' extending her protection over a fleet of ships. Columbus is thought to be among the figures on the left and Hernán Cortés (bearded) on the right.

exploits of Hernán Cortés and Francisco Pizarro? His writings contain two conventional references to Hernán Cortés and the conquest of Mexico and none to Pizarro's adventures in the land of the Incas. In his books there are perhaps as many as three dozen references to such names as America, the Indies, Mexico and Peru, but mostly they are unexceptional allusions to the wealth of the New World. (For example, in one of his stories he created a character named Carrizales who in middle life sailed off to America to recoup his fortune. Twice, at low points in the fortunes of his own middle years, Cervantes applied unsuccessfully for permission to attempt to do the same.) But this is all that can be discovered about the influence of the New World upon his mind and imagination.

With its varied peoples and customs and its constant commerce with the far places of the world, the city of Seville made a profound impression on Miguel, an impression that persisted and was reinforced in later years. Some of his best stories take place within its confines, and it is mentioned some fifty times in his complete works. But Rodrigo did not bring his son and his nephew Juan from Cabra to Seville merely to enjoy the colorful sights and bustling life of the city. They were brought to resume their formal studies.

There were a number of schools to choose from and Rodrigo chose the new Jesuit College, to which Miguel's former teacher, Father Acevedo, had come in 1561 from Córdoba. That Miguel retained pleasant memories of his renewed studies with the Jesuits can be seen from further quotations from *The Colloquy of the Dogs*. For example, Cipión, speaking of the Jesuit teachers in Seville:

'I have heard it said of those saintly ones that in the matter of prudence there is not their like in all the world, while as guides and leaders along the heavenly path few can come up to them. They are mirrors in which are to be viewed human decency, Catholic doctrine, and extraordinary wisdom, and, lastly, a profound humility that is the basis upon which the entire edifice of a holy life is reared.'[7]

His comrade Berganza's account of his association with their students is a tribute to the agreeable character of student life:

'In short, I led the life of a student, without hunger and without the itch – and I can give it no higher praise than that. For if it were not that the itch and hunger are the student's constant companions, there would be no life that is pleasanter or more enjoyable, since virtue and pleasure here go hand in hand, and the young find diversion even as they learn.'[8]

Whatever else Miguel learned in school, he continued to be exposed to Father Acevedo's plays. In view of Miguel's fondness for the theater it must have been a great day for him when Lope de Rueda and his company came to Seville to perform in 1564. When Cervantes writes that as a boy he saw Lope act, one may fairly assume that this was in 1564. Something of his appreciation for the great actor and poet may be felt in these sentences from the

37 Titian's equestrian portrait of Charles V, painted to commemorate the victory of Mühlberg ＞ in 1547. The contrast between this picture of the triumphant 'Christian Knight' and Titian's portrait of a year later (p. 20) is most striking.
Overleaf: 38 The capture of Tunis in 1535, in which Charles V, shown here in the right foreground, fully justified his aspiration to be 'God's standard-bearer' against the infidel.

42 Characters from two of Lope de Rueda's plays (*Eufemia* and *Armelina*), written in close imitation of the Italian style.

prologue he later wrote to a collection of his own plays. He is discussing a conversation on the theater with friends:

'I, as the oldest one there, said that I remembered having seen on the stage the great Lope de Rueda, a man distinguished in both acting and understanding. He was a native of Seville, and a goldsmith by trade, which means he was one of those that make gold leaf. He was admirable in pastoral poetry; and in this *genre* neither then nor since has anybody surpassed him.'[9]

It was clearly Miguel's fate to suffer repeated interruptions in his formal schooling. He had been studying with the Jesuits in his fourth year of grammar for only a few weeks when his father took him off to Alcalá de Henares on family business. His sister Luisa had decided to enter the austere Carmelite convent recently founded in Alcalá by Sister María de Jesús. Rodrigo wanted to talk with his daughter before she disposed so irrevocably of the rest of her life, and there was the matter of her dowry, and perhaps still other items of family business. So Rodrigo and Miguel set off for Alcalá, where they must have arrived around the beginning of December 1564. The effort to arrange for Luisa de Cervantes to enter the convent was successful, and she did so on 11 February 1565, under the name of Luisa de Belén.

The convent belonged to the reformed order called the Discalced Carmelites, and its rule was exceptionally severe. The nuns were required to support themselves only by alms and the work of their hands. They wore habits of coarse linen resembling canvas, and were obliged to go barefoot summer and winter. They observed scrupulously the services of the seven canonical hours beginning at midnight. What sleeping they did was on rough pallets filled with grape-vine clippings. Not all girls could stand such rigorous living conditions. Miguel and his father must have wondered about Luisa, but they need not have worried. She was to remain in this convent for more than fifty years, and enjoy the satisfaction of being elected prioress three times in her long life. Another satisfaction she must have experienced was that of

< 39-41 Four great rulers dominated the known world during the first half of the sixteenth century. Charles V (1500-58) exercised the greatest power of all, but the monarchs of England, France and the Ottoman Empire proved formidable opponents. Above, a European portrait of a Turkish potentate, probably Suleiman the Magnificent (1520-66). Below, Henry VIII of England (1509-47) and Francis I of France (1515-47).

43. Spain in the sixteenth century.

44 St Teresa of Ávila (1515-82), whose career as religious leader, reformer and woman of letters entitles her to world stature.

meeting the future Saint Teresa of Ávila, who visited her friend María de Jesús in the Alcalá convent more than once during the early years of Luisa's residence there.

On the way back to Seville, Rodrigo and his son passed through Córdoba about the time of the funeral of Lope de Rueda, who died in the last week of March 1565. There exists a document attesting to Rodrigo's presence in Córdoba as late as 10 April of that year, and given Lope de Rueda's renown and Miguel's enthusiasm for the theater it is quite possible that father and son attended the funeral.[10]

Back in Seville after an absence of several months, Rodrigo found that his affairs were once again in poor shape. A certain Francisco de Chaves had instituted a suit against him and attached his goods. As though this were not bad enough, it appeared that his daughter was going to have a baby without the benefit of clergy. Nicolás de Ovando, the first-born son of a wealthy Extremaduran family of distinguished jurists, had been courting her, presumably with promises of marriage, but he moved to Madrid without keeping his promise, and probably before their daughter Constanza was born. (Nicolás was a friend of Mateo Vázquez, who later became Philip's secretary and the recipient of a long and moving poetic epistle from Miguel about the plight of the Christian captives in North Africa. It is thus possible that Miguel made the acquaintance of Vázquez at the time when it looked as though Andrea de Cervantes might make a brilliant match with the oldest son of a wealthy and prominent family.)

Usually, Rodrigo had tried to change his luck by changing the scene of his activities, but this time the reasons for his move may have included some new elements, such as Andrea's compelling desire to catch up with her disappearing lover. Also, Doña Elvira de Cortinas, Miguel's maternal grandmother, had recently died in Arganda, and news of her death and of the property she had left to Miguel's mother probably contributed to the decision to move. A legal document connected with this legacy proves that the Cervantes were already in Madrid by early December 1566.[11]

47

45 Sixteenth-century view of Madrid, created his new capital and 'only court' by Philip II in

Alcalá de Henares, Valladolid, Córdoba, Cabra, Seville, and now Madrid. In a way Madrid may have been a disappointment. In 1566 it was a walled city of less than 60,000 inhabitants and with few of the kind of monuments that were ever-present reminders of a long and glorious history in such cities as Córdoba and Seville. The streets were mostly narrow, crooked, dirty, unlighted and without sidewalks. People were well advised not only to look where they set their feet but also to be ready to dodge the refuse thrown from upstairs windows. Accommodations were as poor as they were scarce. The climate, unlike that of the pleasant Andalusian cities, was often harsh and inhospitable. The imposing Sierra de Guadarrama sent down its icy winds in winter; in summer, the sun and dust could be a burden.

But Madrid was now the established seat of the royal court and the bureaucratic center of the largest empire the world had ever seen. It was also soon to become the center of a literary and artistic flowering of great power and originality. Its first printing press was set up in the very year the Cervantes family arrived. Because of the tremendous influx of people attracted by the establishment of the court, Madrid became the fastest growing city in Spain. Little by little, the old was torn down to make way for the new. Soon the medieval walls could not contain the city, and by the end of the century they were gone. The young Miguel de Cervantes was to be an active participant and a gifted observer of the national life that brought the new Madrid into being.

Miguel was now twenty. Once established in his new surroundings, his first concern was probably to continue his education. The City School of Madrid (El Estudio de la Villa, it was called) was closed for lack of a professor during the final months of 1566 and the opening months of 1567. A suitable teacher was, however, finally found in the person of Francisco del Bayo, who taught there from March 1567 to October of the same year. Miguel may have studied under him, but there is no proof. He may just as well have studied

48

1560: during Cervantes' lifetime its population exploded from 5,000 inhabitants to over 60,000.

with private tutors, a luxury that his mother's recent inheritance would have made possible, at least for a while. In any case, there is clear proof that he did finally study for something less than one year in the City School of Madrid, which began to offer classes again in February 1568. The new professor, who won his professorship by competitive examination, was Juan López de Hoyos, a native of Madrid and a learned and prominent priest. On more than one occasion he referred to Miguel as 'my beloved student'. Recognizing Miguel's genius, López de Hoyos may well have devoted extra attention to him. He may even have given him private lessons, since the warmth of his regard for Miguel suggests a relationship of longer duration than can be accounted for by his time in the City School.

Nevertheless, by the most generous estimate that the available facts will allow, young Cervantes cannot have enjoyed much more than six years of formal schooling. In most men this amount of study could not have created a sufficient base for the very considerable literary culture visible in Miguel's later writings, which reveal a good knowledge of the oustanding Latin authors, a smattering of Greek literature, a close familiarity with some of the great writers of the Italian Renaissance and the kind of acquaintance with his own literature that one might expect a boy with strong literary inclinations to possess. What he knew of the Latin language and literature was certainly grounded in his schooling; the rest must have been the product of his own reading. The five years he was soon to spend in Italy contributed decisively to his continuing education and account for his extensive reading in Italian literature.

Some biographers of Cervantes have suggested that one day he will be discovered to have been a student in some notable university like Salamanca or Alcalá. But the known chronology of his life leaves no suitable gaps for a university career. No doubt he dreamed of one while studying with López de Hoyos in Madrid, but, as it happened, an event in his twenty-first year was to motivate his hasty departure for Rome.

46-8 The 'Prudent
King' and his family:
Philip II by El Greco and
Elizabeth de Valois,
portrayed by Alonso
Sánchez Coello; right,
their two daughters,
Isabel Clara Eugenia and
Catalina Micaela, also
by Coello.

4 In Exile

The years 1567 and 1568 brought personal loss to Philip II and grave crises to his empire. On 10 October 1567 Elizabeth de Valois gave birth to her second daughter, Princess Catalina Micaela. This was good news; better news, of course, would have been the arrival of a son, since the son Philip already had was not destined to survive the years under review. Nevertheless the Spanish public received the tidings of Catalina's birth with great joy. Among the verses written to celebrate the happy event, it is probably safe to include a sonnet by Miguel – probably, because the sonnet does not allow the reader to be entirely sure of the occasion that inspired Cervantes' praise of the queen. At any rate the sonnet does belong to the period in question and is Cervantes' earliest known work. One may fairly suppose that a youth with so strong a literary bent would have composed many other poems by the age of twenty, but if he did the results seem not to have survived.

49 Cervantes' earliest known work, his sonnet to the queen.

50-2   The stigma of Don Carlos' death provoked wide-spread hostility in Europe and was an important factor in the growth of the *Leyenda Negra* (Black Legend) about Philip's unnatural cruelty. Top, the prince's effigy appears with those of Philip II and three of his wives on his father's tomb in the Escorial. Left, Don Carlos as a boy and, above, Andreas Vesalius (1514-64), the eminent Flemish physician.

Hard on the heels of this birth came the first of two personal tragedies in the life of King Philip. On the night of 18 February 1568, he ordered the arrest of his only son, Don Carlos. On 25 July of the same year, Carlos died in the Alcázar of Madrid in circumstances that are still mysterious, thus terminating a crisis in the royal family while providing the courts of Europe with occasion for all sorts of gossip and speculation. Did his father have Carlos murdered because of his inclination toward Protestantism or because of his guilty passion for his beautiful young stepmother? Such were the speculative questions that began to circulate and that finally made their way into imaginative literature, notably Schiller's *Don Carlos*. Later historians have demolished these versions of the tragedy.

Don Carlos was the son of Philip and his first wife, Mary of Portugal, both of whom were grandchildren of Joanna the Mad. Such inbreeding was not uncommon among the Habsburgs; but this time the results had been spectacularly bad. Don Carlos turned out to be a kind of monster with a frail body, an enormous head, a permanent stammer, a cruel disposition, and a tendency to madness. Despite early evidence that he was not of such stuff as competent kings are made of, his father did what he could to prepare him to occupy the Spanish throne. He sent him to spend his adolescent years in Alcalá de Henares in the company of his young uncle, Don Juan of Austria, and his cousin Alexander Farnese, destined to become one of Philip's greatest generals. The king doubtless hoped that university classes and the company of those noble youths might improve his mind and character. Apparently they did not.

53 Don Juan of Austria, Charles V's son by the notorious Barbara of Blomberg, 'the washerwoman of Ratisbon', as a young man.

54 Alexander Farnese, who later became the Duke of Parma.

During the Prince's stay in Alcalá, he suffered an accident which aggravated the disabilities under which he already labored. One day in April 1562, while pursuing at breakneck speed the attractive daughter of a porter, he tumbled headlong down a flight of stone steps and seriously injured his head. For weeks his life hung in the balance. Philip could not have shown himself more solicitous for his son's recovery. He sent his own personal physicians to Alcalá at once and lost little time in following them there himself. He summoned as many as nine specialists, including the renowned Vesalius and a Moorish surgeon from Valencia who was famous for cures effected with black and white ointments. A variety of remedies was proposed and tried: Carlos was relieved of eight ounces of his blood; Vesalius and two Spanish doctors performed a trepanation on his skull; the Moor was allowed to try his ointments for several days; and the Duke of Alba had the long-dead but uncorrupted body of saintly Fray Diego de Alcalá (canonized in 1588) brought into the prince's room to intercede with God for a miracle. Something must have worked, for Don Carlos was up and about by mid-July and able to rejoin the royal family in Madrid.[1]

Philip decided to name Carlos president of the Council of State in the hope of encouraging in him the knowledge and responsibility he would need as king. But the prince's behaviour grew more and more erratic and violent. Prone to outbursts of uncontrolled rage, he tried to murder at least six persons who frustrated his desires. Philip tolerated in his son much that he would not have tolerated in anyone else, but the time came when he could bear no more. Carlos began to conspire against him with the rebellious nobles of the Netherlands (whose governor he aspired to be) and with Don Juan of Austria. The latter reported these conspiratorial activities to Philip, who then ordered him imprisoned in the Alcázar. Exactly how he died is not known, but his death left Philip at the age of forty-one without an heir and with unpleasant rumors to combat. In a letter written to Pope Pius V on 9 May 1568, the king went to some pains to make the Pope understand that he had locked up his son, not as a punishment for disobedience or disrespect, but because his numerous defects rendered him not only unfit to govern but an active menace to the State.[2]

The queen survived the birth of her second daughter by one week less than a year. Her death was both a genuine bereavement for Philip and yet another reminder of the problem of dynastic succession. To solve this problem he eventually, in 1570, married Anne of Austria (his fourth and final wife) and by her achieved the desired son and heir (who reigned as Philip III). In the meantime, Miguel's teacher, López de Hoyos, was commissioned by the City Council of Madrid to publish an account of the illness, death and exequies of the queen, together with the sermons, poems and epitaphs inspired by her death. The book appeared in Madrid in 1569, and is of interest here because it contains four poems by Miguel de Cervantes.

The first two poems are presented in these words by López de Hoyos: 'First epitaph in the form of a sonnet, with some Castilian verses, composed by Miguel de Cervantes, my beloved student.' Some idea of Miguel's early

55 Anne of Austria, Philip II's last
    wife and the mother of Philip III

poetic efforts may be gleaned from even this rough translation of his sonnet-epitaph:

ON THE DEATH OF THE QUEEN
DOÑA ISABEL DE VALOIS

Here the worth of the Spanish land,
Here of France's people the very flower,
Here she who harmonized all difference,
Crowning with olive branch that war;
Here in brief space you see confined
The clear morning star of the West;
Here lies enclosed the excellent
Cause that banishes all our good.
Consider the world and its power,
And how over a life most gay
The victory death always wins.
But consider too the blessedness
Our illustrious queen doth enjoy
Forever now in glory's realm.[3]

As though the burden of his personal grief were not heavy enough, Philip now had to contend with new and serious outbreaks of familiar trouble on the international scene. Like his father before him, Philip could count on recurring crises resulting from the spread of Protestantism in Europe and

Moslem pressures from North Africa and the eastern Mediterranean. Several Protestant sects were beginning to gain a foothold in the Netherlands, the most important and aggressive of these being the Calvinists. Determined to stop their encroachment upon his lands, Philip had in October 1565 ordered the strict application of anti-heresy laws by the Inquisition. The severity of the measures taken gave rise in August 1566 to outbreaks of rioting and destruction in many cities of the Low Countries. Although the majority of the Netherlanders were Catholics, they were not organized to resist the 'Calvinist fury' which swept the country. More than four hundred churches and monasteries were left in ruins, including the great cathedral of Antwerp, whose irreplaceable artistic treasures were all destroyed or stolen.

In order to retain control of this part of his empire, Philip was obliged to send thither the Duke of Alba with ten thousand soldiers who had previously been stationed in Italy. Of course the king's problems in the Low Countries were not exclusively religious; they were compounded by questions of local autonomy – especially as it related to taxation – and of intrigues by the local nobility, whose expectations of preferment and power had not been fulfilled. Two of these nobles, Counts Egmont and Horne, were beheaded in the main square of Brussels on 5 June 1568; Cervantes refers to this event when he makes the Captive Captain in *Don Quixote* tell how he journeyed from Italy to Flanders in the duke's army and found himself present at the execution.

56   The execution of Counts Egmont and Horne in 1568, which served only to inflame hatred in the Netherlands against Spain.

56

57   Moors being baptized in the time of Ferdinand and Isabella.

While all this was going on in the Low Countries, Philip decided to issue, on 1 January 1567, an edict designed to hasten the full conversion and assimilation of the Moriscos of Andalusia. By the terms of the edict, the Moriscos were given three years to learn Spanish and abandon the use of Arabic; they were also required to give up their native costumes, ceremonies and customs, including even their splendid baths. The proclamation of the edict brought to a head a situation which for sixty years had been looking more and more dangerous to Spanish eyes.

When Ferdinand and Isabella had completed the conquest of the Moorish Kingdom of Granada in 1492, the terms of capitulation allowed the Moors to practice their religion, their laws, and their customs in freedom. But it was not long before the Spaniards had second thoughts about tolerating an alien nation which professed an alien religion within their borders, and they initiated a policy of forcible conversion. When in 1502 the Moors were given a choice between conversion and expulsion, most of them had chosen conversion. It was widely, and for the most part accurately, believed that these 'Moriscos' were only nominal Christians, adhering in secret to their ancient beliefs and customs. Further, while they were growing in numbers and prosperity, their co-religionists of the Ottoman Empire, aided by the Barbary pirates of North Africa, threatened to convert the Mediterranean into a Moslem lake. This is the way the situation looked to Philip when he issued his edict, which was intended primarily as a security measure.

For almost exactly a year the Moriscos tried to negotiate a liberalization of the new restrictions imposed upon them; but Philip was adamant, and so on Christmas Eve 1568 the Moriscos rebelled. The city of Granada would have fallen on the first day if the Moriscos of the Albaicín quarter had risen with the others, and the revolt rapidly assumed serious proportions, occasioning acts of the utmost cruelty on both sides. Fernando de Valor, a descendant of the caliphs of Córdoba, was proclaimed king under the name of Aben Omeya. He was killed within a year, but the war raged on. The Moriscos were particularly hard to deal with in the mountain fastness of the Alpujarras, south of Granada and accessible to help from the sea. Considerable help was in fact received from Mohammedan lands. Thus El Uchali, the viceroy of Algiers of whom we shall hear more later on, sent troops to their assistance in 1569. For a time the Spanish situation was grave. The Morisco insurrection, after all, occurred at a time when Spain had weakened her position in the Mediterranean by sending troops from Italy to the Netherlands, and the Ottoman Empire probably saw in the uprising of their fellow Moslems in Andalusia a new opportunity to attack Spain under favorable conditions. Until 1570, when the revolt was put down, Philip had no way of knowing how much his Turkish enemies were prepared to invest in prolonging the war.[4]

At home, the court was still in deep mourning for the death of the queen and buzzing with talk of the crisis in the Netherlands when an episode in Miguel's life necessitated his hasty departure from Madrid. Late in 1568, Cervantes had wounded a certain Antonio de Sigura in a duel. This individual seems to have been a construction foreman who for a number of years found prominent employment in the royal palaces of Aranjuez, Madrid and El Pardo. No one really knows what caused the quarrel, although Cervantes' biographers almost without exception have assumed that a woman must have been at the heart of it. There is a faint possibility, however, that an insult to Miguel's sister Andrea occasioned the duel.

In 1568 an Italian gentleman named Giovanni Locadelo had appeared before a notary with Andrea to arrange for her to receive for her own exclusive use a long and valuable list of personal clothing, household linen, rugs and furniture, in addition to three hundred gold coins.[5] The goods given to Andrea amounted to a better than average wardrobe with enough linen and furniture to furnish a house, and the coins that rounded out the gift must have been a rare sight in Rodrigo's household. Locadelo declared before the notary that he was making this gift to Andrea because of her many attentions and kindnesses and because she and her father had cured him of certain illnesses. The property bestowed upon her was also intended as a dowry. Locadelo's action may have been his generous way of putting an end to a love affair. If this is true, it represents a second liaison for Andrea without benefit of marriage, and it is possible that the girl was sometimes the object of unflattering gossip in this connection, and that Miguel's fight in or near the royal palace was provoked by some insulting remark made in his presence by Antonio de Sigura.

However that may be, the National Archives at Simancas contain a royal order (dated 15 September 1569) requiring the arrest of Miguel de Cervantes for having wounded Antonio de Sigura.[6] Two specifications in this order are of particular interest. The first is the extreme rigor of the penalty to be imposed on Miguel: his right hand was to be cut off in public and he was to be exiled from the kingdom for ten years. As Sigura's wound was not mortal, one may wonder at the severity of this sentence. An old Spanish law still in force at the time of the duel suggests an explanation, however. This law calls for the amputation of the hand of anyone caught drawing a dagger or a sword in the royal court, and it is because of this that we can infer that Miguel and de Sigura must have fought in the royal palace or its grounds.

The other interesting item in the order of arrest is the statement that Cervantes had been seen in several parts of Spain, special mention being made of Seville. It is not hard to imagine why Miguel fled to Andalusia to escape the rigors of the law while his family tried to reach a settlement with the wounded man. He had relatives in more than one Andalusian town – notably in Cabra, where his uncle Andrés was mayor. But Andalusia was clearly not the best place to ride out the storm. The revolt of the Moriscos was at its height, which spelled hazards of two kinds: travel was dangerous, and the cities and towns were full of royal agents attempting to recruit soldiers for the war. Their presence sharpened the probability of Miguel's being seen by someone who knew of the order for his arrest. At any rate, the next thing we know with any certainty is that in the fall of 1569 Miguel arrived in Rome.

58   The warrant for Cervantes' arrest in connection with the wounding of Antonio de Sigura.

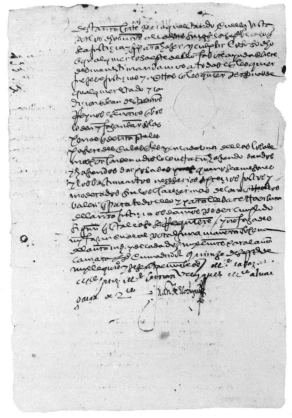

Several characters in Cervantes' stories make their way to Rome from one part or another of Spain. Since there is no documentary evidence about the route followed by Miguel, his biographers have tried to find some clue to his itinerary in his fiction. Most of the fictional characters sail for Italy from Cartagena, a seaport on the south-eastern coast of Spain. But an expeditious journey such as a fugitive would hope to make from any principal Andalusian city to Cartagena would lead directly through the territory where, at the very time Cervantes was making his escape, the revolt of the Moriscos was at its height. Given the hazards of a raging war and the strong possibility of being seen by royal agents, Miguel would hardly have chosen to depart via Cartagena.

Periandro and Auristela, two characters in Cervantes' novel *Persiles y Sigismunda*, travel overland from Spain to Italy via Barcelona and southern France. This is a route Cervantes shows great familiarity with, and it may well have been the one he followed. By back roads and paths, he could have made his way north-east from Cabra to Valencia. This leg of the journey would not have been free from danger, but once he reached the Mediterranean coast at Valencia he would have been well beyond the war zone and the probability of encounter with Castilian agents of the law. Even if it were not known that much later Cervantes returned from his captivity in North Africa by way of Valencia, one would be seriously inclined to suppose he had visited that city because of the numerous references to it in his works. Whether or not, like Periandro and Auristela, he passed through Valencia in his flight to Rome, it is almost certain that, like them, he did visit Barcelona. There are even more references in his works to Barcelona than to Valencia. Some of them reveal personal observation, and the time of Miguel's escape is the only occasion in his life when he could plausibly have been there.

Toward the end of *Don Quixote*, the hero delivers himself of a tribute to Barcelona that seems to go beyond what his experiences in that city would warrant. He calls it 'the treasure house of courtesy, the refuge of strangers, the hospital of the poor, the country of the valiant, the avenger of the injured, and the abode of firm and reciprocal friendships, unique in its position and beauty'.[7] One would be justified in sensing in Don Quixote's eloquent words some of the gratitude young Cervantes felt at the hospitable treatment he received in that great port, especially since he makes more than one reference to it as 'the refuge of strangers'.[8]

By following more or less closely the route of Periandro and Auristela, Miguel would have entered France at Perpignan, left it by the ancient province of Dauphiné, and crossed the Piemonte to Milan, where he would have wondered at 'the grandeur of the city, its infinite wealth, its golden treasures, since gold in the singular would not do it justice, its warlike smithies that looked as though Vulcan himself had moved them there, the infinite abundance of its products, the greatness of its temples, and finally the shrewdness of its inhabitants'.[9] Thence to Lucca, 'a small city but beautiful and free, which, under the wings of Spain and the Empire, excelled and saw itself exempt from the princes who wanted it. There, better than elsewhere,

Spaniards are well regarded and received, because in it they do not command but request, since they stop there no longer than a day and hence do not reveal their characters thought to be arrogant...';[10] then perhaps to Florence,[11] and on by the main road to Rome (Acquapendente near Lago di Bolsena is the last town mentioned before Rome).

When Periandro and Auristela, traveling with a band of pilgrims, came in sight of the Eternal City, they knelt down in thanksgiving while an unknown pilgrim stepped forth to recite these verses:

O powerful, grand, thrice-blessed, and passing fair
City of Rome! To thee I bend the knee,
A pilgrim new, a lowly devotee,
Whose wonder grows to see thy beauty rare!
The sight of thee, past fame, beyond compare,
Suspends the fancy, soaring though it be,
Of him who comes to see and worship thee,
With naked feet, and tender loving care.
The soil of this thy land which now I view
Where blood of martyrs mingles with the clod,
Is the world's relic, prized of every land;
No part of thee but serves as pattern true
Of sanctity; as if the City of God
Had been in every line its model grand![12]

59 Sixteenth-century engraving showing pilgrims visiting the seven basilicas of Rome, ending with St Peter's; this pilgrimage is still made today.

The words of the unknown pilgrim probably express something of Miguel's reaction to his first sight of the Eternal City.

The young fugitive had, of course, to find a way to feed and shelter himself in Rome, but no doubt he spent a few days, like the hero of his story *Man of Glass*, getting his bearings and seeing the famous sights of 'that queen of cities and mistress of the world'.

'He visited its temples, adored its relics, and marveled at its grandeur. Just as from the claws of a lion one may judge the size and ferocity of the beast, so was his opinion of Rome formed from its marble ruins, the statuary whether whole or mutilated, its crumbling arches and baths, its magnificent porticos and huge amphitheaters, the renowned and sacred river that washes its banks to the brim and blesses them with countless relics from the bodies of martyrs that are buried there, its bridges which appear to be admiring one another, and its streets whose very names invest them with a dignity beyond those of all other cities in the world: the Via Appia, the Via Flaminia, the Via Julia, and others of that sort. He was no less pleased by the manner in which the city was divided by its hills: the Caelian, the Quirinal, and the Vatican, along with the other four whose names show forth the greatness and majesty that is Rome. He likewise remarked the authority that is exerted by the College of Cardinals, as well as the majesty of the Supreme Pontiff and the great variety of peoples and nations that are gathered there. He saw and made note of everything and put everything in its proper place.'[13]

Little wonder that Miguel was impressed with the monumental splendor of Rome, which had fallen on evil days during the long years when Avignon was the papal See but which now gloried in the enlargements and beautifications undertaken by the powerful and opulent Renaissance popes. The city was far from abandoning the dissolute ways that had characterized it in the early sixteenth century, but the papacy no longer set an example of licentiousness. On the contrary, Pope Pius V was a devout and ascetic priest dedicated to reform. Under his rule, the papal court distinguished itself by its sobriety; prostitutes were driven from the city or confined to a special quarter; decrees and ordinances were issued against profanity and animal baiting; and monastic orders were required to live according to their vows. A firm advocate of strict orthodoxy, Pius V revitalized the Inquisition, expelled the Jews from the Papal States, ordered the extermination of the Huguenots, conspired to dethrone Queen Elizabeth of England, encouraged Philip II to put down Protestant revolts in the Netherlands and played a key role in the creation of the Holy League to stem the tide of Islam in the Mediterranean.

In the dedication to his pastoral novel *La Galatea* Cervantes refers to his service in Rome as chamberlain to Cardinal Giulio Acquaviva. Acquaviva had been in Madrid in 1568 while Miguel was still in residence there, and it is possible that the two men met at that time; but even if they did not Miguel must have been confident of gaining an audience with him in Rome through the good offices of his distinguished relative, Don Gaspar de Cervantes y

60   Pope Pius V (1566-72).

61   The Roman Forum in the sixteenth century.

Gaete, who was a friend of Acquaviva – in 1570 both of them were to be named cardinals by Pius V on the same day.[14]

But more was required than a mere introduction. Miguel discovered that one was not acceptable in the household of a nobleman unless one could produce evidence of what was then called purity of blood (that is, having no Jewish or other non-Christian ancestry). There is a satirical reference to this requirement in the already quoted *Colloquy of the Dogs*, where one of the dogs remarks:

'The lords of earth are very different from the lord of Heaven. The former, before they take a servant, must investigate his pedigree, test his abilities, note his appearance, and even pry into his wardrobe; whereas when it comes to entering God's service the poorest is the richest and the humblest is the highest born, providing only he be disposed to serve Him with a pure heart, in which case he is at once entered in His book of wages . . . .'[15]

However irksome it may have been, Miguel wrote to his father in Madrid, who on 22 December 1569 was able to secure the proper legal document

63

attesting to his son's legitimacy, untainted ancestry and good reputation (despite the duel that had occasioned his hasty departure from Madrid).[16] Miguel must have received the testimonial and been taken into the household of Monsignor Acquaviva several months before the latter's elevation to the rank of cardinal, which occurred on 17 May 1570. So now our young fugitive had a comfortable place to stay and a means of earning a living. His duties as chamberlain cannot have been onerous. In the sixteenth century, a chamberlain in a noble or royal household was usually a kind of head *valet de chambre*. It was an honorable post. Acquaviva was himself chamberlain to the Pope.

Miguel remained in Acquaviva's employ for only a few months. Since there is some evidence that he enjoyed the confidence of the cardinal and no indication of a falling-out between them, one may be inclined to ask why the relationship was to end so soon. A sufficient answer might be that the twenty-three-year-old Miguel's adventurous spirit was not satisfied with the humdrum life of a chamberlain, and he may already have had in mind the doctrine so often enunciated by Don Quixote:

'For there is nothing on earth more honourable or more profitable than to serve God first, and then your king and natural lord, especially in the profession of Arms, which may not gain you more riches than Letters, but wins you more honour, as I have very often said. For though Letters may have been the foundation of more estates than Arms, still soldiers have an indefinable superiority over men of letters and a certain splendour about them which puts them above everybody.'[17]

If his mind entertained thoughts like these, a developing crisis in the Mediterranean would soon offer him a chance to carry them into the realm of action.

Charles V had been plagued throughout his reign by the growing naval power of the Ottoman Empire and its allies in North Africa. His son initially fared no better. In fact, during the first decade or so of his rule the problem took a turn for the worse. In the 1560s the Barbary corsairs, aided and protected by their Turkish allies, swarmed over the western Mediterranean and even raided Spanish shipping along Spain's Atlantic coast. In 1560 Philip tried to teach his North African foes a lesson by striking at Tunisia. His expedition was a disaster, ending with the loss of 42 ships and 18,000 men killed or captured on the island of Djerba. Philip took the lesson to heart, launching a systematic building up of naval strength in the Mediterranean. As his strength increased, it was inevitable that he would eventually seek a major confrontation with the Turks.

The year 1569-70 could scarcely have seemed less opportune for such a confrontation, since Spain was at war with the Moriscos in Andalusia and unrest persisted in the Netherlands. In that year, however, awareness of Spain's problems encouraged the Turks to step up their offensive in the Mediterranean. Their attack on the Venetian possession of Cyprus in July 1570 resulted in the bloody fall of Nicosia on 9 September of that year.[18]

62-4 In the early years of his reign Philip II's problems with the Ottoman Empire were no less acute than his father's had been. Above, the signing of the treaty establishing the Holy League against the Turks, 1571: Pius V with the Spanish and Venetian ambassadors. Below, a suit of armor which belonged to Philip II and a detachment of Spanish infantry, crack troops which remained virtually undefeated for nearly a century.

What the Turks did not realize was that this victory would contribute to the success of Pius V's efforts to form with Venice and Spain a Holy League against Islam and that the conditions which made it difficult for Spain to join such a venture were about to change with the victorious termination of the war against the Moriscos and the temporary achievement of stability in the Netherlands under the iron rule of the Duke of Alba.

Cervantes would not have been unaware of the threatening power of the Ottoman Empire and of Spain's insatiable need for ships and soldiers to contain it. Like Don Quixote he knew that 'by arms states are defended, kingdoms preserved, cities guarded, the roads kept safe, and the seas swept free of pirates'.[19] As a sixteenth-century Catholic and a patriotic Spaniard, he could see a campaign against the infidels as a crusade; as a spirited young man he could imagine adventure in the dangerous life of a soldier. In the summer of 1570, he enlisted. Some writers have supposed that he joined at once the company of Diego de Urbina, under whom in about a year he would fight in the battle of Lepanto, but at the time of his enlistment Captain Urbina was still fighting Moriscos in Spain. All that is known for certain is that Cervantes began his military career in a Spanish regiment in Naples.

5 Lepanto and the Career of Arms

Precisely when Cervantes reached Naples is not known, but it is evident that he spent considerable time there on this and other occasions. He was fond of the city and paid repeated tribute to it in his writings. In his *Journey to Parnassus* (1614), he remembered:

> There's no deception here,
> 'Tis Naples' self, that city of great fame,
> Whose streets I paced for better than a year.
> Italia's pride, that sets the world aflame,
> For of all famous cities near and far
> Not one possesses such a glorious name![1]

Here, some time late in 1570, Miguel was joined by his brother Rodrigo, who was to share his military adventures and the terrible years of Algerian captivity.

It was in Naples that Cervantes began to learn the trade of a soldier. He was trained to be a harquebusier, a gunner whose fire power was perhaps as important in naval warfare as in land engagements. It was his fate to do the fighting he remembered best in the naval battle of Lepanto, which towards the end of his life he still called 'the greatest occasion which any age, past, present, or future, ever saw or can ever hope to see',[2] and which few people would now remember if Cervantes had not been there.

In that battle he fought aboard the galley *Marquesa*. It may be useful to recall that, in the tricky winds and waters of the Mediterranean, galleys such as the *Marquesa* were the most important warships of the day. They were propelled by both sails and oars, and although they often mounted as many as twelve cannon, they were appreciated especially for their speed and maneuverability, since the crucial phase of a naval battle still came when the attacking ships closed and grappled with one another and the soldiers fought with harquebus, sword and pike. Lepanto was the last great naval battle fought in this style.

On 20 May 1571 a treaty was signed establishing the Holy League against the Turk, which was solemnly proclaimed five days later in the basilica of Saint Peter in Rome. The treaty stipulated that for three years the Papacy, Spain and Venice would assemble annually by the first of April 200 galleys, 100 sailing vessels, 50,000 troops and 4,500 cavalry, the expenses of which were to be borne in three parts by Spain, in two by Venice, and in one by the

Papacy. As Spain was the major partner in the alliance, it is not surprising that a Spaniard, Don Juan of Austria, was named commander-in-chief.[3]

Don Juan was born in Regensburg, Bavaria, in the same year as Miguel de Cervantes. He was the illegitimate son of the Emperor Charles V and (presumably) of Barbara of Blomberg, a Bavarian lady of good family and ambitious character. The emperor tried to keep secret the birth of his bastard son, entrusting his upbringing to Don Luis de Quijada and his wife Doña Magdalena, whom, although Quijada was wealthy and one of the most distinguished officials in Charles' government, he charged with raising Juan in seclusion and in ignorance of his royal birth. It was not until 1559 that the boy learned who his father was. At that time his half-brother the king officially recognized him, invested him with the Order of the Golden Fleece, and incorporated him into the royal family. Educated as a prince from that time on, he had attained a position of prominence and popularity by the age of twenty-four. Slender, graceful, handsome, brave, ambitious, fresh from his victory over the Moriscos, and already named captain-general of the Holy League, he was eager to meet the Turk and add new luster to his growing fame.

The assembly point of the Christian forces was the Sicilian seaport of Messina, where Don Juan arrived on 23 August 1571. Part of the papal fleet was already there under the command of Marco Antonio Colonna. On 2 September, the Genoese admiral, Gian Andrea Doria, and his Spanish counterpart, the Marquis of Santa Cruz, entered the port. Miguel and his brother Rodrigo came with the ships of the marquis. Never again would they see such a spectacle as Messina offered on this occasion. In fact, in all its history Messina itself probably never sought to honor a mightier gathering of naval forces or a more imposing collection of notable men. The commander of the papal forces belonged to a family of Roman nobles who had played a prominent part in the life of Rome for four centuries. Although Marco Antonio was now supporting the Pope the Colonnas had often opposed the

68

66, 67 Gian Andrea Doria (left) and the Marquis of Santa Cruz (right), the Genoese and Spanish commanders of the Christian fleet.

Papacy in the turbulent days when the Renaissance popes were trying to re-establish its prestige and authority. Gian Andrea Doria was from an ancient Genoese family of famous statesmen and seamen. His uncle had been the greatest admiral in the service of Charles V. The Marquis of Santa Cruz is generally regarded as the foremost fighting seaman in Spanish history. He was the leading proponent of a naval attack on England, but he did not live long enough to lead what might have proved to be, under his command, the Invincible Armada.

The Christian fleet sailed from Messina on 16 September, heading for the island of Corfu. There it was learned that the Turkish fleet under the command of Ali Pasha was in the Bay of Lepanto at the narrowest part of the Gulf of Corinth, not far from Missolonghi – where some 250 years later Lord Byron was to lose his life in another war against the Turks. After a final council of war, the allied fleet put to sea on the morning of 3 October to seek the enemy. On 4 October, the Christians received belated news of the fall of Famagusta, the last stronghold on the island of Cyprus, and of the flaying alive of the Venetian commander Bragadino. The Turks' treacherous and inhuman treatment of Bragadino inflamed the passions of the Christian forces and sharpened their impatience to come to grips with their enemies. They had not long to wait. At sunrise on 7 October the two armadas sighted one another at the entrance to the Bay of Lepanto. Face to face along a line some five miles wide, they could at last calculate with some accuracy the magnitude of each other's forces. The Christian fleet contained about 208 galleys plus auxiliary ships, the Moslem fleet about 230. On the average, the allied galleys were better than the Turkish ones, and the well-armed Spanish infantry had no peers in all of Europe.

Although some twelve miles apart, the two fleets began at once to assume their battle formations. Don Juan divided his fleet into four squadrons in line of battle: the left wing under the Venetian admiral Barbarigo, the right wing under the Genoese admiral Doria, the center under his own command, and the fourth under the Marquis of Santa Cruz as a kind of roving rearguard. The Turkish forces were disposed in similar fashion with Ali Pasha facing Don Juan, Mahomet Sirocco opposing Barbarigo, and El Uchali confronting Doria.

The Moslem leaders were for the most part as prominent as the Christian leaders already described. Ali Pasha was the brother-in-law of the Turkish sultan, Selim II; Mahomet Sirocco was the governor of Alexandria; El Uchali was the Dey of Algiers. Of the three, El Uchali had enjoyed the most unpredictable rise to power and prestige. He was born in southern Italy and destined by his parents for an ecclesiastical career, but in his youth he was carried off in a raid by the Barbary pirates. According to Cervantes, who seems to have respected him, he was

'at the oar as a slave of the Great Turk for fourteen years, and when he was over thirty-four turned renegade, in his fury at a Turk who had given him a slap on the face while he was rowing. In fact he renounced his faith to get his revenge. He had such character too that he came to be king of Algiers and, afterwards, Commander of the Sea – which is the third post in their empire – without resorting to the base methods by which most of the Great Turk's favorites rise. He was a Calabrian by birth, a good moral man, and treated his prisoners with great humanity.'[4]

The left wing of the Christian forces under Barbarigo, being slightly ahead of Don Juan's squadron, was the first to join battle. Some of the bitterest fighting of the day took place on this sector of the line, and here was where the galley *Marquesa* held its place. Sick with fever on the fateful day, Miguel had been ordered to remain below deck in bed. This he refused to do, saying to his friends and officers:

'Gentlemen, on all occasions in his Majesty's wars that until now have offered themselves and I have been under orders, I have served well, like a good soldier; and so now I will do no less, even though I am sick and feverish; it is better to fight in the service of God and King and to die for them than to stay below deck. Captain, post me where the danger is greatest and there I shall remain and fight to the death.'[5]

His wish being granted, he was put in command of twelve soldiers stationed beside a longboat lashed to the deck of the *Marquesa*. What the fighting was like can be gathered from Don Quixote's account of a head-on collision of two fighting galleys at sea:

68 Ali Pasha, depicted on a broadsheet of the battle of Lepanto.

'For when ships are locked and grappled together, the soldier has no more space left him than two feet of plank on the beak-head. But though he sees in front of him countless pieces of artillery threatening from the enemy's side, each a minister of death, and no more than a spear's length from his body; and though he knows that at his first careless step he will go down to visit the deep bosom of Neptune, nevertheless with undaunted heart, sustained by the honor that spurs him on, he exposes himself as a mark for all their shot, and endeavors to pass along the narrow causeway into the enemy's ship.

And, most amazing of all, no sooner does one man fall, never to rise again this side of Doomsday, than another takes his place; and if he, in his turn, falls into the sea, which lies in wait for him like an enemy, another, and yet another, takes his place, without a moment passing between their deaths: the greatest display of valour and daring to be found in all the hazards of war.'[6]

Something of the horror and confusion of the fierce struggle is also captured in the chaotic style of a near-contemporary historian of Philip II:

'Never was a more confused battle seen, the galleys being joined one with another or two or three with another, however their luck would have it, grappled by the prows, gunwales, sterns, or prow to stern, if so it turned out. The aspect was terrifying because of the wild cries of the Turks, the shots, the fire, the smoke, the laments of the dying. Turned to blood, the sea was the grave of dying bodies tossed by the waves, upset and foaming from the shock of the galleys and the horrible blows of the artillery, pikes, spears, swords, fires, hail-like clouds of arrows that converted the masts, yards and hulls into veritable hedgehogs and porcupines. Frightful was the confusion, fear, hope, furor, stubbornness, grit, courage, rage, fury; the pitiful dying of friends, the encouraging, wounding, killing, capturing, burning; the throwing into the water of heads, arms, legs, torsos, miserable men: some already dead, some about to give up the ghost, some gravely wounded and receiving the *coup de grâce*, some swimming to the galleys to save their lives at the cost of their freedom, grabbing oars, rudders, cables, asking with pitiful voices for mercy . . . , only to have their hands cut off without pity . . . .'[7]

69 Detail of a contemporary engraving of Lepanto, giving a vivid picture of the turmoil and devastation on both sides.

Barbarigo's forces gave a good account of themselves in the ferocious *mêlée*, but Barbarigo himself did not live to see the victory. When he lowered his shield to observe what new orders were needed, a Turkish arrow struck him in the eye and killed him almost instantly. His place was taken by his nephew, Marco Contarini, who was killed soon after. Frederigo Nani took his place, and the left wing held firm. Cervantes maintained his exposed position and when his part of the battle was over he was found standing at his post, a sword in his right hand, his left hand and chest bleeding from deep wounds. Some six years later as a captive in North Africa, he remembered this moment with deep satisfaction in a verse epistle addressed to King Philip's secretary, Mateo Vázquez:

> At this sweet moment I, unlucky, stood
>> With one hand buckled firmly to my blade,
>> The other dripping downward streams of blood;
> Within my breast a cruel thrust had made
>> A deep and gaping wound, and my left hand
>> Was bruised and shattered, past all human aid;
> Yet such was the delicious joy and grand
>> That thrilled my soul, to see the faithless foe
>> Crushed by the valor of the Christian band,
> I hardly knew if I were hurt or no,
>> Although my anguish, cutting and unkind,
>> At times with mortal swooning laid me low.[8]

The center squadrons were the next to make contact. The opposing flagships, the *Sultana* and the *Real*, made straight for each other and grappled. The fight raged for nearly two hours on the narrow battlefield of these pre-eminent galleys locked in a mortal embrace. Ali Pasha's flagship held some 400 janissaries, 300 with harquebuses and 100 with bows; Don Juan's flagship contained some 300 Spanish harquebusiers. Both were reinforced as needed, and both fought gallantly. The turning point came when Ali Pasha, wounded by gunfire, fell before a Spanish soldier, who cut off his head and exposed it on a pike to the view of the Moslems.

The Christian right flank was almost turned by El Uchali, by all odds the most skillful captain of the Turkish forces. Only the alert and decisive line-backing of the Marquis of Santa Cruz, whom Cervantes called 'that thunderbolt of war', averted disaster in Doria's squadron. As it was, El Uchali was able to escape with many of his ships and thus prevent the total destruction or capture of the Turkish fleet. So ended the greatest naval engagement since the battle of Actium, where in 31 BC (and not far from Lepanto) Octavian and Agrippa vanquished the fleet of Anthony and Cleopatra.

Among the bizarre incidents connected with Lepanto was the appearance in the battle of a female dancer known as María la Bailadora. Having stowed away in one of the galleys, on the day of the battle she appeared on deck with a harquebus and demonstrated that she could fight as well as she could dance. Despite his prohibition of women with the fleet, Don Juan commended

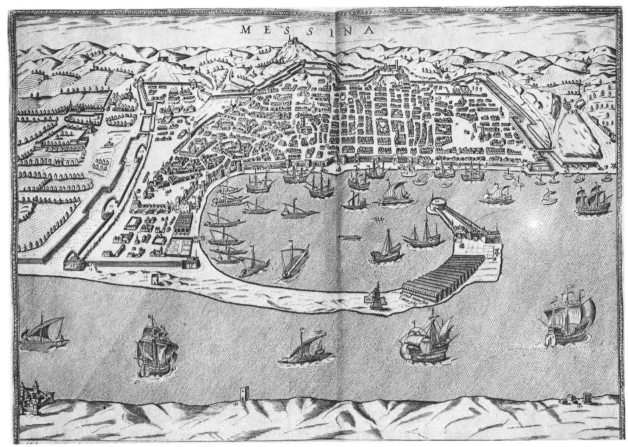

70 View of Messina, the Sicilian port in which the Christian fleet mustered for the 1571 campaign.

her bravery and enlisted her in the famous regiment of Don Lope de Figueroa, whose standing in Don Juan's forces may be judged by his being chosen to carry the news of the great victory to Philip II.[9]

All Christendom rejoiced at this resounding victory over the sea power of the Ottoman Empire, showing all nations, in words penned by Cervantes, 'how wrong they were in supposing that the Turks were invincible on the sea'.[10] The Turkish losses were tremendous: all but 35 of their galleys were captured or sunk; 30,000 men were killed or wounded and 3,000 taken prisoner. The Christians may have suffered nearly as many casualties, but they rescued 15,000 Christian slaves and captured an immense amount of booty.[11] Despite the losses suffered, however, the Turks were able rapidly to rebuild their naval strength and to remain for another ten to fifteen years a sea power to be reckoned with.

On the day after the battle, Don Juan visited the sick and wounded men of his armada. It is likely that he saw and spoke to Miguel or at least heard some account of his bravery, for it appears that an increase in his pay was authorized on that very day.[12] As soon as the most pressing needs of the wounded men and damaged ships were taken care of, the allied fleet moved in stormy weather to Corfu and finally on to Messina, where it arrived at the end of October. Don Juan and his men were accorded a triumphal reception followed by festivities compared to which their send-off had been a pale affair. Cervantes was too ill to participate in the celebration. No doubt he was taken at once to the Messina hospital.

There are good reasons for believing that Miguel arrived at the hospital in critical condition. One can begin to understand how critical by remembering that he had been declared too sick to fight before the battle started, that his left hand was smashed and his chest severely wounded by gunfire, and that approximately three weeks had elapsed between the battle and his admission to a hospital where he might expect to receive the best professional care available. It would not have been extraordinary if Miguel had died in the hospital at Messina. He survived, however, and after hospitalization for six months was discharged in the middle of April 1572 and assigned to the company of Don Manuel Ponce de Leon. Given his fondness for literature, it is possible that he was able to devote some portion of his long convalescence to reading the important Italian writers of the day. It seems certain that he did so at some time during his stay in Italy.

The several squadrons of the Holy League were slow in gathering for the 1572 campaign against the rebuilt Turkish fleet, and when by midsummer they had finally assembled they were able to do little more than play hide-and-seek among the Ionian islands with the Turks, now under the expert and evasive command of El Uchali. Although nothing significant was accomplished in this final campaign of the Holy League, an incident that took place on the anniversary of the battle of Lepanto is worth recording. As Don Juan's armada sailed past the Gulf of Messenia, El Uchali came out to fight. The Turks soon changed their minds, but before they could withdraw the Marquis of Santa Cruz in his flagship the *She-Wolf* captured the galley commanded by the grandson of the Algerian pirate Barbarossa. Miguel was with the fleet; he may even have been aboard the *She-Wolf*. At any rate in *Don Quixote* he has something to say about this engagement:

'In this expedition the galley called *The Prize* was taken. Her captain was a son [in fact, a grandson] of the famous pirate Barbarossa. The flagship of Naples, the *She-Wolf*, took her, under the command of that thunderbolt of war and father to his soldiers, that fortunate and unbeaten captain, Don Alvaro de Bazán, Marquis of Santa Cruz. I do not want to leave out what happened at the capture of *The Prize*. The son of Barbarossa was so cruel, and treated his slaves so badly, that as soon as the rowers saw the *She-Wolf* nearing them and about to board, they all dropped their oars at once and seized hold of him, where he stood at his station shouting at them to row hard. Then they tossed him from bench to bench, from stern to prow, biting him again and again, so that he had hardly gone farther than the mast before his soul had passed into hell; so cruelly did he treat them, as I said, and so bitterly did they hate him.'[13]

The dispersal of the Christian squadrons at the end of October 1572 turned out to be the effective end of the Holy League. One of the principal causes of its

71 Medal commemorating
Don Juan of Austria's
easy capture of Tunis
in 1573.

demise was that before the season for a new campaign came round the Venetians
had signed a separate peace with the Turks.

Miguel and his brother Rodrigo were garrisoned in Naples during the
winter of 1573, and we can only imagine the life they led. When it became
apparent that the annual allied campaign against the Turk would not come
off in 1573 King Philip again directed his thoughts towards North Africa,
which lay much closer to Spanish interests than Turkey itself. It was finally
determined that Don Juan should be sent against Tunis.

Don Juan was enthusiastic about the project, both because it afforded a
chance to repeat his illustrious father's victory at Tunis in 1535 and because
he entertained some hopes of finding there a throne for himself. In early
October, therefore, his forces finally reached Tunis, whose defenders sur-
rendered without a fight on 11 October 1573. Miguel was present at what
soon became a hollow conquest. The following summer El Uchali brought the
rebuilt Turkish fleet to Tunis and recaptured the city on 13 September 1574.
Don Juan tried to go to the relief of the Christian garrison, but Philip was
slow in authorizing the attempt and a series of violent storms caused such
further delay as to render rescue impossible. Miguel was still with the
Christian forces, but on this occasion neither glory nor profit attended their
efforts. Understandably, he was beginning to yearn for a new life back in
Spain. Although he had no way of knowing it, his fighting career was already
finished. He was once more garrisoned in Naples, where he was to remain for
nearly a year.[14]

What love affairs Cervantes may have had before his twenty-eighth birthday may never be known. Most biographers, as we know, have assumed that the duel that sent him fleeing from Spain in 1569 involved a lady, but nothing is certain. It is reasonably certain, however, that in Naples he did fall in love with a beautiful girl, whose memory was to last as long as his life. She appears in his first novel, *La Galatea*, under the name of Silena. They seem to have had a son, whom they chose to call Promontorio and who grew up to be a soldier. That Cervantes never forgot her is clear from a passage in his *Journey to Parnassus*:

> My friend embraced me with a hug full dear,
>   And, holding me, to question he began
>   Whether 'twas I myself he held so near;
> He called me 'father', and I called him 'son',
>   And so the truth was placed in sudden light,
>   Or sunny light, to use a homely pun;
> Said Promontorio: 'Tell me if I'm right
>   That some misfortune, father, brings thee here,
>   With hairs so grey, and in this half-dead plight?'
> 'My son,' I said, 'I trod this country dear
>   In happier hours, and in a merrier vein,
>   While yet my powers were fresh, my vision clear,
> But that same will, that doth all wills constrain,
>   I mean the will of heaven, hath held me bound
>   To seek it now with greater joy than pain.'[15]

'Silena' has never been identified.

72 Neapolitan noble-woman, mid-sixteenth century.

73 Cervantes aged 53, a portrait purporting to be by Juan de Jaurigui, but probably a forgery. >
Overleaf: 74 The battle of Lepanto, described by Cervantes as 'the most memorable and sublime occasion that past ages have known or those to come may hope to know'.

6 Captivity

Having spent six years of his early manhood away from Spain, six years during which he had visited the famous cities of Italy, sailed the Mediterranean from Albania and Greece to the Barbary States and fought in several celebrated battles, Miguel was more than ready to go home. Early in September 1575, he and his brother boarded the galley *Sol* and set sail with three other vessels for Spain.[1] Some time in the third week of September, the little flotilla was scattered by violent storms. The *Sol* was separated from its accompanying ships, and while sailing somewhere between the Rhône estuary and the Catalan coast she was attacked by three or four Algerian galleys under the command of Arnaut Mami. The lone Spanish ship resisted fiercely for several hours but after many casualties was finally overcome. Most of the surviving Christians, including Miguel and his brother Rodrigo, were already aboard the Algerian galleys when the *Sol*'s companion ships hove into sight. At this, the corsairs abandoned the *Sol* and headed at full speed for Algiers. The date was 26 or 27 September 1571. Two years later Miguel memorialized this unhappy event in his verse *Epistle* to King Philip's secretary Mateo Vázquez:

> For in the galley *Sol*, whose lustre fell
> By my ill-fortune, I was doomed to see
> My comrades' ruin, and mine own as well.
> At first our valour shone in high degree,
> Until by sad experience we awoke
> To see how mad was all our bravery!
> These two long years I've born a foreign yoke,
> And my o'erburdened neck hath felt the gall
> Of an accursed sacrilegious folk.[2]

When the corsairs reached Algiers, they divided up the plunder. In the division, Miguel fell to the lot of Dali Mami, who found on Miguel's person letters of recommendation from the Christian commander-in-chief and the Duke of Sessa, and confiscated them. Although Miguel never recovered these letters, he was later able to establish their existence and contents. In 1578, at the request of his family, the Duke of Sessa testified to soldier Cervantes' exemplary conduct under fire and in captivity and to the fact that he, the duke, had given him letters of recommendation to His Majesty.[3] In a similar piece of sworn testimony the same year, a friend and former comrade in

< 75   View of Seville, showing the Guadalquivir in the foreground, part of the city wall and the prominent Giralda Tower.
< 76   View of the Plaza Mayor in Madrid during the reign of Philip III.

Pellerins mores, reue-
nans
de la Mecque

Fille Moresque esclaue   en Alger
ville de Barbarie

Marchant   Juif

77-9 Ottoman cosmopolitanism: left to right, Moorish pilgrims returning from Mecca, a
Moorish slave girl in Algiers and a prosperous Jewish merchant.

arms, Gabriel de Castañeda, declared that he had witnessed his friend's brave
conduct at Lepanto, had been with him in Algiers, and had read letters of
recommendation by Don Juan of Austria recommending to Philip II that
Miguel de Cervantes be given command of one of the new infantry companies being formed in Spain for service in Italy.[4] That such famous Christian
leaders as Don Juan and the Duke of Sessa should write in behalf of a
common soldier and even recommend him for a captaincy induced Dali
Mami to believe that his new slave was not the common soldier he appeared
and claimed to be; he therefore set his ransom at 5,000 escudos,[5] a sum so
grossly miscalculated that it contributed much to the length of Miguel's
enslavement. If he had been privileged to earn his own ransom at the rate he
was later to be paid as a royal commissary, it would have taken him over
thirteen years, working 365 days per year!

In Moslem hands since 1516, Algiers had become the leading port of
North Africa and the most active base of the Barbary pirates. It was governed
by a viceroy known as a Dey, who at the time of Cervantes' arrival was
Ramadan Pasha. Within its walls were crowded more than 12,000 houses; its
streets were for the most part narrower than those of the Santa Cruz quarter
of Seville; it supported something like a hundred mosques, of which at least
a half a dozen were major temples; its public baths were both numerous and
luxurious; its bazaars and markets constituted one of the principal trading
centers of the Mediterranean world. The population in 1575, leaving aside
transients and about 25,000 Christian slaves, consisted mostly of three

80, 81 Janissaries. The one on the right is ready for battle, with his sword and powder horn girded, robe tied back and musket-fuse alight.

groups: Turks, Moors and Jews. Among those usually thought of as Turks were the European renegades, who, partly because of their superior education, were among the most influential residents of Algiers. Good examples of such people would be the already familiar naval commander, El Uchali, and Arnaut Mami, who had led the attack on the galley *Sol* and was an Albanian by birth. The most impressive figures to walk the street of Algiers were the dreaded janissaries, that strange corps of the Turkish army whose ranks were filled by forced levies of Christian youths trained to be the *élite* fighting men of the Ottoman Empire. Because of their origins, their early segregation from the population at large and their exceptional physical training, they constituted a separate and potentially dangerous element within the Empire, one capable on occasion of making and breaking sultans. Superb on the battlefield, they were often irresponsible and quarrelsome in times of peace. Father Diego de Haedo, writing at the end of the sixteenth century, had this to say about their arrogance and special status:

'If anyone not a janissary were to strike a janissary or even push him merely to get him out of the way or lay hand on his chest or arm, the penalty is to have the hand cut off; to kill a janissary means for the offender to be burned alive, or impaled, or hooked, or to have his bones smashed with a mace, as we have seen done to so many ....'[6]

It goes without saying that the inhabitants of Algiers tried to keep clear of such privileged and brutal men.

Some of the 25,000 Christian captives were kept at home by their masters; others were held in large prison houses called *bagnios*. The royal *bagnio*, where Miguel was to be confined on two separate occasions, was a rectangular building 70 feet long by 40 feet wide. It contained many rooms on upper and lower floors around a central patio where there was a cistern of good water. One of the lower rooms was a kind of chapel. Since there were always priests among the Christian slaves, it was possible to hear mass and sermons all year long. On Church holidays so many Christians wanted to hear mass that it had to be said in the patio, where the Moorish guards made money charging admission. The religious services held in the *bagnios* and an occasional play were about the only consolations in the captives' lives.[7]

Father Haedo's account of how these captives were treated renders more than understandable Miguel's repeated attempts at escape, even though the consequences of failure were usually mutilation or death.

'They loaded them with so many chains and irons that they could scarcely move; some with thick fetters, others with heavy cross-irons, others with great iron shackles, others with frightful chains, which some carry on their shoulders and others around their bodies or their necks.... Most of them are locked up in houses or *bagnios*, in dark, damp, stinking rooms, and even underground in narrow caves and gloomy dungeons. There they make them grind continuously by the light of a lamp, if they have one, with hand-operated mills, which for this purpose they make and keep in all houses.... For food and drink they are given only water and two little loaves of bran or barley bread.... If some of them are allowed out of doors, it is only to labor in public works or building houses or repairing walls.... Domestic service, who performs it but these wretched men and with their chains on their backs? They supply the houses with firewood, fetch water, carry bread to the ovens, go to the mills, sweep the houses, wash the corridors, patios and vestibules, cure the horses, plough the fields, pasture the cows and other cattle, tend the vineyards, plant, cultivate, water and protect the gardens and orchards.... And in all these labors they have almost always at their heels some Moor or vile Negro as a guard, who with a tough stick or cane is constantly beating them and treading on their heels, without letting them rest or wipe the sweat from their brows. And if perchance, exhausted by the immense labor as well as by the cruel weight of their irons and chains, they should ease up a little and let their chains fall from their shoulders (to give some relief to their tired and afflicted members), this is in no wise permitted them; on the contrary, the sad and miserable Christian (as though he were made of marble or steel) must carry the heavy irons on his back as well as the hoe in his hands.... Most of them go barefoot, naked and hungry under the sun, the moon, the rain, the wind, the cold and the heat.... All the streets of the city are filled with numberless Christians so sick, so emaciated, so worn, so consumed and so disfigured that they can hardly stand or be recognized.'[8]

This was a Christian's life in the city where, as Cervantes wrote in the Prologue to his *Exemplary Novels*, he 'learned to be patient in adversity'.

84

Miguel had not been long in Algiers when he met some old friends, one of whom was Gabriel de Castañeda, who had been with him at Lepanto and was later captured by the Turks in the fort that guarded the Gulf of Tunis. To Gabriel and other fellow slaves Cervantes revealed a plan of escape by land to the Spanish-held port of Oran. The plan was accepted and left to Miguel's direction, even though he was outranked by several soldiers in the group. His own words tell the story in brief:

'Desiring to do good and set some Christians free, he [Cervantes here speaks of himself in the third person] sought a Moor to lead him and them by land to Oran. The aforesaid Moor travelled with them for several days and then abandoned them; and so they were obliged to return to Algiers, where Miguel de Cervantes was badly treated by his master and kept with more chains, more guard, and more confinement.'[9]

This ill-fated attempt at escape must have taken place in the late winter of 1576, when Miguel was 29. Early the next spring two of Miguel's companions were ransomed and returned to Spain. They were Gabriel de Castañeda and Antonio Marco, and both carried letters to Miguel's father in Madrid, who was moved to seek with all haste the ransom for his sons.

About this time the Order of Our Lady of Mercy undertook a campaign to raise money to ransom in Algiers as many Christian slaves as possible. In charge of this charitable undertaking were Friar Jorge de Olivar, Friar Jorge de Ongay and Friar Jerónimo de Antich, all of whom sailed in due time to Algiers to negotiate the redemption of the Christians. Aware of this venture, the Cervantes family redoubled their efforts to raise money for the deliverance of their sons. First Rodrigo senior appealed to the Royal Council for a subvention. The Council turned him down, partly, one suspects, because they were flooded with similar appeals. Then his wife, feigning widowhood, petitioned the Council of the Crusade, describing the present plight of her sons and detailing the record of their services to the king. Doña Leonor was luckier than her husband, but the 60 escudos granted to her by royal decree on 6 December 1576 were but a small fraction of what was needed. Next, the family tried, but without avail, to collect a debt of 800 ducats owed to them by a certain Pedro Sánchez de Córdoba.[10] Finally, as a measure of their devotion and despair, they sold all their goods. How much money they realized on this sale is not known, but all of it, along with the modest royal subvention, was turned over to the three Mercedarian friars, who on 30 March 1577 sailed from Valencia and reached Algiers three weeks later.

Notified by the friars of the ransom money available, Rodrigo and Miguel began to negotiate with their respective masters. Rodrigo's negotiations went better than Miguel's, mostly because his master, Ramadan Pasha, was not a man driven by greed. On the other hand, Dali Mami, the Greek renegade into whose hands Miguel had fallen, was excessively greedy and would consider nothing less than 500 escudos for Miguel. When it became apparent that he would not reconsider this price, Miguel renounced his share of the ransom money in favor of his brother, whose freedom was thus

EL REY

C. 53

Iuan san dy caguirre nro criado y rreceptor delas ymposiciones y de
pensaçiones que por el commissario general dela cruçada se haçen enesta corte
sabed que doña leonor decortinas vezina desta villa demadrid nos hi
zo relaçion que ella tiene dos hijos que se llaman miguel y rrodrigo dez
rbantes los quales nos han seruido en ytalia y en flandes y en las
galeras y enlas demas ocaçiones que se han ofreçido y finalmente
se hallaron en la batalla naual donde al vno dellos le cortaron vna
mano y el otro mancaron y que viniendose a estos Reynos enla galera
sol deque venia por capitan carrillo los captiuaron los moros de argel ado
nde alpresente estan captiuos y pues como nos podia constar porçierta
ynformacion quel enel nro consejo dela cruçada auia presentado y nos
supp.co que atento aloque los suso dichos nos auian seruido y aque no te
nia con que poder los rrescatar por ser muy pobre le hiçiesemos m.d de
le mandar dar algunos mrs para ayuda al rrescate delos dichos sus
fijos delos que en vro poder estauan depositados Para redempçion
de cautiuos loqual visto por el commissario general dela dicha cruça
da y enel nro consejo della atento aque por la dicha ynformacion con
sta del dicho catiuerio y seruicio delos dichos miguel y rrodrigo dezr
bantes hemos tenido por bien delesmandar librar en vos para
ayuda al dicho su rrescate sesenta escudos deoro que valen veinte
y quatro mill mrs Por ende os mandamos que delos mrs que en vro
poder estan depositados para redempçion decautiuos deis y paguei
ala dicha doña leonor decortinas oaquien supoder ouiere los dich.s
sesenta escudos para ayuda al rrescate decada vno dellos trey
nta scudos los quales le mandamos librar por quanto se ha ho
bligado y dado fianças deque dentro devn año primero segui

assured and on whom Miguel pinned some of his hopes for the success of a second plan of escape now germinating in his mind. At this point, his thoughts might have run on similar lines to those of the Captive Captain in *Don Quixote*, who, speaking of his own enslavement, said: 'For I never gave up hope of gaining my liberty, and when the result did not shape with my design in such plans as I contrived, worked out and put in practice, I never gave up, but immediately devised some new hope, never mind how slender and weak, to keep me going.'[11]

In the late spring of 1577, negotiations for the release of Christian prisoners were interrupted by the naming of a new viceroy of Algiers, a certain Hassan Pasha (known to Cervantes as Azán Agá). He is important to our story, for Miguel became his slave for five months and had to endure his rule until 1580. It is a kind of miracle that Miguel survived this new relationship. Again some words of the Captive Captain are pertinent:

'Nothing disturbed us so much as to hear and witness, wherever we went, the unparalleled and incredible cruelty which my master practised on Christians. Every day he hanged someone, impaled another, and cut off the ears of a third; and this on the slightest excuse or on none at all, so that even the Turks acknowledged that he did it only for the sake of doing it, and because it was in his nature to be the murderer of the entire human race. The only one who held his own with him was a Spanish soldier, called something de Saavedra; for his master never so much as struck him, nor bade anyone else strike him, nor even spoke a rough word to him, though he did things which those people will remember for many years, all in efforts to recover his liberty, and the rest of us were afraid that his least actions would be punished by impaling, as he himself feared they would be more than once. And if it were not for lack of time I would tell you something about that soldier's deeds, which you would find more entertaining and surprising than this story of mine.'[12]

Ramadan Pasha left Algiers two months before the new viceroy arrived on 29 June 1577. As soon as possible, the three friars tried to resume with Hassan Pasha the negotiations suspended when Ramadan Pasha left. But the greed of the new Dey put in jeopardy the fate of some of the 106 Christians who had been given to believe that ransom money had arrived for them. In the end, heroic Friar Jorge de Olivar volunteered to remain in Algiers as a slave so that the others would be allowed to leave; this they did on 24 August 1577, landing on Spanish soil near Valencia on the 29th. Rodrigo was one of the fortunate 106 Christians who in the cathedral of Valencia on 1 September gave heartfelt thanks to God for their deliverance.

During his long years of captivity in Algiers, Miguel became acquainted with many of the Christian slaves. He took a special interest in the various writers whose unhappy fate deposited them there, and it is not venturesome to suppose that on propitious occasions there was much lively talk of literature and exchange of literary pieces. One of Cervantes' companions in confinement later testified that Miguel often devoted himself to the compo-

< 82 Part of the royal letters patent granting Cervantes' mother 60 escudos towards the ransom of her sons from Algerian captivity.

sition of verses in praise of the Lord and the Virgin Mary. It is highly probable that some of the poetry scattered through the early works published after his return to Spain was written in Africa. One of his most celebrated poems, the verse *Epistle to Mateo Vázquez* (already quoted with reference to the battle of Lepanto), was certainly composed in Algiers. In fact, it was among the papers carried back to Spain by Rodrigo in behalf of his brother's personal campaign to help his fellow prisoners. In the poem he pleaded with King Philip to rescue them:

> Thou hast the keys, within thy hand they lie,
>   To unlock the prison, dismal and profound,
>   Where twenty thousand Christians pine and die.
> They all, as I, are groaning on the ground,
>   Pressing with hands and knees the cursed place,
>   With most inhuman tortures girdled round!
> Most potent Sire, they beg thee of thy grace
>   To turn, and that right soon, thy pitying eyes
>   On theirs, whence tears do run in endless chase.
> Since now from out thy land pale Discord flies,
>   Which hitherto hath wearied out thy heart,
>   And peace unbroken all around thee lies,
> Be thine the task, good King, with fitting art
>   To end the work, in which with courage high
>   Thine honoured father took the foremost part.[13]

83 Sixteenth-century knight of the Order of St John, wearing the Order's distinctive version of the Maltese cross.

But Rodrigo carried papers that held more promise of prompt results than the *Epistle* to Philip's secretary. They were letters addressed to the viceroys of Valencia, Mallorca and Ibiza written by two prominent knights of the Order of Saint John: Don Antonio de Toledo and Don Francisco de Valencia. The purpose of the letters was to request that a rescue ship be directed to a certain spot on the Algerian coast on a specified night in late September. At this place, about three miles from the city of Algiers, there was a cave where Miguel had hidden some fourteen Christians to await rescue by sea. That he was able to do such things while himself a prisoner and penniless to boot is in itself a minor miracle.

Many of the Christian slaves held for ransom were allowed on occasions to wander about the city with some freedom. The punishments meted out to anyone helping them to escape were too horrible to make it likely that very many people would be tempted to do so. And then the slaves usually wore chains and other irons calculated to render flight extremely difficult if not impossible. During the critical weeks in September when Miguel was completing plans for the second attempt at escape the fortunate absence at sea of his master seems to have afforded him more freedom than usual to move about. He arranged that the Christian gardener of an estate near the cave should keep watch over it and warn of approaching danger and that an ex-renegade Christian from Spanish Morocco known as 'El Dorador' should buy provisions and deliver them at night. Miguel's role, aside from being chief

88

instigator and planner, was to collect the money required to buy provisions. How much money he begged and borrowed for this purpose can only be guessed, but he succeeded in keeping his companions fed until the fateful night of the rendezvous.

Eight days before the appointed arrival of the frigate, that is, on 20 September 1577, Miguel disappeared from Algiers and joined his friends in the cave. On the night of the 28th no message came to the worrying prisoners. They spent the 29th in deepening anxiety, and on the 30th Hassan Pasha sent armed guards to arrest them and lead them back to Algiers.

Rodrigo had faithfully discharged his mission in Valencia; a suitable frigate was found and outfitted, which sailed from Mallorca in time to meet the secret schedule. The frigate did appear off the African coast on 28 September but was seen and had to withdraw. It returned the following night only to be captured. 'El Dorador', realizing the plan had failed and that he might be implicated, hurried to Hassan Pasha with two items of intelligence: one, that he wished to become a Moslem again; the other, that Miguel de Cervantes had hidden some Christians in a cave and arranged for a Spanish boat to come to their rescue. For his part in the affair, the Christian gardener was strung up by one leg until he died. Hassan Pasha called Cervantes into his presence. Speaking of himself in the third person, Cervantes described his interview with the Dey as follows:

'Presented thus before King Hassan, tied, alone, without his companions, the aforesaid King, with threats of death and torture, wishing to know how the business came about, he [Cervantes] with much constancy said that he was the author of the whole affair, and beseeched his Highness, if someone had to be punished, that it should be he alone, since he alone was to blame for everything'.[14]

Once more, however, Cervantes evaded the common fate of escapees.

Father Haedo's report of this affair, after mentioning that on four occasions Cervantes found himself in imminent danger of execution by impalement, hooking, or burning alive, concludes with these words:

'One could write a separate history of the things that happened in that cave during the seven months the Christians were there and of the captivity and exploits of Miguel de Cervantes. Hassan Pasha, King of Algiers, used to say that if he could keep that maimed Spaniard under guard, his Christian slaves, his ships, and even his whole city would be safe; so much did he fear the scheming of Miguel de Cervantes....'[15]

There may be more than an exaggerated expression of irritation in Hassan Pasha's statement about keeping his city safe by keeping the maimed Spaniard under guard. There are indications that Cervantes had been scheming to organize a great uprising of Christian slaves in Algiers. Haedo seems to be hinting at such a possibility when he writes of Cervantes and his activities: 'If good luck had corresponded to his courage, industry and schemes, today would be the day that Algiers belonged to Christians, for his designs aspired to nothing less....'[16] In any case, Hassan Pasha loaded him with irons and locked him up in the royal *bagnio*, where he was to remain for some five months.

Some time towards the end of these five months, Miguel planned another escape by the overland route to the port of Oran. Secretly he sent a trusted Moor with a letter to the Spanish commander of that port. Unhappily, the Moor was intercepted and sent back to Hassan Pasha along with the incriminating letter signed by Cervantes. Hassan was enraged and ordered cruel penalties for both offenders: impalement for the Moor, who died bravely without confessing anything, and two thousand blows for Cervantes, which meant certain death. Happily, the blows were never administered. Influential friends interceded for the brave but troublesome Spaniard. Both they and present-day readers of his biography have marveled that he escaped the brutal fate of so many other Christian slaves, especially as his master was notorious for his cruelty. One circumstance that tended to protect him was the belief that he was a personage who would bring a high ransom. To kill him would be to throw away treasure. Still, other men of substantial ransom had been killed with less provocation. What, then, saved him? It may have been the unique example he set of courage, steadfastness and generosity — some quality of the man himself that imposed restraint on a master noted for his lack of it. In any event, all that Hassan did this time was to have Miguel thrown out of the royal *bagnio* and returned to his owner, Dali Mami.

The *Epistle to Mateo Vázquez*, sent in the hope that it would come to King Philip's notice, apparently attracted no attention at all, or if it did, it produced no help for Miguel and his fellow captives. Meanwhile the Cervantes family continued their search for the ransom money. In her petitioning for government assistance, his mother resumed her intermittent role as widow. His sisters Andrea and Magdalena gave up their dowries to contribute to the ransom fund. Learning that Trinitarian friars (under the leadership of Friar Juan Gil, procurator general of the Trinitarian Order) were preparing a rescue trip to Algiers, Doña Leonor redoubled her efforts to raise more money in time to take advantage of their rescue mission. On 31 July 1579, Friar Juan Gil and Friar Antón de la Bella acknowledged receipt of 250 escudos from Doña Leonor, plus the promise of 50 more from Andrea, to buy Miguel's freedom.

Some two months after the Trinitarian friars received money for Miguel's ransom and about a year before his release was finally effected, he was actively plotting a fourth attempt at escape. He had made friends with a Spanish renegade who as a Christian had been called Licentiate Girón but was now known in Algiers as Abderráhmen. As a renegade of good standing, he could buy a frigate without incurring suspicion. This he agreed to do for Cervantes with money which the latter had obtained from a Valencian merchant by the name of Onofre Ejarque. The boat was duly purchased and preparations for the escape of Miguel and many of his friends were well under way when once more Hassan Pasha learned of the plot. This time the informer was a captive Dominican friar named Juan Blanco de Paz. This despicable friar belonged to Hassan Pasha himself. No motive for his perfidy is known beyond the desire to win favor with his master. His treachery earned him a gold coin and a jar of butter from Hassan, the bitter enmity of Cervantes and the angry contempt of the Spanish colony.[17] Onofre Ejarque, aware that the Dey knew of the plot and that he might attempt to torture Miguel into revealing the names of his accomplices, offered to pay Miguel's ransom so that he could leave Algiers at once. Cervantes, who was then in hiding, assured the Valencian merchant that under no circumstances would he ever implicate anyone but himself. Then Hassan issued a public proclamation to the effect that anyone caught hiding Cervantes would forfeit his life, and, afraid that his friends might be made to suffer on his account, Miguel came out of hiding and turned himself in. The Dey had his hands tied and a noose put around his neck and again threatened him with torture in an effort to discover his associates, but to no avail. Miguel assumed full responsibility for this attempt at escape as he had for the three previous ones. This time the Dey loaded him with shackles and chains and locked him in the Moorish jail, where he was confined for about five months. It was probably March 1580 when he was released from jail. At about this time, Hassan Pasha purchased him from Dali Mami and put him for the second time in the royal *bagnio*.

84 Part of a document signed by Friar Juan Gil in Algiers testifying to Cervantes' good character; it is dated 22 October 1580.

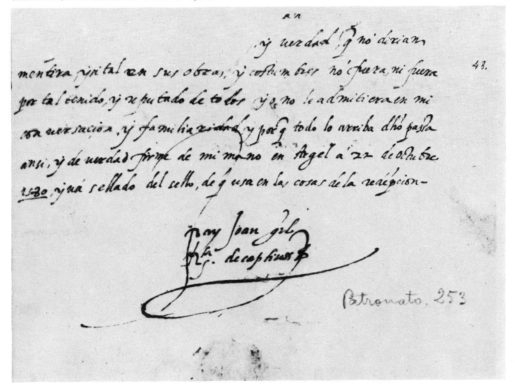

In his play *The Bagnios of Algiers*, Cervantes wrote of a defiant Christian whose ears were cut off in punishment for his attempt to escape by the overland route. Taunted by a Moor, the Christian replied:

> If you don't double my shackles,
> Bear in mind I'll be gone:
> If you lop off everything
> And leave me even worse
> Than I see myself now,
> I desire so to be free,
> That I'll settle for flight
> By land or by wind
> By water and by fire,
> Because with freedom in mind
> I'll try anything at all
> That offers me that joy.[18]

It is easy to imagine Miguel in such a mood and pleasant to remember that he was spared the mutilations he had seen inflicted on so many slaves caught in attempted flight.[19]

Miguel had spent more than four and a half years of his young manhood in captivity when Friar Juan Gil and his companion set sail on their rescue mission to Algiers, where they arrived on 29 May 1580. The two friars began at once to seek out the Christians for whom they had collected ransom money. This was not easy or, in some cases, possible, since some of the slaves had been taken out of the city by their owners. In the months of June and July, however, Friars Juan and Antón did locate 108 Christians whose ransoms they were able to negotiate successfully. With these Friar Antón sailed in early August for Spain.

As one of the most celebrated and respected Christians in Algiers, Miguel was not hard to locate. Friar Juan had met him soon after his own arrival and had already tried unsuccessfully to negotiate his release. Since Hassan Pasha had paid 500 escudos for Cervantes, he was naturally unwilling to accept the 300 escudos offered by Miguel's family. Remaining in Algiers to continue his efforts in behalf of his captive compatriots, Friar Juan tried again to persuade the Dey to set Miguel free, but the Turk was adamant.

Meanwhile, the three years of the Dey's corrupt and intemperate rule of Algiers had brought the city to the verge of famine. So many complaints were received in Constantinople that Hassan was finally recalled. On the morning of 19 September 1580, he was ready to sail out of Algiers with his entire retinue of servants and slaves. Miguel appeared to be doomed to slavery for the rest of his life, since few Spaniards ever escaped from Constantinople. His feelings as he boarded Hassan's galley must have been gloomy indeed. But once again the tides of fortune turned before it was too late: Friar Juan came aboard prepared to add to Miguel's ransom some money which he had collected for other Christians not yet located. The Dey at last agreed to accept 500 escudos provided they were all paid in coins of

85   Obverse and reverse of an eight-real piece of Philip II.

Spanish gold. Given the shortness of time, this demand created severe new difficulties for Friar Juan, but he overcame them and Miguel finally attained that liberty to which, in Don Quixote's words, 'no treasures the earth contains or the sea conceals can be compared to'.[20] In passing, it should be said that Friar Juan Gil suffered many personal indignities and risked his life repeatedly during the long months he spent in Algiers working for the release of Christian slaves.

However longingly 'the eyes of desire' were fixed on Spain, Miguel had to wait more than a month for a ship to take him home. But he had a number of things to occupy his time. For example, he had to post bond to cover the amount of money added by Friar Juan to his ransom. The most important thing he did, however, was to collect and prepare a lengthy testimonial (known as the *Información de Argel*) describing his conduct during his five years of Algerian confinement. The testimony collected in this document was given by the most respected Christians in Algiers, some of whom had shared in Cervantes' military campaigns as well as in his captivity. These Christians were asked to answer twenty-five questions formulated by Cervantes, each of which concerned one of his activities during his Algerian captivity, including his role in the four attempts at escape narrated in this chapter. The witnesses were invited, in effect, to confirm the truth of Miguel's statements. The questions and answers might prove useful in at least two ways: in seeking preferment from the Royal Council in Madrid, and in defending himself against possible calumnies by his enemy Juan Blanco de Paz, who had already tried unsuccessfully to promote unfavorable reports about him.[21] When completed, the testimony was notarized in the presence of Friar Juan, who could be said to represent in Algiers both the Church and the Spanish king.

This testimonial is one of the prime sources of information about Cervantes' life in North Africa, and it records the warm and widespread esteem in which he was held by the Spanish colony. Don Diego de Bonavides, who arrived in Algiers only two months before Cervantes was ransomed, found him so kind and helpful to a newcomer that he was moved to testify that he had found in Cervantes both a father and a mother.[22] Lieutenant Luis de Pedrosa spoke of the fortitude with which Miguel had faced the probability of torture and death while assuming entire responsibility for frustrated schemes of escape: 'He won great fame, praise, and crowning honor, and was worthy of great reward, because, although there were other gentlemen no less deserving, Cervantes excelled in doing good to captives and in matters of honor. He showed a very special grace in everything, being so discreet and wise that few were his equals.'[23] Friar Juan Gil himself crowns the *Información de Argel* with his own sober testimony:

'I have dealt and conversed and communicated on private and familiar terms with the aforesaid Miguel de Cervantes, in whose behalf this testimonial was made, and I know him as a very honorable person who has served His Majesty for many years; particularly in his captivity has he done things for which he deserves His Majesty's favor, as is fully testified by the witnesses recorded above... If in his acts and customs he were not as described and if he were not so reputed and regarded, I would not have admitted him to my conversation and intimacy....'[24]

On 24 October 1580, the brave comrade in arms and faithful companion in captivity was able to make a second start for home. For the first time in twelve years he was to set foot on Spanish soil. He landed, late in the same month, in the Valencian town of Denia. From there he made his way promptly to Valencia, whence he sent a letter to his father informing him of his freedom and of his need for money to pay back the Trinitarian friars and the Valencian merchants who had advanced extra money to complete his ransom. Whether to settle such business matters or for other reasons, he remained something more than a month in Valencia, and it was early in December when he set out for Madrid. He was thirty-three now, and had seen a good deal of life and the world. Both he and Madrid had changed since 1568. He had left it a fugitive from justice and re-entered it with the credentials of a hero. But would they be recognized in the bureaucratic capital of Philip II?

7 Petitioner at Court

It seems somehow fitting that the soldier of Lepanto should have been born in the days of that Christian knight, Charles V, while his new career as civil servant and man of letters should unfold mostly in the second half of the reign of the Prudent King, Philip II. If one believes that kings may sometimes stamp their character on the ages in which they live, one can almost distinguish the character of the two halves of the sixteenth century in Spain by contrasting Titian's equestrian portrait of Charles V with El Greco's painting often called *The Dream of Philip II*. Titian, representing the jutting-jawed emperor clad in armor and astride a spirited Spanish horse caparisoned in scarlet, gives his subject the air of a knight about to enter battle confident in his stout lance and strong right arm. El Greco's painting (inspired by a verse from St Paul's letter to the Philippians, 2.10-11: 'that at the name of Jesus every knee should bow, in heaven, on earth, and in the depths') represents in the most brilliant lights and colors of a painter noted for his chromatic brilliance the hosts of Heaven, Hell and Earth subordinated to an anagram of Jesus Christ shining in the unearthly golden light of the Zenith. In the approximate center of the lower half of the picture, attired in black, Philip kneels in prayer, his eyes turned upwards toward the heavenly host. The contrasting portraits may serve to remind us that Philip was not a warrior but a deeply religious man who put his trust in God and in his own unending devotion to administration. He was, as Garrett Mattingly put it, 'the chief clerk of the Spanish Empire'.[1] Since his empire was the largest ever to be ruled by one man and since he was unwilling to delegate any decision of administration or government to his subordinates, he must have dealt personally with more state papers than any monarch in history. His willingness to assume this Herculean task no doubt saved him from most of whatever disloyalty or irresponsibility a ruler may expect from his subordinates, but it made his court a very slow place to dispatch business. Cervantes would soon have occasion, and more than once, to discover this for himself.

Miguel reached Madrid sometime in December. After twelve long years of separation, his homecoming was a joyous occasion. His brother Rodrigo had re-enlisted in the army and was not in Madrid. His sister, Sor Luisa of Bethlehem, was still living in the Carmelite convent in Alcalá de Henares, so he probably did not see her at this time. But his sisters Andrea and Magdalena, still unwed, were in the capital and eager to see him. His old teacher López de Hoyos continued to run the same City School of Madrid, and he probably

86 King Sebastian of Portugal (1557-78), whose death at Alcázarquivir effectively brought his kingdom under Philip II's control.

87 English engraving of 'the rare and straunge bataille' of Alcázarquivir in 1578. >

conversed with other literary friends whom we know to have been in Madrid at the time. One of them, Luis Gálvez de Montalvo, wrote a laudatory sonnet intended to be prefixed to the pastoral novel Miguel was then working on. It is pertinent to reproduce it here, because it salutes his safe return to Spain as well as suggesting that Cervantes already enjoyed a reputation as a poet:

TO CERVANTES

What time the Moormen held thy body chained,
　　And pressed thy captive neck beneath their feet,
　　Whereas thy soul, with rigour more complete
Bound fast to Faith, a higher freedom gained,
All heaven rejoiced; but this our land remained
　　Without thee widowed, and the royal seat
　　Bewailed the absence of our Muses sweet,
While in its halls a cheerless silence reigned;
But now thou bringest to our country dear
　　An unchained body, and a healthy mind,
　　Freed from the trammels of a savage host,
Heaven draws the veil that hid thy merit clear;
　　The land receives thee with a welcome kind,
　　And Spain regains the Muses she had lost. [2]

But Miguel had serious business to attend to, such as the tasks of finding money to pay his ransom debts and of finding gainful employment. His family, poor as ever, had already spent on him more than they could afford. It seemed to be the time to use at court the testimonials to his conduct in captivity as well as his military record in the hope of procuring a livelihood. But the court was where the king was, and the king was not in Madrid.

A year after Philip II ascended the Spanish throne, his cousin Sebastian had become king of Portugal. Imbued with fanatical religious fervor, Sebastian considered himself another Christian knight and dreamed of winning glory by a crusade against the Moslem infidels of North Africa. In 1577 a disputed

96

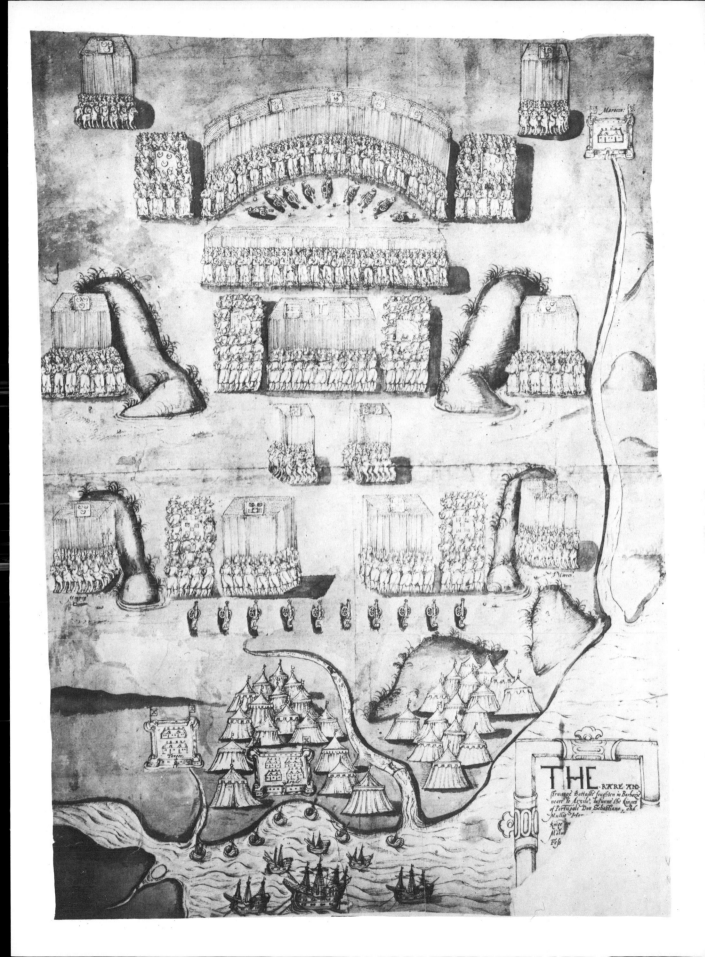

Marocco:

Maroco

Tunggr

THE RARE AND
straung Battaile foughten in Barbaria
neare to Arzile, betwene the Kinges
of Portugale Don Sebastiano, and
Mullie Soldon
Anno Do
M D
LXXviij

succession to the Moroccan throne appeared to provide him with the opportunity he had been waiting for. Against the advice of his ministers, his cousin Philip II, and the Pope, he prepared an expeditionary force of about 17,000 men and set sail across the Straits of Gibraltar in the summer of 1578. The sultan of Morocco, aided and advised by a substantial number of Moriscos from Granada, allowed Sebastian to march inland for five days, thus exhausting the Portuguese army and rendering rapid communication with their fleet impossible. Then, on 4 August 1578, the Moroccans with vastly superior forces attacked and destroyed the Portuguese army at Alcázarquivir, and only about 1,000 men escaped. This engagement is sometimes called the 'battle of the three kings', since in it the sultan of Morocco, the Moorish pretender to his throne and Sebastian all lost their lives.

Sebastian was succeeded by his aged great-uncle, Cardinal Henry, whose reign ended with his death on 31 January 1580, leaving some seven claimants to vie for the Portuguese throne. Of these, the two strongest were Philip II and Don Antonio, the Prior of Crato. They were both direct descendants of the Portuguese King Manuel I, but Philip's claim was stronger, because he commanded more power and because Antonio was illegitimate. With the help of a Spanish army under the Duke of Alba and a Spanish fleet under the Marquis of Santa Cruz, it took Philip only a few months to persuade the Portuguese nation that he was indeed the rightful heir to the throne. When Cervantes was ready to present himself to Philip, therefore, the latter was in the Extremaduran city of Badajoz waiting to proceed to the Portuguese town of Thomar to receive the oath of allegiance from the Cortes before passing on to Lisbon for his coronation.[3]

Miguel must have caught up with the court in Thomar, for it was in that town that, on 21 May 1581, he received a royal order by which he was to earn 100 ducats for undertaking a confidential mission to North Africa. Mateo Vázquez was probably responsible for this modest commission, which, despite its modesty, Miguel was glad to accept. Two reasons have been alleged for the mission: one has to do with the king's concern over disobedience on the part of Portuguese officials in Africa, the other is his desire to discover why El Uchali had mobilized the Turkish fleet.[4]

Miguel set out at once for the North African coasts he had so recently left. His assignment took him to Oran and to Mostaganem. In Oran he talked with the Spanish general Martín de Córdoba, that same friend to whom he had secretly sent a Moorish messenger on the occasion of his third attempt to escape from Algiers. No copy of Cervantes' report to the king has been found; some day it may be discovered among the still uncatalogued papers in the Escorial. One may suppose however, that his mission was successful. There is every reason to think that Don Martín de Córdoba received him cordially and informed him fully on the situation in North Africa. The general was a veteran of many a battle in North Africa between Moslems and Spaniards, and, like Miguel, he had been a captive in Algiers. He and his brother Alonso had distinguished themselves in the heroic defense of Oran and Mazalquivir early in 1563. So, quite apart from Cervantes' mission, he and Don Martín had a lot of African experience about which to compare notes. Cervantes seems to have remembered much of their conversation, for many years later he wrote a play called *The Gallant Spaniard* which tells a romantic story set against the background of the siege of Oran. Two of the characters in the play are Don Martín of Córdoba and his brother Don Alonso.

Cervantes discharged his assignment promptly. By 26 June 1581, a little over a month after his departure, he was back in the Spanish port of Cartagena, where he received the final payment on the 100 ducats promised him. He headed straight for Lisbon, into which city the king had made his solemn entrance on 29 June 1581 but which Miguel could not expect to reach from the other coast of Spain until late July.

Back in the Portuguese capital, Cervantes made his report on what he had learned from his talks in North Africa. Then for something like seven months he remained in Lisbon petitioning for employment, either in the form of another temporary commission like the one he had just completed or a position in the Spanish colonies in America. But he had no luck. It was a bad time for a Castilian to expect notice at court. King Philip was trying hard to ingratiate himself with his new Portuguese subjects, and he and his officials had time only for them. And then, as usual, there were grave problems demanding the royal attention, such as the threatened insurrection in the Azores – a revolt that could not under any circumstances be tolerated by Spain since these islands were essential to communication with the colonies in America.

The problem of the Azores was partly resolved by the great Spanish naval victory in July 1582 in which the Marquis of Santa Cruz defeated the French

89 Preparations being made in Cádiz for the departure of an expedition to the West Indies.

forces sent by Catherine de Medici to support Don Antonio, the Prior of Crato, in his continuing struggle for the Portuguese throne. It was another spectacular victory for the Marquis, who won it with only 25 warships against the 60 of Don Antonio. Some biographers have suggested that Miguel participated in this battle, but there is no evidence to support this view. His brother Rodrigo, on the other hand, almost certainly did take part in it.

Soon after Miguel got back to Lisbon from his trip to North Africa what had finally looked like a promising love affair between his sister Magdalena and a Basque gentleman named Pérez de Alcega was drawing to the kind of unhappy end that seemed to be the destiny of the Cervantes girls. Pérez de Alcega, faced with the prospect of a suit for breach of promise, proposed a settlement of 300 ducats, which Magdalena finally accepted. Deeply hurt by this disappointment in love, Magdalena donned, at the age of twenty-nine, the somber garb of a lay sister, and resolved to devote the rest of her life to piety and good works.

Although Miguel's quest for employment was unsuccessful, he may still have enjoyed his stay in Lisbon. An active trading center for two great overseas empires, the city was bustling, prosperous and entertaining:

'Here love and modesty join hands and walk together, courtesy does not suffer the presence of arrogance, and bravery does not consent to the approach of cowardice. All its residents are agreeable, are courteous, are liberal and are lovers, because they are discreet. The city is the greatest of Europe and the one of greatest commerce; in it are unloaded the riches of the East, which from it are distributed throughout the universe; its port can contain not only such ships as can be counted but movable forests of masts; the beauty of its women provokes wonder and love; the gallantry of its men is, as they say, beyond belief; in short, this is the land that pays to Heaven abundant and holy tribute.'[5]

But Cervantes was rapidly running out of funds. The 100 ducats paid him for his mission to Africa could not support him indefinitely. Now it was rumored that the court might soon return to Madrid. If so, a Spanish veteran might stand a better chance there, and Miguel decided to return to the Spanish capital. It is certain that he was there by 17 February 1582, for on that date he sent to Lisbon a letter addressed to the secretary of the Council of the Indies. The secretary was Antonio de Eraso, and the letter shows that Miguel had been counting on Eraso's help to find a post in America:

'Illustrious Sir:
Secretary Valmaseda has shown toward me... the kindness I expected, but neither his solicitude nor my diligence can offset my meager luck, which in this business amounts to my learning that the office I applied for is not conferred by His Majesty; and so I must wait for the dispatch boat to see if it brings news of an opening, because all those that existed on this side of the water are already filled, as I have been told by Señor Valmaseda, who I know has truly tried to discover something that I might apply for. For his good will I beg Your Grace to give him the thanks he deserves, so that he will understand that I am not ungrateful. In the meantime, I entertain myself rearing *Galatea*, which is the

book I told Your Grace I was composing. When she has grown a bit more, she will go to kiss Your Grace's hands and to receive the correction and emendation I may not have known how to give her. May Our Lord in His power keep and prosper the illustrious person of Your Grace. From Madrid, 17 February 1582.'[6]

After the failure of his pretensions to royal preferment, Miguel devoted himself for a time wholeheartedly to literature. In Algiers (and perhaps even earlier) he had begun to write the pastoral romance called *La Galatea*, which, as the letter just quoted suggests, was now well advanced. He had probably already completed at least four of the six books into which the romance is divided. In any case, it may be fair to use a poem from Book IV of *La Galatea* to discover something of Cervantes' state of mind and spirit on his return from Lisbon. In his pastoral romance, as in many others, the names of the shepherds and shepherdesses were to knowledgeable contemporaries only thin disguises for real people. The poem of interest here was sent by Lauso (Cervantes) to Larsileo (probably Mateo Vázquez), and so constitutes a kind of second verse epistle to Philip's secretary. It tells how disillusionment with the false promises of the world has put an end to the author's hopes for royal favor and set his tired hand to writing again. It describes also the unkindness of the fates towards him and contrasts the good and simple life of the shepherd close to Nature with the ambitions and flatteries of the courtier dancing attendance on the mighty. A rough translation of a fragment may serve to suggest the mood:

> Who shall hold that life in low esteem?
> Who shall not say that life alone is life
> That truly leads the soul to peace?
> The fact the courtier esteems it not
> Commends its goodness to the mind
> Of him who aspires to good, and evil doth decline.
> Oh life where accompanied pleasure
> In solitude is refined!
> Oh shepherd's low estate
> Higher than the Highness
> Of scepter most sublime!
> Oh fragrant flowers! Oh shady
> Woods! Oh crystal rivers!
> Would that I might enjoy ye yet
> A while before misfortunes mine
> So pure a pastime do disturb![7]

If it is true that such sentiments as these are characteristic of the pastoral *genre*, it is also true that they were particularly congenial to Cervantes' spirit. Were they not it would be difficult to understand why he not only completed and published *La Galatea* but also cherished for the rest of his life the often expressed intention of writing a sequel to a work which had brought him neither fame nor fortune.

. nan — Risselo

e de vera — Belardo

o flereb Ussano

merub. — Rissardo   on Feliseo

ernantel — ausso

Guinea   Rubelio   Jos eta

figueroa —   Tirssi   2

330 130   Salus

Salus

8 Man of Letters

Early in the seventeenth century, the great satirist Francisco de Quevedo wrote that there were four thousand poets on every street corner in Madrid. The number of recognized poets in the city in 1583 might not have inspired quite such an exaggeration, but it was nevertheless very large. For Book VI of *La Galatea* Cervantes composed a poem called 'Calliope's Song', in which he listed and characterized in laudatory terms an even hundred poets who were his contemporaries. It is difficult to say how many of these poets were new friends, like Pedro de Padilla, who despite the newness of their friendship asked Miguel for a dedicatory sonnet for his forthcoming *Romancero*, and how many were friends of long standing, like Juan Rufo Gutiérrez, who had been Miguel's schoolmate in Córdoba and fellow soldier at Lepanto and who was now preparing his epic poem, the *Austriad*, on the exploits of Don Juan of Austria. Some of Cervantes' literary friends dated from his soldiering in Italy and his captive years in North Africa, but a hundred Spanish poets known even casually to a young Spaniard who had been abroad for twelve years are hard to account for. It seems likely that he already knew a substantial number before his flight from Madrid in 1568. Perhaps he had met some of them through his teacher, López de Hoyos. Perhaps, too, like some others, he had in those days frequented the royal palace. Likely examples of such pre-Lepanto friends are Pedro Laínez, who had been *valet de chambre* to the ill-starred Prince Carlos; and Luis Gálvez de Montalvo, whose frustrated love affair with one of the queen's beautiful ladies-in-waiting made him an *habitué* of the palace. The possibility that Miguel knew these courtier poets in his youth and that he often accompanied them to the palace would fit very well with the circumstances of his hasty departure from Madrid in 1568, since it was probably in the palace precincts that he wounded Antonio de Sigura.[1]

If the conditions under which Cervantes became so well acquainted with the Spanish literary world of his day are conjectural, his poet friends were real enough. He mentions them repeatedly in his works. One of them, Pedro Laínez, besides having been with Miguel at Lepanto, may have been one of his early masters in poetic composition. There is a passage in *La Galatea* in which the shepherd Damon (thought to be Laínez) begs the shepherd Lauso (Cervantes) to recite some more of his verses because he finds them so pleasing. Lauso replies: 'That must be, Damon, because you were my master in them, and your desire to see how much you have profited me is what makes you want to hear them.'[2] But beyond their literary companionship lies another

< 90 Late sixteenth-century manuscript listing the pseudonyms used by various Spanish poets. Cervantes is 'Lausso' (as in *La Galatea*) and Lope de Vega 'Belardo'.

91 Cervantes' friend the poet Luis Gálvez de Montalvo.

92 'The age abounds in poets', an allegory of Spain's literary burgeoning in the later sixteenth century.

connection worth noting. In 1581, while Miguel was getting ready to leave on his mission to Oran, Laínez married a young lady called Juana de Gaitán. She was living in Madrid at that time, but she seems to have come originally from the nearby country town of Esquivias and to have been instrumental later in Cervantes' own courtship of a girl from her home town. Another of Cervantes' poet friends, Luis Gálvez de Montalvo, whose sonnet celebrating Miguel's return from captivity has already been noted, had just published in Madrid his romance *Filida's Shepherd*. Interestingly enough, Pedro Laínez was chosen by the Council of Castile to examine the new book and to write the approbation required for its publication. The opinions he expressed about his friend's work were, of course, very favorable. *Filida's Shepherd* was a celebrated *roman à clef* relating in suitable disguise the love affair of the author with Doña Magdalena Girón, the queen's lady-in-waiting. Cervantes appreciated the book and knew its secret. Many years later he caused it to be saved from the fire to which the Priest and the Barber condemned so many of Don Quixote's books.

To some readers it has seemed strange that a writer as gifted as Cervantes in the portrayal of real life should have devoted so much time to a *genre* as artificial as they judge the pastoral romance to be. Evidently it did not seem so artificial to Cervantes and this was not for lack of familiarity with the *genre*. In *Don Quixote* he was to mention the Italian Jacopo Sannazaro, whose *Arcadia* (1504) became the model for the first pastoral romance in Spanish, that is to say, for the *Diana* (1559) of Jorge de Montemayor. He stocked Don Quixote's private library with it and at least seven others, three of which were judged good enough

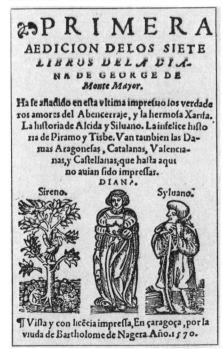

93-6 Spanish literature of the golden age expressed itself in a variety of *genres*, as this selection of title pages indicates. Above left, Juan Rufo Gutiérrez' epic poem the *Austriad* (Madrid, 1584), and, right, Cervantes' own pastoral romance *La Galatea* (Lisbon edition, 1590). Below left, Jorge de Montemayor's *Diana*, first published in 1559, started an influential vogue for love stories in bucolic settings. In *Amadis de Gaula* (Seville edition, 1531) Garcia Ordóñez de Montalvo retold a traditional tale as a prose romance, the first in the long line of chivalric romances which Cervantes satirized in *Don Quixote*.

97, 98 Illustrations to *Don Quixote* by Jean-Honoré Fragonard (1732–1806): 'The pleasant scrutiny which the curate and the barber made of the library of our ingenious gentleman', and the Knight with Sancho Panza.

to escape the flames to which most of his books of chivalry were consigned. Being familiar with the pastoral tradition, he must have known that its heyday had already come and gone. He seems to recognize as much in the Prologue to *La Galatea* when he writes: 'The occupation of writing eclogues at a time when, in general, poetry is not much favored, I fear will not be considered a laudable exercise....' And yet, from the last page of *La Galatea* to the last words he ever wrote, Cervantes continued to promise publication of a second part. Furthermore, he continued to use pastoral themes in his later works, including his masterpiece. The evidence of his writings, then, suggests that in his own inner world the Arcadian strain was as genuine and vital as the heroic had been in his life as soldier and captive.

What was it in these novels of make-believe shepherdry that pleased him? For one thing, they contained a great deal of poetry, and he was passionately addicted to poetry: 'From tender years I've loved, with passion rare, The winsome art of Poesy the gay....'[3] For another, their setting was like that of the Golden Age which Don Quixote evoked before the fascinated and bewildered goatherds:

'In that blessed age all things were held in common. No man, to gain his common sustenance, needed to make any greater effort than to reach up his hand and pluck it from the strong oaks, which literally invited him to taste their sweet and savoury fruit. Clear springs and running rivers offered him their sweet and limpid water in glorious abundance. In clefts of the rock and hollow trees the careful and provident bees formed their commonwealth, offering to every hand without interest the fertile produce of their fragrant toil.... All was peace, then, all amity, all concord....'[4]

For a man who had lived so intimately with the vicissitudes of war and bad luck, it was pleasant to dream of a world of beauty, serenity and abundance and to people it with shepherds and shepherdesses possessing all the attributes of musicians, poets and lovers.

But Cervantes knew very well what the world of real shepherds was like. One of his talking dogs makes that clear enough:

'The greater part of the day they spent in hunting fleas on their bodies or in mending their sandals; nor did I hear any of them mention such names as Amarilis, Filida, Galatea or Diana, while none of these swains was called Lisardo, Lauso, Jacinto or Riselo, but instead were all Antones, Domingos, Pablos or Llorentes. This confirmed me in the belief, which I think others should share, that all those books, though well written, are full of things that have been dreamed up for the amusement of persons with nothing better to do, and there is not a word of truth in them; for if there had been, there surely would have been among those shepherds of mine some vestige of that happy life, those pleasant meadows, spacious groves, sacred mounts, lovely gardens, clear running brooks, and crystalline fountains, as well as of those decent, poetically avowed love affairs, with a shepherd swooning here and a shepherd lass over there, now to the sound of a flute and now to that of a flageolet.'[5]

In writing *La Galatea*, Cervantes began – somewhat timidly, as one might expect in a first book – his lifelong experimentation with mixing the perceived and the imagined; he began to see how myths could be deflated with injections of real life and real life ennobled in mythical robes; he began to explore the possibility of catching the complexity of human life in a net of ambivalence.[6]

It took Cervantes only four or five more months to finish his first novel. On 29 March 1583 Philip II and his court returned to Madrid, after a long stay in Lisbon, and shortly after this date Miguel put the final touches to *La Galatea*. If he proceeded to seek a Maecenas and a publisher, he didn't find them at once. But, disappointed though he may have been, he realized that he had not produced a masterpiece. Perhaps his most accurate estimate of what he had achieved is expressed in the words spoken by the Priest during the famous scrutiny of Don Quixote's library. When the Barber hands him Don Quixote's copy of *La Galatea*, the Priest remarks:

'That Cervantes has been a great friend of mine for many years, and I know that he is more versed in misfortunes than in verse. His book has some clever ideas, but it sets out to do something and concludes nothing. We must wait for the second part he promises, and perhaps with amendment he will win our clemency now denied him. In the meantime, neighbour, until we see, keep him as a recluse in your room.'[7]

In the summer following the completion of his first novel, Cervantes learned two items of news that must have affected him deeply. On 28 June 1583, his old friend and teacher López de Hoyos died. And in late July the last stronghold of rebellion in the Azores was conquered by Spain. The commander of the Spanish forces was, once again, the Marquis of Santa Cruz, and the first Spanish soldier ashore in the first assault on the island was Rodrigo de Cervantes, whose exemplary conduct on that occasion was recorded by more than one eyewitness.[8]

Cervantes' first novel, still awaiting a publisher, could not be counted on to contribute anything to his support, and he remained without remunerative employment. In an attempt to make a living by the use of his literary talents Cervantes turned to the theater, which was becoming daily more popular in the growing city of Madrid. Not that plays in the 1580s had reached the level of excellence they were soon to attain in the golden age of the Spanish theater. Nevertheless, they drew capacity crowds to the two thriving outdoor theaters of the capital: the Corral de la Cruz and the Corral del Príncipe.

The early theaters known as *corrales* (comparable to the inn-yards of London) were primitive, open-air sites, usually occupying courtyards or patios rented for a specific number of days. The stage was an uncovered board platform improvised for the occasion. Scenery and stage effects were almost non-existent, and plays were ordinarily performed only on Sundays and holidays. Little by little, however, the theatrical arts matured, the frequency of performances increased and the locales became fixed and better equipped. Some fifteen or more years before Cervantes began to write for the stage, two charitable fraternities (*cofradías*) had acquired a monopoly of the *corrales* in Madrid, devoting to the support of hospitals for the poor the income derived from renting them to companies of actors.

By 1584 there were theatrical performances nearly every day in one or both of the two theaters. The Corral del Príncipe was the newer (inaugurated on 21 September 1583) and better equipped. It occupied a rectangular space in Príncipe Street bounded on the longer sides with grated windows, and with a raised stage at the farther end. Most of the area was left uncovered, since natural light was needed for the performances, but the stage itself was covered, as was a section of terraced seats that ran along the left wall of the courtyard. Ninety-five portable benches were placed in the open space in front of the stage, and these were rented by men. Most of the rest of the open space was occupied by a standing audience composed of those impatient and boisterous groundlings known in Spain as *mosqueteros*. At the end of the courtyard farthest from the stage was the gallery set aside for the women of the lower classes. The upper classes occupied the covered terraced seats and the rooms and balconies of the enclosing houses.

The spectacle that people flocked to the *corrales* to see consisted of a number of items. It began with a *loa*, which might be a monologue intended to prepare the audience for the play about to be represented or a slight dramatic sketch or some other kind of attention-catching piece. After the first act of the play proper, there was usually a comic interlude (*entremés*) – a *genre* in which Cervantes is the acknowledged master. Between the second and third act, it was common to perform a dance. The whole spectacle usually lasted about

99   The Corral del Príncipe in Madrid, c. 1582.

two and a half hours, and the public of Madrid acquired an insatiable appetite for it. It took a galaxy of the world's most prolific playwrights to satisfy that appetite.[9]

Cervantes had been strongly attracted to the theater since his early schooldays. Some words spoken by Don Quixote in the presence of a company of players fairly represent his creator's attitude: 'For from boyhood I have been a lover of pantomimes, and in my youth I was always a glutton for comedies.'[10] In his youth Cervantes had seen and conceived a lasting admiration for the outstanding comic actor and author Lope de Rueda. Given, then, his fondness for the theater, the expanding market for dramatic works and his precarious economic condition, it was almost inevitable that he should try his hand at writing plays.

In the prologue to a collection of plays and dramatic interludes published the year before he died, Cervantes tells of a conversation with literary friends on the question of who may have been the first Spaniard to take the national theater out of its 'swaddling clothes' and reveal it in all its splendor. He reports that as the oldest in the group he remembered seeing the great Lope de Rueda act, and goes on to produce a thumb-nail history of the Spanish theater, including an assessment of his own place in that history. Here are a few of his remarks pertinent to this stage of his career:

'The theaters of Madrid saw performed *The Manners of Algiers, The Destruction of Numantia* and *The Naval Combat*, in which I dared to reduce comedies to three acts, from the five they used to have; I showed, or rather, I was the first to represent the imaginings and secret thoughts of the soul, setting moral figures on the stage to the general and pleasurable applause of the listeners. I composed at this time up to twenty or thirty plays, all of which were received without cucumbers or other things suitable for throwing; they enjoyed their run without whistling, shouting or hubbub. I had other things with which to busy myself; I put aside my pen and my plays; and then that monster of nature, the great Lope de Vega, entered the scene and made off with the crown of the comic monarchy.'[11]

The first period of Cervantes' dramatic production ran from some time in 1583 to 1586 or 1587. It is in this brief period that he wrote the 'twenty or thirty plays'. In the Appendix to his *Journey to Parnassus*, he mentions the titles of some of these works:

'*The Manners of Algiers, Numancia, The Grand Sultana, The Naval Combat, Jerusalem, Amaranta or the May-flower, The Amorous Grove, The Rare and Matchless Arsinda*, and many others that have slipped from my memory. But that which I most esteem, and still pride myself upon, was and is one styled *The Confused Lady*, which, with peace be it spoken, may rank as good among the best of comedies of the "Cloak and Sword", which have hitherto been represented.'[12]

Unfortunately, all but the first two of the plays listed are now as lost to us as the titles Cervantes claims to have forgotten.

Cervantes' first play is the one whose title has been translated into English, not entirely satisfactorily, as *The Manners of Algiers*.[13] It is a four-act play which tells the story of the Christian lovers, Aurelio and Silvia, who are captured and sold to Yzuf and his wife Zahara in Algiers. The Moslems fall in love with their Spanish slaves and seek to satisfy their desires by using the slaves as go-betweens. The play ends happily with the ransoming of the Christians. It is not one of the author's best plays, but it is of exceptional documentary value, being full of verifiable historical incidents and plausible descriptions of life in Algiers during the late 1570s. Of special interest is a soldier named Saavedra, who acts as the firm friend and sustainer of other Christian captives. Like Velázquez in the *Maids of Honor*, Cervantes has painted his own portrait but not in the center of the canvas.

Miguel's second play, *The Destruction of Numantia*, presents the heroic resistance of the inhabitants of the ancient city of Numantia (high on the Castilian plain near Soria) under siege by Scipio the Younger in 134-133 BC. The protagonists of the play are the entire population of the city. Every last man, woman and child accepts death in preference to Roman domination. The last person to die is a young boy who, bidden by Scipio to surrender, hurls himself from a high wall to his death. The final words of the tragedy are spoken by Fame. From atop the desolate walls of Numantia, she proclaims the unequalled heroism of its inhabitants, and prophesies the valor which unborn generations of Spaniards will derive from such a heritage. The play was evidently a success in its day and it came to act as a source of national inspiration in times of crisis, as, for example, during the siege of Saragossa by Napoleon's forces in 1809. Some part of the fierce defense put up by the Saragossans on that occasion may be attributed to their having attended a performance of *The Destruction of Numantia* at the height of the seige.

Despite his literary genius, Cervantes was not a great dramatist. His early success in the theater can probably be explained not only by the novelty and human interest of his first plays but also because the state of Spanish dramatic art allowed more freedom in the 1580s than it would after Lope de Vega had perfected the dramatic formula that was to make him the most popular playwright of all time. When Cervantes began to write, all the thematic veins that would be exploited in the Golden Age of the Spanish theater had already been tapped: the Bible, the sacraments, the lives of saints, the literature of Greece and Rome and of the Italian Renaissance, national history and legend, even contemporary events. All this material and more was available, but it was not yet clear which of these veins would stand the best chance of pleasing the Spanish public. Accordingly, nothing that Cervantes wrote about in his plays collided with anything in the dramatic tradition of their day.

It was not yet apparent just what the characteristic form of the Spanish *comedia* would be. How many acts would it have? Would it be written in verse or in prose or in both? Would it combine the tragic and the comic? Would it observe the unities of time, place and action? In a word, would it be a romantic or a classic theater? Hindsight indicates the former, but in the 1580s there were writers who favored the latter. Cervantes was one of them, and at the time he could implement his preference without bucking an unmistakable trend.

Most important of all, there were no dramatists of genius to rival him. Since the death of Lope de Rueda in 1565, the only precursor of Lope de Vega that need be considered is Juan de la Cueva, who is still studied because his exploitation of the medieval epic pointed the way to some of Lope's later triumphs. But Juan de la Cueva strikes modern readers as dull, and there is no evidence that he was ever popular. Of course, Lope himself had already begun to compose *comedias*, but in 1583 he was only twenty-one and not yet the arbiter of theatrical fashion.

Perhaps it was Cervantes' success in the theater that helped him to find a publisher for *La Galatea*. At any rate, in 1584 he sold the rights of his novel to Blas de Robles (father of the publisher of *Don Quixote*) for 1,336 reals.[14] With this money and whatever his plays brought in he may have enjoyed a little relief from the constant pressure of penury.

During this period of relative prosperity Miguel, now thirty-six, was involved in a love affair with a young woman by the name of Ana de Villafranca. Her identity was a complete mystery until about twenty years ago, which allowed some of Cervantes' biographers, who called her Ana Franca de Rojas, to give free reign to their imaginations. Now it is possible to say exactly who she was.[15] She was the daughter of Juan de Villafranca and Luisa de Rojas, and her father was a vendor of the thin rolled wafers called *barquillos* in Madrid. Around 1580, at the age of seventeen or eighteen, she was married to an illiterate Asturian trader named Alonso Rodríguez, whose interest in her dowry was probably greater than his love for Ana. She had been married about four years when she and Miguel met. Nothing at all is known about their affair, except that it produced a daughter, born on 19 November 1584 and named Isabel.

While this love affair was in progress, and before Isabel's birth, Cervantes' good friend, the poet Laínez, died. His wife, Juana de Gaitán, remarried almost at once and settled in the little town of Esquivias, to which she soon summoned Miguel to help her arrange for the publication of her late husband's poetry. Miguel is known to have been in Esquivias on this business in late September 1584. It turned out to be a fateful trip, for it was in this small country town, which he would probably never have had occasion to visit without Juana's summons, that he found a wife.

Cervantes travelled from Madrid to Esquivias by the main Toledo road as far as Illescas and the rest of the way by an unimproved secondary road. Although this is not yet that part of central Spain usually thought of as La Mancha, it borders on La Mancha and is very similar to it. Monotonous, gently rolling, semi-arid and brownish gray, the high plain stretches off into distances that seem both endless and beyond time. Despite the olives, vineyards and winter wheat cultivated there, it speaks somehow of desolation and potential madness – a place where an Alonso Quixano might have to convert himself into Don Quixote merely to survive. The town of Esquivias, some twenty miles

101 El Greco's *Dream of Philip II*; the victors of Lepanto (Philip, the Pope and the Venetian >
Doge) kneel with St Paul in the foreground of a teeming canvas which brilliantly combines
the world, heaven and hell, temporal statecraft and eternal truth.
Overleaf: 102 The Escorial, created by Juan de Herrera (1530-97), served Philip as royal
residence and art gallery, monastery and mausoleum. It was also the central super-ministry
from which the 'chief clerk of the empire' strove to rule his domains through a cumbrous
bureaucracy.

103 El Greco's dramatic *View of Toledo*, painted between 1606 and 1614.

104 The house where Catalina Cervantes was born and brought up in Esquivias.

south of Madrid, had about 255 householders in 1584. A quieter place so near the heart of empire could hardly be imagined. It would certainly be difficult for a man who had seen the world and lived close to the bustle and excitement of the court to live in such a cultural backwater. But for a while perhaps he might be happy, especially if he were tired of the struggle to earn a precarious living by writing for the theater.

In the prologue to his last novel, Cervantes wrote that Esquivias was famous for its illustrious lineages and for its even more illustrious wines. Among the respected Esquivian gentry were the Palacios and the Salazars. On 12 November 1565 Catalina de Palacios and Fernando de Salazar Vozmediano had baptized their daughter, Catalina de Salazar y Palacios, who as a young woman was to catch Miguel's eye on his brief visit to her town in the fall of 1584. It is scarcely necessary to ask how they met in a town as small as Esquivias. To judge by the brevity of their engagement, they must have been attracted to each other at once. Catalina's prospects of inheriting wealth were dim. Although she belonged to one of the more distinguished propertied families in town, her father, who died in February of 1584, had mismanaged the family estate sufficiently to reduce it to very modest proportions. Catalina's dowry consisted principally of about six small vineyards, an enclosed orchard and a fairly complete but modest set of household furnishings. When her mother died in 1588 Catalina inherited part of the substantial family residence in addition, but properly administered the bride's estate would still provide only a modest rustic living. It seems clear, then, that Miguel could not have courted her for her wealth. Perhaps his thoughts were comparable to those once expressed by Don Quixote:

117

Pineda, Notari.

105 Sixteenth-century Spanish wedding ceremony.

'If a prudent man wants to take a long journey he seeks a safe and peaceful companion to go with him, before setting out on the road. Why then should he not do the same when he has to travel all his life, right up to the resting place of death; all the more so since his companion must be with him at bed and at board and everywhere....'[16]

About the end of September, Miguel had to return to Madrid. Whether he and Catalina became engaged during this first short visit or later in the fall is uncertain. In any event, they were married on 12 December 1584 in the Esquivian church of Santa María de la Asunción. The officiating priest was Catalina's uncle, Juan de Palacios, and this, plus the fact that Miguel's father named Catalina's mother as one of the executors of his estate, suggests that the two families were on good terms.

Many of Cervantes' biographers have assumed (without direct evidence) that Catalina was not very attractive and that the marriage was not very successful. It is true that she was eighteen years younger than her husband and that he was soon to spend the better part of thirteen years travelling about Andalusia without her; it is also true that after his Andalusian years they lived together almost constantly until his death. In her first will, dated 16 June 1610, Catalina makes certain bequests to her husband 'because of the great love and good company we have had together'.[17] In a later will dated some ten years after her husband's death she asked to be buried, not in Esquivias as she had specified in her first will, but in the Trinitarian convent in Madrid where Miguel had been interred.[18] These testamentary dispositions hardly support the notion that the marriage, which began in 1584 and lasted until Miguel died thirty-two years later, was a failure.

Cervantes spent as much time as he could with his young bride in Esquivias, but on numerous occasions during 1585 his affairs carried him to

118

Madrid and elsewhere. Sometime during the period of his engagement or early marriage, he found a patron to whom to dedicate his forthcoming novel, *La Galatea*. The patron was the distinguished young ecclesiastic Ascanio Colonna, born in Rome, educated at Alcalá and Salamanca, and soon to be a cardinal. Ascanio was the son of Marco Colonna, commander of the papal squadron at Lepanto, and at this time he was residing in Alcalá de Henares. While Miguel was there to call on him, he probably visited his sister Sor Luisa of Bethlehem and maybe his publisher Blas de Robles, who would then have been able to tell him that *La Galatea* was to be published in March.

On 5 March 1585 Miguel was in Madrid, where he signed an agreement with the well-known theatrical impresario Gaspar de Porres. For forty ducats Cervantes promised to provide Porres with two plays: *The Confused Lady* (within two weeks) and *The Manners of Constantinople and Death of Selim* (by the week before Easter). *The Confused Lady* must have been a great success that spring, for, as already noted, its author continued to remember it with pride nearly thirty years later, when he published his *Journey to Parnassus*.

On 13 June 1585, Miguel's father died in Madrid at the age of seventy-five. His will is a valuable, even a touching, document. Among other things, it shows the trust and respect he still felt for his wife after more than forty years of a married life that had seen much heartbreak and poverty. He left to her good judgment the number of priests and friars who would accompany him to his grave as well as the number of masses to be said. Unable to remember how much her dowry had amounted to, he specified that she was to receive from his estate without question whatever amount she claimed. He declared that he had no debts. (If this is true, it shows that somehow the debts incurred to ransom his sons had finally been paid.) He stipulated that the rest of his property be divided equally among his surviving sons and daughters, all of whom are mentioned except Luisa, who as a nun could not inherit property. One wonders how much property there can have been to divide.

Miguel surely went to Madrid for his father's funeral. He probably stayed there for a few days to help and console his mother before returning to Esquivias.[19]

With his successful plays and the publication of his novel, Miguel might with reason have thought of himself as a well established figure on the literary scene. He was beginning to understand, though, how very difficult it was to live by writing for the stage. Too many good writers were competing and some were wealthy enough to write without requiring payment. Besides, he had, as he said, 'other things with which to busy myself'. As Miguel contemplated abandoning the city of the court for the peace and quiet of Esquivias he may have felt some of the disenchantment he later put into the words of one of his characters:

'O court, you who more than fulfil the hopes of audacious pretenders and cut short those of the competent, you provide in abundance for shameless mountebanks and let the wise who have a sense of shame die of hunger.'[20]

106 El Greco's *Burial of Count Orgaz* (1586), called by the artist 'my sublime work'.

9 Rustic Interlude

It took but a scant day to travel from Madrid to Esquivias, and Miguel had good reasons for making the trip with some regularity: his new wife lived in the country town; his mother, his sisters, and his literary friends in the capital. It is not clear in which town he made his headquarters during the second half of 1585. To complicate matters, in early December he appeared in Seville to borrow 204,000 maravedis for a period of six months.[1] His childhood friend Tomás Gutiérrez, who had been a famous actor and producer and now kept the best inn in Seville, was one of the witnesses to his loan. There is record that he cashed the draft for the 204,000 maravedis in Madrid on 19 December 1585. One wonders how he was able to borrow so large a sum of money and to what use he intended to put it. If, as has been conjectured, he invested it in some business deal, the nature of the transaction has never been discovered.[2] Since he was able to return to Seville in six months to pay off the debt, it is clear that at least he did not lose the money.

In January 1586 Miguel probably settled down in Esquivias for a stay of about sixteen months, interrupted only by a June trip to Seville to repay his loan, by a journey to nearby Toledo in August, and possibly by brief sojourns in Madrid. In Esquivias he helped to manage the estates of his wife and his mother-in-law. Indeed, on 9 August 1586 the latter named him administrator of all her property[3] and sent him soon after that date to Toledo to pay certain debts of her dead husband and to collect back rent on a house that she owned in that city.

Miguel's mission to Toledo was not in itself an agreeable one, but he liked the city, which he would later use as the setting for two of his *Exemplary Novels*. Having seen some of the most impressive cities of Europe, he could yet be impressed with Toledo, which he has one of his characters call the 'glory of Spain and light of her cities'.[4] Continuously inhabited since before the Christian era, capital of Spain under Visigoths, Moors and Christians for over a thousand years, a bishopric since the sixth century and See of Spain's cardinal primate, at the time of Cervantes' August visit Toledo remained a more populous city than Madrid and incomparably richer in noble churches, convents, mosques, synagogues, palaces and other monuments to a long and varied history.

Some of Doña Catalina's forebears had lived in Toledo as long ago as the beginning of the fifteenth century, and a fair number of her relatives were residents of the city in 1586. In August one of them, Gonzalo de Guzmán Salazar,

was planning to marry the niece of Don Andrés Núñez de Madrid, who happened to be the curate of the little Toledan church of Santo Tomé. Don Andrés deserves to be remembered, since it was he who commissioned El Greco to paint *The Burial of Count Orgaz*. El Greco had settled in Toledo and was actively at work on this masterpiece at the time of Miguel's visit. Either through his wife's relatives or his own Toledan literary friends, Cervantes could easily have met this highly original and talented contemporary, and he may even have seen his great painting. If he did, he would have been particularly interested in the way El Greco attempted in *The Burial of Count Orgaz* to represent and integrate two worlds: the world of perception and the world of faith and imagination. Cervantes himself was to become a master of such integrations in the literary art.

There was much talk that summer in Toledo, Madrid and elsewhere about the completion of another artistic project of truly monumental proportions: the monastery of San Lorenzo del Escorial, which included, besides the monastery itself, a church, a royal apartment, a mausoleum, a museum and a library. Nothing in sixteenth-century Europe could touch it for size and magnificence except St Peter's and the Vatican.

108   English engraving of 'the King of Spaynes Hows at the Escorial in Process of Building'.

The history of the monastery had begun soon after the Spanish victory over the French in the battle of St Quentin on 10 August 1557. Philip decided both to commemorate that victory and to provide a suitable burial place for his august father, himself and his royal descendants. After much thought and investigation, he chose a site on a bleak spur of the Guadarrama Mountains about thirty miles north-west of Madrid. The overall plan settled on by Philip and his architects represents a huge grill, symbolizing the martyrdom by grilling of St Lawrence, whose day chanced to coincide with that of the victory of St Quentin. On 23 April 1563, the first granite stone was laid. 'From then on', as Garrett Mattingly wrote, 'Philip seemed obsessed with the fear that he might not live to see his tomb. He pressed the work so urgently that his councillors grumbled about a king who spent as much time on one monastery as he did on all his kingdoms.'[5] But now at last, after twenty-three years of intensive efforts, the vast edifice was complete, except that the king's agents continued to enrich its interiors with the best paintings, sculptures, tapestries, manuscripts and holy relics to be found in all of Europe. It became Philip's favorite residence at once. From his austere apartment within the granite pile, he was soon to issue the dispatches that would accelerate the final preparations for launching the Invincible Armada against England. Although the Escorial is now regarded as one of Spain's greatest artistic treasures, in the sixteenth century it did not enjoy the universal approval of Philip's subjects. Some of them could think of better ways to spend the untold millions it cost – such as outfitting an expedition to free the 25,000 Christian slaves languishing in the *bagnios* of Algiers.

It seems likely that Cervantes returned to Esquivias in September; there is clear evidence of his presence there at a baptism in late October.[6] In April of the following year he began a long sojourn in Andalusia. What did he do between fall and spring, apart from keeping an eye on the business affairs of his wife and mother-in-law? The only evidence is what his works show that he assimilated in Esquivias, but that is considerable and convincing.

Although Cervantes had lived in some of the great cities of his day, had observed the life of the court and associated on occasions with people of the upper classes, the very best of his writing does not deal with high-born lords and ladies in urban settings but rather with humbler folk in towns, villages, crossroads and country inns. His best remembered characters are the village barber and priest, the innkeepers, the serving maids, the farmers, the muleteers, the vagabonds and rogues, the galley slaves and students. The co-protagonist of his greatest work is the earthy peasant, Sancho Panza, whose sententious and salty speech is one of the major delights of the novel. Cervantes lets us see these people in village scenes of insuperable charm and authenticity. But beyond such general knowledge, he seems in Esquivias to have acquired some specific information of use to him in his later writing.

In the famous literary discussion between the Canon of Toledo and Don Quixote, the Canon tries to persuade Don Quixote that most of the knights he believes in and emulates never existed. To Don Quixote this is tantamount to blasphemy. In defending the reality of the chivalric world in which he

109 Sixteenth-century woodcut of a reveller.

believes so passionately, he adduces without discrimination a multitude of knightly examples ranging from the strictly historical to the purely fictitious. Toward the end of his harangue, he remarks sarcastically: 'They will also deny the adventures and challenges also performed in Burgundy by the valiant Spaniards Pedro Barba and Gutierre Quixada – from whose stock I am descended in the direct male line – when they beat the sons of the Count St Pol.'[7] These two Spanish knights belong to the strictly historical category of Don Quixote's examples, and of course it is the second one that excites our interest. Noting that Cervantes' hero claims direct descent from the fifteenth-century Gutierre Quixada, one should remember what Cervantes wrote about his name in the first chapter of his novel: 'Finally he resolved to call himself Don Quixote. And that is no doubt why the authors of this true history, as we have said, assumed that his name must have been Quixada and not Quesada, as other authorities would have it.'[8] How did Cervantes happen to call his hero Don Quixote and to make him a descendant of the particular historical family that included Gutierre Quixada, so celebrated for his knightly exploits? Would it not be because a branch of Gutierre's family lived in Esquivias and was in fact the most prominent family there?

In a town like Esquivias, conversation was one of the few forms of social entertainment available. In the late afternoon, under the portico of the town hall or over a glass of wine at the inn, Miguel would join the village priest and the local hidalgos to talk about whatever there was to talk about: such news from the wide world as might drift that way from the nearby court; the births and deaths and marriages of Esquivias and its surrounding towns; whether the harvest had been good or bad; the current price of olive oil and wine and bread. Miguel might reminisce about his adventures in Italy and North Africa, or about the great naval battle of Lepanto.

Personalities and fragments of family histories would be staple items of conversation. The Esquivian Quixadas and Salazars were not on good terms, but this would be more of an incentive than a deterrent to conversation. Cervantes could scarcely have failed to hear a lot about the Quixadas, and he may have heard something of capital importance to the creation of Don Quixote. During the first half of the sixteenth century there had lived in Esquivias a certain Alonso Quixada, who was the nephew of Doña Catalina's grandfather and who eventually became an Augustinian friar. The potential value of this man to Cervantes' imagination becomes clear when one learns of his inordinate fondness for books of knight errantry, which he took to be true histories.[9]

But Miguel discovered other things he was later to use in *Don Quixote* in his Esquivian days besides the tempo and the tenor of the kind of village life that drove Don Quixote to his chivalric addiction. In the time of Alonso Quixada there had lived in Esquivias a priest called Pero Pérez (the name of Don Quixote's good friend, the Curate). A certificate of baptism has been found, bearing the date of 1 February 1529, which reveals that Pero Pérez baptized the son of Francisco Chamiso and his wife Mari Gutiérrez.[10] Readers of *Don Quixote* will recognize the second name as that given on one occasion to Sancho Panza's wife. They will remember, too, the prankish Sansón Carrasco when they are informed that there were Carrascos in Esquivias, and they will recall Sancho Panza's encounter with the Morisco Ricote on his return from the governorship of Barataria when they are told that in Esquivias there had lived Moriscos by the name of Ricote. It is difficult not to begin to suspect that Esquivias was the prototype of that village in La Mancha whose name Cervantes chose, quite understandably, not to remember.[11] In any event, Cervantes indisputably gathered in his memory seeds for future artistic germination during the rustic interlude between his first attempt at a literary career and his peregrinations as one of King Philip's long-suffering commissaries.

In the late afternoon of 23 April 1587, a procession bearing the remains of St Leocadia stopped in Esquivias to spend the night. St Leocadia's remains had been brought to Spain from Flanders and were to be deposited with great pomp and a ceremony, which Philip and his family attended, in the Toledan hermitage called the Cristo de la Vega, built on the site of the seventh-century Visigothic basilica of St Leocadia. On the following day, numerous residents of Esquivias accompanied the procession to Toledo to witness the colorful proceedings and see the assembled notables. It is better than a fair guess that Cervantes went along, since there is record of his presence in Toledo on 28 April 1587, which is the date of an extensive power of attorney drawn up in that city in favor of his wife. It bestows on her ample powers to handle any and all of their joint or separate business affairs, and it suggests that Miguel anticipated a long absence from home.[12] He may have decided days or even weeks before on a trip to Seville in search of the employment that was soon to hold him for so many years in Andalusia. The apparent suddenness of his decision to journey to Seville may have been only the result of a chance encounter at the well-attended fiesta in Toledo, which offered the possibility of transportation or at least of good company.

How many times in his life Miguel was to make the ten-day trip from the center of Spain to the capital city of Andalusia! If there were nothing but his fiction to document his travels between Castile and Andalusia, we could still be sure of his intimate acquaintance with the route and its bordering territory.

The Royal Road by which he travelled south is studded with Cervantine associations. It passed somewhat to the west of the modern highway, because the picturesque mountain defile of Despeñaperros was not opened until the eighteenth century. The most important towns on the way between Toledo and Córdoba were Ciudad Real and Almodóvar del Campo, each of which is mentioned three times in Cervantes' fiction. On occasion he may have spent the night in one of these towns, but for the most part he had to put up at the country inns, of which more than thirty were distributed along his route. In his writings he mentions at least three of these: the Venta del Molinillo, the Venta del Alcalde, and the Venta Tejada. But he does much more than merely mention names of real places; he also exhibits an accurate knowledge of topographical features and distances which he was to use many times in his later writing.

110 Knight holding a banner with an allegorical representation of Castile.

125

Antonio de gueuara Del consejo de Hazienda del Rei.

Prou.or y proueedor general desus galeras Armadas y frontes.

del proueedor Ant.o guevara
y a los en eçija y uaeça &.a
de azeite

C. 66.

Por quanto para prouision Delos galeones del rrei n.o s.r ydelas demas Naos de harmada que p[or] su mandado seban aprestando y juntando este p.te año para cosas de su R.l ser.o es Necesario se tomen ysaquen quatro mill arrouas de azeite en la ciudad de eçija de poder de quales quier p[er]sonas que lo tubieren por ser parte donde mejor se podra auer y hallar y que todo ello se traiga y conduzga a esta ciudad de seuilla a poder de g.mo maldonado tenedor de bastimentos y municiones en ella por el Rei n.o s.r y conuiene nonbrar una persona de diligencia y cuidado que se requiere para ello por la platica y expiriencia que tiene de semejantes cossas y por la satis-faccion q[ue] tengo de su persona por la presente le nonbro Ordeno y mando que luego q[ue] esta mi comis.on... sepa... a la dicha ciudad de eçija ysaque en ella las dichas quatro mill arouas de azeite de poder de quales quier p[er]sonas que lo tubieren dando les certi-ficaçion firmada de su nonbre A cadauno de lo cantidad que les tomare ysacare Para que con ella Acudan antemi que les mandare librar y pagar luego lo que por ello hubieren de auer y todo ello... a toda priesa Sin p[er]dida ora de t[iem]po los arateles... y conduzir a esta dicha ciudad a poder del dicho m... maldonado para el dicho efeto y para la dicha conducta tome... y enbiar para los bagajes carros y caretas que sea Neces A... la dicha ciudad de eçija como en las demas partes que conuenga don-de se hallaren y de quales quier p[er]sonas quesean qual los d.hos vagd.ros y les mandare pagar lo que quisieren de auer por su trauajo ya... y todo ponga mucha diligencia y cuidado de manera que se haga con la breuedad qual ser.o del rrei N.r señor conuiene que para todo lo que es y pendiente le doi poder y comis.on tan bastante como yo lo e y tengo del Rei n.o s.r y por ser cosa de su Real seruicio y tan inportante ael de su parte exorto y Requiero A todas e quales q[uier] Juezes y demas fuere No le inpidan ni perturben lo suso dicho antes le den el ayuda q[ue] les pidiere y fuere menester sopena de g.s ducados para gastos de guerra en que des-de luego les doi por condemnados lo contr[ario] haziendo y poder y facultad al dicho miguel de cerbantes A quales quier e... hagan con el los autos y dilig.as que conbenga y de todo lo quante ello par-... Ase le de... En manera quehaga... sopena de cinq... ... y la dicha pena pecuniaria A su suso d.ho la pueda executar en cada Uno q[ue] lo contr[ario] hiciere fecho en seuilla veinte y tres dias del mes de set.e 1588 a.s A.nt.o de Guevara. Por m.do de d Ant.o de Guevara Prou.or General Pero Gomez.

Concertado con la comis.on original que se boluio al parte... ... de med[iad]o junio de mile e q.tos y nouenta y dos anos

10 Commissary

By the end of March 1587, Philip had at last made up his mind to invade England. His great sea-fighter, the Marquis of Santa Cruz, had proposed such an invasion as long ago as August 1583 – a proposal which he renewed in 1586. Philip neither accepted nor rejected the marquis' suggestion; he waited and pondered. In the meantime, England continued to provide him with substantial provocations to hostility. Just as the Duke of Parma was beginning to reassert Spain's weakened authority over the Netherlands, Queen Elizabeth sent the Earl of Leicester with 6,000 troops to help the enemies of Spain. On 18 February 1587 her Catholic Majesty Mary Stuart was beheaded at Fotheringhay. Philip honored her with solemn funeral services at El Escorial, no doubt remembering that he had considered her a likely bride for his son Don Carlos when in 1560 she had become at the age of eighteen the dowager queen of France. At the end of April, Sir Francis Drake made a successful surprise attack on the Spanish port of Cádiz, destroying or capturing some twenty to thirty ships and taking much valuable cargo. It was too much. Philip was at last impatient to act.[1]

Not two weeks after Drake had 'singed the king's beard' in Cádiz bay, Miguel arrived in Seville. He stopped, for a while at least, with his good friend Tomás Gutiérrez at his famous inn in Bayona Street near the cathedral. If it were not for his friendship with Tomás, Miguel would probably have stayed in a less expensive hostelry; but presumably he could reconcile himself to occasional exposures to luxury. And he would be much interested in the conversation of the distinguished and influential transients who put up at Tomás' inn.

The most exciting recent topic of conversation was of course Drake's bold raid on Cádiz, a topic that could easily be related to the feverish activity observable in Spanish shipyards, to the gathering of naval strength in Lisbon harbor, and to many other signs that something portentous was afoot. It would be to Spain's advantage to keep the invasion plans a secret, but Philip could clearly not hope to hide or disguise so much significant activity, especially in Seville, which had been designated headquarters for the provisioning of the fleet. In this last matter Cervantes took a particular interest. In fact, what brought him to Seville was probably the news picked up in Toledo that Antonio de Guevara had been named chief purveyor of the Spanish fleet and would soon be sent to Seville.[2]

< 111 Cervantes' commission from Antonio de Guevara to obtain 4,000 arrobas of oil in Ecija (dated Seville, 22 January 1588).

112 Sir Francis Drake
(c. 1540-96), aged 43.

Miguel hoped to obtain a commission from Guevara, but the chief purveyor had not yet arrived and did not in fact reach the city for several months. The problem was money. Philip was not able simultaneously to raise money for ships, for recruiting and paying seamen and soldiers, and for supplies – not to mention money for the administration and defense of his vast dominions. Meanwhile, Guevara appointed a judge of the Royal Tribunal, Diego de Valdivia, as his deputy in Seville, and it was probably from Valdivia that Miguel finally got his first commission to procure wheat for the Armada.[3] But the commission did not start until the middle of September, which left Cervantes with the considerable expense of living in Seville without income for about four months. If he had left Esquivias in the hope of contributing something to family finances this period of financial loss must considerably have distressed him. Had he known in advance that he would remain idle for four months, he might have gone back to Esquivias for a while, but he had no way of knowing when he would be called to his new duties. How did he spend the idle summer? Since he had friends and relatives in the nearby Andalusian towns of Córdoba and Cabra (where his uncle was still mayor), it is likely that he paid them brief visits. Perhaps he was writing, too, though there is no way of telling what.

Cervantes' first commission was to collect wheat and barley in Ecija, an important Andalusian city about halfway between Seville and Córdoba. For this he was assigned a salary of twelve reals a day, payable whenever money became available. Though not a princely salary, it would still buy a little over three bushels of wheat, for example, or six live hens, or close to fifteen gallons of table wine![4] In theory, at any rate, his commission empowered him to do whatever might be necessary to collect and transport the quotas of grain allotted to him. When occasion demanded, he could break into granaries, seize grain, commandeer vehicles for transportation and arrest and imprison anyone who tried to interfere with the accomplishment of his mission. He had no money to pay for the grain he collected. All he could give to the owners was a certificate showing the date and the amount of grain taken. These certificates entitled their holders to fair payment when the king's paymaster in Seville had funds, which he often did not.

128

113-15 Cervantes' years as a commissary in Andalusia cannot have been entirely pleasant, but the value of the experience he gained during them – and particularly its contribution to the vitality of *Don Quixote* – cannot be questioned. Left, Cristóbal Mosquera de Figueroa, Cervantes' friend and the outgoing corregidor of Ecija. Below, Ecija, 'the frying pan of Andalusia', and Marchena, two of the many southern towns in which Cervantes found himself in the course of discharging his invidious duties.

129

Miguel arrived in Ecija on about 20 September. At that time a certain Cristóbal Mosquera de Figueroa was finishing a term as corregidor of that city. That he happened to be a good friend of Miguel's (who had praised him in *La Galatea*) helped the latter to begin his difficult mission under friendly auspices. But if this was a piece of good luck, it was the only one. The king's agents had seized much grain the previous year, and its owners still went unpaid. Although Ecija was the center of a very fertile region, the last harvest had not been good. For these reasons, the inhabitants were in no mood to hand over still more of their property in exchange for promises to pay that recent experience had rendered dubious. And there was another circumstance not favorable to the rapid discharge of Cervantes' assignment; the annual fair with its accompanying fiestas started on 21 September and would continue for two whole weeks.

In October Cervantes held several conferences with the town council, which consulted Valdivia in Seville and stalled in as many other ways as they could think of. Finally, under renewed orders from Guevara, Cervantes proceeded to take possession of something over three thousand bushels of wheat. Among the owners of the wheat were several influential ecclesiastics who protested vociferously over this outrage. The vicar general of the archbishopric of Seville declared Miguel excommunicate and ordered his name so posted in Ecija. In a country like Spain, where nationality and religious affiliation were inseparable, being excommunicated was a handicap in every aspect of daily life. Cervantes knew this of course, and eventually took steps to have his unjust excommunication lifted.

If one wonders how excommunication affected Cervantes himself, one has only to remember Don Quixote's reaction to the threat of the same punishment. It is expressed in the words he speaks after his nocturnal encounter with a group of priests who are taking a dead body to Segovia for burial:

'I did not suspect that I was injuring priests or Church property, which, good Catholic and faithful Christian that I am, I respect and adore, for I thought they were phantoms and spectres from the other world. But if it comes to the worst, I remember what happened to the Cid Ruy Díaz, when he broke the chair of the king's ambassador in the presence of his Holiness the Pope, who excommunicated him for it; notwithstanding which the good Rodrigo de Vivar bore himself like a very honourable and valiant knight that day.'[5]

If Don Quixote was not overly intimidated by the prospect of excommunication, perhaps his creator would not have been either.

By 20 November Cervantes had moved on to the Cordovan town of La Rambla. After the usual resistance had been overcome, Miguel managed to collect between 700 and 800 bushels in that town. From the city of Córdoba, Valdivia next sent word that Miguel was to proceed to the nearby town of Castro del Río, where he was able to attach over 2,600 bushels. Some of this wheat also belonged to an ecclesiastic, and, worse still, Cervantes had to jail a sacristan for resisting his orders. At once the vicar general of the bishopric

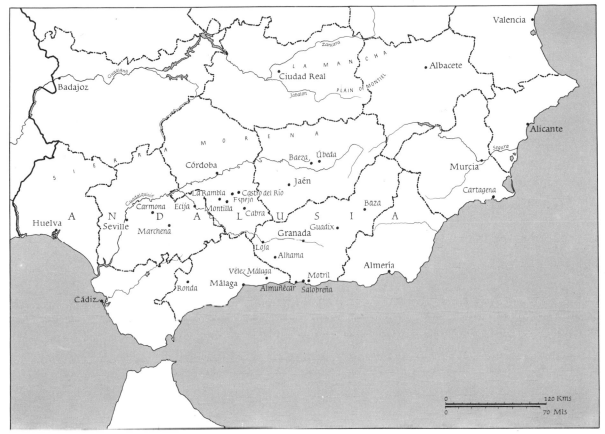

116 Cervantes' Andalusia.

of Córdoba fulminated a second excommunication against him! From Castro del Río, Miguel went to Espejo; from Espejo he returned to La Rambla, where he succeeded in attaching around 2,000 more bushels; and at last in early January 1588 he was able to go back to Seville, having completed his first commission and earned 1,344 as yet unpaid reals. To a sensitive person like Miguel, a commissary's duties must have been irksome in the extreme.

Cervantes was not destined to rest very long in Seville. On 22 January 1588 he received another commission: to return to Ecija in search of 4,000 arrobas of olive oil. How popular he must have been on his second visit to that beleaguered agricultural center! The town council petitioned the king not to send any more commissaries to reduce their sustenance beyond all endurance. Unwilling to use more force, Miguel resigned himself to collecting only half the quota before returning to Seville.

A few weeks later news reached Seville that the Marquis of Santa Cruz had died on 9 February. It was a bad omen for the Invincible Armada. Shortly after the arrival of this news, Miguel was ordered to Ecija for yet a third time. His mission was to complete the quota of olive oil and to inspect the wheat that had been attached and stored there. This business seems to have retained him in Ecija until late in May.

131

Back in Seville in the final days of May, he probably found sad news waiting for him at the inn of Tomás Gutiérrez: the death of his mother-in-law in Esquivias on 1 May 1588. Even if he had received the news promptly, he could not have reached Esquivias in time to attend the funeral. Besides, he had no money for personal travel. His salary was still unpaid, and he must have owed his friend Gutiérrez a sizable bill.

Soon after Cervantes returned to Seville, the great Armada sailed from Lisbon for the English Channel. Its commander was the Duke of Medina Sidonia, a grandee of Spain and a man of considerable administrative experience but of none at all as soldier or seaman. Indeed, he asked Philip to relieve him of this command because, among other things, of his propensity to seasickness. But Philip insisted that he go to sea and follow the plan that had been set. Unfortunately for Philip's hopes, the plan was as weak as the duke's stomach for seafaring. The heart of the plan was a rendezvous off Calais between Medina Sidonia with his naval force and the Duke of Parma (Alexander Farnese), who had assembled a tough expeditionary army in the ports of Dunkirk and Nieuport. The rendezvous was virtually impossible, though, because the Spanish fleet commanded no port on or near the Channel, and the Duke of Parma had no shallow-draught warships to break the Dutch blockade of his embarcation ports. Parma had mentioned this problem to Philip repeatedly but to no avail.

By early August – after storms, delays for repairs and much harassment from English ships – the Armada finally made Calais, unbroken and ready to protect Parma's crossing of the Channel; but of course the great Spanish galleons could not move into the shallow coastal waters and Parma could not come out of his ports. During the night of 7-8 August, the English sailed fire ships into the Armada, which had no choice but to scatter. The next day off Gravelines the swift English ships were able at last to inflict serious

117　The Armada at bay in the Channel; the smaller, swifter English ships were able to inflict crippling damage on the lumbering galleons of the Spaniards, which were also hard pressed to maneuver out of the way of fire ships.

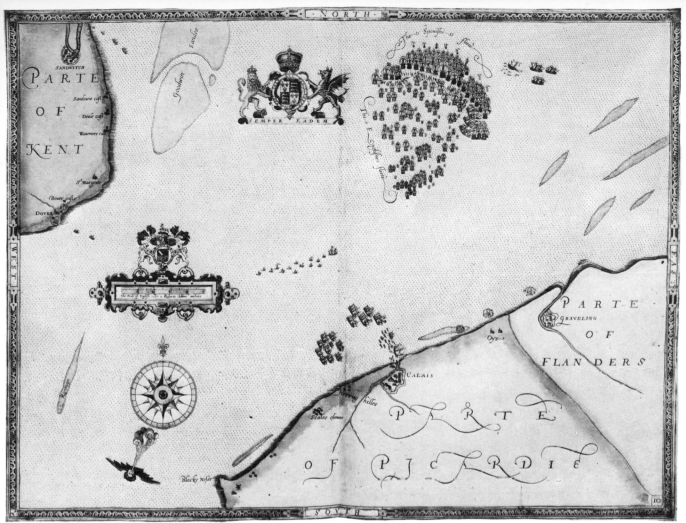

118 English representation of the engagement off Gravelines; the fire ships being sent into Calais harbour are also shown.

damage on the galleons before storms dispersed the fleets, driving the Armada into the North Sea. It could do nothing now but try to beat its way home around Scotland and Ireland. Only about half of the Spanish ships ever got back to Spanish ports.[6]

It was not until the second half of October that the outcome of the Armada's venture into the English Channel was widely known in Spain, but toward the end of the summer false reports of its success began to circulate. Miguel registered his reactions to both the unfounded rumors and to the delayed report of the truth in two long poems. The first poem bears the wordy title 'Song Born of the Varied News That Has Come of the Catholic Armada That Went Against England'. In it, acknowledging the uncertainty and confusion that beclouded the fate of the Armada, he yet dared to hope for and almost prophesy victory. The other poem is called 'Second Song on the Loss of the Armada That Went to England'. In this one he accepts the popular Spanish belief that it was the wind and the sea that defeated the Armada; he reminds Philip of the continuing depredations by English corsairs at home and in the colonies; and he urges him to renew the attack on England. As for Philip himself, he accepted the bad news with his usual iron self-control and set about analyzing the circumstances that had led to defeat. He was confident he could rebuild what he had lost, and, although Spanish power had passed its zenith, the nation did in fact remain dominant in Europe for a few years longer. What Philip may not have realized was that he would never command sufficient power to impose Catholic regimes on an increasingly Protestant Europe.

Except for one brief commission in September to buy olive oil in the Sevillan town of Marchena, and a couple of quick trips to Seville, Miguel spent most of the ten months between July 1588 and May 1599 in the now excessively familiar town of Ecija. Even under otherwise favorable circumstances, Ecija was not a pleasant place to spend the summer months. Known as 'the frying pan of Andalusia', its temperatures often reached truly African levels. During this period, one of Miguel's assignments was to produce large amounts of olive oil; another was to make arrangements for and supervise the milling of the collected wheat. Unfortunately, a substantial part of it had become wormy, which fact had to be reported to Seville and ultimately to the king, who was already disturbed by reports of the rotten foodstuffs supplied to the Armada. In the end Antonio de Guevara was to lose his position as chief purveyor to the Spanish fleet because of the poor quality of some of the supplies sent to the fleet and because of the dishonesty of some of his subordinates. Miguel had seen enough of the behaviour of some of his fellow commissaries to conclude, as he caused one of his loquacious dogs to remark, that they were 'the bane of our commonwealth'.[7]

But even honest commissaries found it difficult to maintain their reputation for honesty. Given the natural inclination of people to protect their property, it was almost inevitable that they would sometimes resort to the expedient of trying to discredit the commissaries. Cervantes had ample opportunity to observe in Ecija and elsewhere such attempts on his own reputation. He was usually able to combat them successfully, as was evident on two occasions in the fall of 1588. Agents of the town council of Ecija had persuaded the king that their commissary was not leaving them enough grain for food and seed and was in other ways abusing his office. Philip sent Antonio de Guevara a royal cedula containing unfavorable references to Cervantes. Of course, Miguel protested and in the end was completely exonerated. At a meeting of the town council on 30 September 1588, even the mayor spoke in his behalf:

'The aforesaid royal cedula was not obtained at the request of this city, nor was such a thing agreed upon by it, because the report which it contains and which apparently was used to obtain it, is false and sinister; because, as is well known, the aforesaid Miguel de Cervantes, during the past year of 1587 when he was present in this city commissioned by Antonio de Guevara, used his office in the collection of wheat with great rectitude, and he has done the same in this present year of 1588.'[8]

134

A few days later, as though to clinch the matter, the corregidor of Ecija had this to say: 'He has not seen nor heard that the aforesaid Miguel de Cervantes has done anything improper; on the contrary, he has exercised his office of commissary well and diligently....'[9] It takes a man of exceptional skill in human relations to win such testimony as this while discharging the thankless duties of a commissary.

On 26 June 1589, Miguel seems to have spent most of the day in notarial offices, since there exist four legal documents signed by him on that date and in the presence of four different notaries. So much legal business on one day suggests that he was pushing ahead preparations for a long absence from Seville. Two of the documents are of great interest. The first represents the settling of his very substantial bill with Tomás Gutiérrez, and makes specific reference to Miguel's having lodged with him. The second document confers on one of his commissarial associates, Miguel de Santa María, power of attorney to collect property and money owed him in Seville, to render an accounting of the milling of wheat in Ecija, and to collect Miguel's still largely unpaid salary. Since he had not received most of his salary, it is something of a mystery how he was able to pay his bills and get ready for a trip north. At least one scholar has suggested that he may have made a killing playing cards for money. This notion is supported only by the recognized popularity of gambling in Seville (with its three hundred gaming houses) and by Cervantes' evident familiarity with card games, as revealed in his fiction.[10]

119   Sixteenth-century Spanish playing cards.

There is no documentary evidence of Miguel's whereabouts from 26 June 1589 until he shows up in Seville again in February 1590. Had he continued with his commissions in Andalusia, there would be the usual public records. It seems altogether probable, therefore, that he headed for Esquivias and Madrid.

It is not difficult to find motives for this trip: Miguel had not seen wife, mother or sisters for nearly two years; additionally, it would have been a pleasure after such mundane pursuits to get in touch again with the literary life of Madrid, and he may well have had business with his publisher or with theatrical impresarios. Aside from these obvious possibilities, there are at least two other motives that look persuasive.

On 23 October 1587, Alonso Rodríguez, Ana de Villafranca's husband, had died.[11] There is no way of knowing when Miguel first heard this news, but presumably he knew it by the time of his trip north. His illegitimate daughter Isabel was over five years old. Now that her putative father was dead, Miguel may at this time have begun to assume some responsibility for her welfare. In view of the full responsibility he later assumed, this does not seem unlikely.

A final motive for a trip to Esquivias and Madrid may have been Miguel's inclination to try again for a post in America. Despite his unusual talents and his acknowledged achievements in war, in captivity, and in the literary world, he had reached the age of forty-two without securing a dependable livelihood. His commissions in Andalusia did support him, but they were uncertain, wearisome and vexatious. Besides, they kept him constantly separated from his family and the center of his deepest interests. If he had to be so much away from home, why not in America, where so many Spaniards had made their fortunes? But the decision to sail off to another world was not one to be taken lightly. One would want to talk it over with family and friends. Also, during this six-month period of unemployment, it would have been odd if he devoted no time to writing.

When Miguel got back to Seville in February of 1590, he was surprised to learn that Antonio de Guevara had not yet returned from Madrid (he was in the process of losing his job). His substitute, Miguel de Oviedo, offered Cervantes a commission to buy 4,000 arrobas of oil in Carmona. And so he spent a good part of the late winter in yet another important Andalusian city. Carmona, situated on the main road to Córdoba between Seville and Ecija, had been a major town since Roman times. Both its agricultural wealth and its archeological treasures may have appealed to Cervantes, but he does not mention the city in his works. And he was unable to find there anything like his assigned quota of olive oil.

In the late spring, still unpaid and tired of the bickerings and the endless comings and goings of the commissary's life, Miguel decided to make application to the Council of the Indies for one of four vacancies known to exist in America in 1590. He composed a formal petition to the king, known as a 'memorial', and sent it to Madrid along with his military service record and the testimonial from Algiers. It was presented to the Council of the Indies on 21 May 1590. The memorial is of sufficient interest to warrant reproducing it here.

120   Cervantes' Memorial applying for a post in the West Indies. $>$

Miguel de cerbantes Sa hauedas dice q ha seruido a V. M. muchos años en
las jornadas de mar y tierra q se han ofrescido de V. ydosanios desta parte
particularm.te en la Batalla Naual donde le dieron muchas heridas de
las quales perdio una mano de un arcabuçaco - y el año siguiente fue
a Nauarino - y despues a la de tunez y a la Goleta y viniendo a esta con
te con cartas del señor Don Joan y del Duque de Seza para q V. M.
le hiciese md. fue cautiuo en la galera del Sol el y un hermano
suyo q Tambien ha seruido a V. M. en las mismas jornadas y fueron
lleuados a argel Donde gastaron el patrimonio que tenian en Resca
tarse y toda la hazienda de sus padres y las dotes de dos hermanas
donzellas que tenia las quales quedaron pobres por Rescatar a sus her
manos. y despues de libertados fueron a seruir a V. M. en el Reyno de
Portugal. y a las terceras con el marques de S.ta cruz y agora al pre.te
estan siruiendo y siruen a V. M. el uno dellos en flandes de alferez
y el miguel de cerbantes fue el que traxo las cartas y auisos del Alcayde de
Mostagan y fue a oran por orden De V. M. y despues ha asistido siruj
endo en seuilla en negocios de la Armada por orden de Antonio de
gueuara como consta por las informaciones q tiene y en todo este tpo
no se le ha hecho md. ninguna Pide y supp.ca humilmente q.to puede a
V. M. sea seruido de hazerle md. de un off.o en las yndias de los
tres o quatro q al pre.te estan Vaccos q es el uno la contaduria del
nuevo Reyno de granada. O la gouernacion de la probincia de
Soconuzco en guatimala. O contador de las galeras de cartagena
o corregidor de la ciudad de la Paz y con qualquiera destos
officios q V. M. le haga md. La Resceuira por q es hombre auil
y suffi.ciente y benemerito para q V. M. le haga md. porq su de
sseo es a continuar siempre en el seruicio de V. M. y acauar su
vida como lo han hecho sus antepassados q en ello Resceuira
muy gran bien y md.

busque por aca en que
se le haga
md. en madrid a 6 de Junio 1590

'Sire: Miguel de Cervantes Saavedra says that he has served Your Majesty for many years in the sea and land campaigns that have occurred over the last 22 years, particularly in the Naval Battle, where he received many wounds, among which was the loss of a hand from gunfire. The following year he went to Navarino and then to the campaign of Tunis and La Goletta. Returning to the Court with letters from His Lordship Don Juan and from the Duke of Sessa so that Your Majesty might grant him favor, he was captured on the Galley *Sol* (he and a brother of his who also served Your Majesty in the same engagements), and they were taken to Algiers, where they spent what patrimony they had and their parents' estate and the dowries of two maiden sisters, who accepted poverty to ransom their brothers. After they were freed, they went to serve Your Majesty in the Kingdom of Portugal, and to the Azores with the Marquis of Santa Cruz. At present they are still serving Your Majesty: one in Flanders as a lieutenant, and Miguel de Cervantes, who is the one who brought letters and information from the Mayor of Mostaganem and went to Oran by order of Your Majesty. And he has since continued to serve in Seville on business of the Armada, under the orders of Antonio de Guevara, as is on record in the testimonials in his possession. In all this time he has received no favors at all. He asks and begs as humbly as he can that Your Majesty be pleased to grant him the favor of a position in America, of the three or four currently vacant, namely, the accountant's office in the new Kingdom of Granada, or the governorship of the province of Soconusco in Guatemala, or the office of ship's accountant in Cartagena, or that of corregidor in the city of La Paz. He will accept any one of these offices with which Your Majesty may favor him, because he is skillful, competent and worthy enough to receive Your Majesty's favor. His desire is to continue always in the service of Your Majesty and end his life in it as have his ancestors, because in it he will be greatly favored and rewarded.'[12]

Influence and money won more jobs than merit, it seems. On 6 June 1590, an official of the Council of the Indies scribbled on the back of Cervantes' memorial: 'Let him look on this side of the water for some favor that may be granted him.' Perhaps the sympathetic reader will console himself with the proverb about the ill wind that blows no good. The action of the Council of the Indies unwittingly favored the birth of Don Quixote.

Unable to carry his hopes and dreams off to the New World, Miguel had little choice but to continue in his present service to the king. It was to last longer than he ever imagined – long enough, in fact, to survive the tenure of three chief purveyors to the Spanish navy. It has already been noted that Antonio de Guevara had been summoned to Madrid to answer for the poor quality of the foodstuffs collected for the Armada. Although the judicial investigation ordered by Philip did not reveal dishonesty on the part of Guevara, it did uncover dishonesty among a number of his chief subordinates. The upshot of the judicial proceedings was that Guevara lost his job and his guilty associates were hanged (in December 1592).

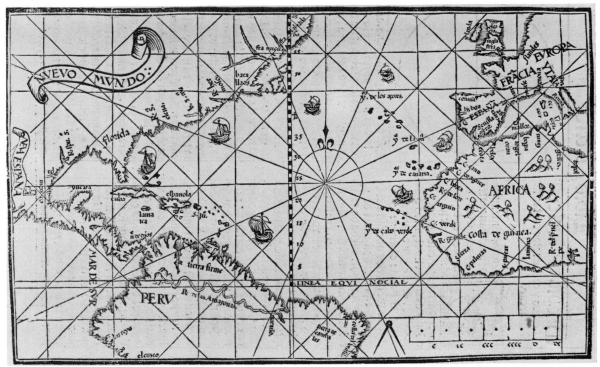

121 Map of the Old and New Worlds, 1545.

At one time or another, Miguel had been obliged to have dealings with most of the men thus executed. Although he was never a party to any of the misappropriations of money or grain, the atmosphere of mistrust created by the conduct of the executed officials did make the periodic rendering of his accounts more exacting. The minor discrepancies sometimes found in his accounts could usually be explained in one of two ways: either the king's accountants were trying to spare the public exchequer by short-changing him or his arithmetic was faulty. In the second case, he sometimes inadvertently cheated himself.[13]

One indication of Miguel's honesty and dependability is that each new purveyor proceeded to renew his commission. Guevara's successor, Pedro de Isunza Lequeitio, was appointed in the spring of 1591. Even before Isunza assumed his office, Miguel was given a new commission in his name by his deputy, Miguel de Oviedo. The following year, having occasion to write the king in defense of his commissaries, Isunza mentions Miguel de Cervantes Saavedra among his 'honorable and trustworthy men'.[14] But no amount of honorable conduct and official backing could fully insulate a man from the kind of suspicions engendered by a commissary's functions. On 19 September 1592, Miguel was arrested and jailed in Castro del Río, that same Cordovan town where he had earlier been excommunicated for arresting a sacristan! Soon released on bail, he was fully exonerated before the end of the fall.[15]

As was evident in the case of Antonio de Guevara, the chief purveyor of the fleet could also run into difficulties arising out of the exercise of his functions. Pedro de Isunza was no exception. Early in 1592, one of Cervantes' assistants had taken some 1,800 bushels of wheat from one Salvador de Toro of the province of Málaga. Tired of waiting for his pay, Toro finally sued Isunza, who late in November had to go to Madrid to defend himself. This is of interest here mostly because Isunza took Miguel with him as a witness. Toro continued litigation with Isunza until the latter's death on 24 June 1593.

Cervantes testified on behalf of his chief in the first days of December 1592,[16] and then presumably had some time for his mother, his sisters, his daughter Isabel, and whatever old friends happened to be in town. Isabel's mother and her mother's husband had kept a quality tavern in Tudescos Street at least since 1585 and perhaps before. The mother was still running the tavern in the winter of 1592. It is possible that she and Miguel may have met there in the days of their love affair, and it was there that he would have had to go to see his daughter. Before the end of December, he was back in Seville.

Despite his commissarial duties, Cervantes never abandoned his interest in writing. The record of the writing he actually did is meager but not blank. A curious document, dated 5 September 1592, testifies to his continuing (or renewed) inclination to write for the theater.[17] On that date, he signed with the successful impresario Rodrigo Osorio an agreement to compose six plays at a price of fifty ducats each. One of the conditions of the agreement was that Osorio was required to put each play on the stage within twenty days of receiving it. Another condition stipulated that Osorio was obliged to pay nothing at all for any of the plays that did not turn out to be among the best ever represented in Spain. The price was very good by the standards of the day. In the 1580s, Cervantes had received forty ducats for the highly successful play *The Confused Lady*. That he should now offer to waive payment for any of the plays not well received says something about his self-confidence as a writer. So far as is known, he never delivered any of the plays to Osorio. No doubt he was prevented from doing so by the endless distractions of the life of a commissary, beginning with his arrest in Castro del Río only about two weeks after he signed the agreement.

Before his commissions finally ended in the spring of 1594, Cervantes was to know, as a muleteer or carter might, the highways and byways of at least six Andalusian provinces – Badajoz, Córdoba, Huelva, Jaén, Málaga and Seville – not to mention the considerable stretch of territory over the Sierra Morena Mountains and across La Mancha to Toledo, Esquivias and Madrid. It is perhaps natural to dwell on the privations and harassments attendant on these commissarial travels: the bad roads, the inclement weather, the rough lodgings and poor food, the ill-will of people understandably reluctant to exchange their wheat for certificates of payment, and the shortage of money to live on when, as usual, wages were in arrears. But, of course, there was another and more agreeable side to all this. The weather was often good, the lodgings acceptable and the food sometimes savory.

122 Courtyard of a sixteenth-century inn in Toledo.

123 Woodcut of a guitar-player.

It can be no exaggeration to say that Cervantes spent hundreds of nights in country inns during the almost thirteen years he travelled about the southern half of Spain on His Majesty's business, and what he saw and learned must have been worth more to him as a writer than the university education fate had denied him. Some notion of how he and his fellow guests may have whiled away their idle hours at the hostelries to which their travels led them can be fairly inferred from his writings. What went on in the inns was as varied as the people who frequented them, and, as the inns were not large, most of what went on came sooner or later to everybody's attention.

In the rest periods between stages of a journey, travellers looked to the inns not only for food and lodging but also for recreation. There was often a deck of cards available for those who liked to play. If a traveller carried his own deck, however, it might be a sign that he was a professional gambler. Two of Cervantes' amusing young rogues, Rinconete and Cortadillo, liked to pick up some extra change by luring unwary muleteers into a game of 'twenty-one' played with marked cards. Cervantes shows them at work at the Venta del Molinillo, one of the real inns mentioned in the last chapter. If there was a guitar in an inn there was usually someone who could play it and thus increase the possibility of singing and dancing as well. In a story called *The Illustrious Kitchen-Maid*, Cervantes animates an impromptu fiesta of singing and dancing at the door of the historic Posada del Sevillano in Toledo. The dancers who took advantage of the music were stable boys, scullery maids and the like. Some of the customers of the inns were just as rough and

124 Sancho Panza tossed in the blanket: an illustration from a nineteenth-century American edition of *Don Quixote*.

ready as the stable boys and scullery maids and even more disposed to amuse themselves with the kind of horseplay Sancho had to endure on a certain occasion:

'But, as ill fate would have it, among the people in the inn were four wool-combers from Segovia, three needle-makers from the Colt Square in Cordova, and a couple from the Market of Seville, cheerful, well-meaning, playful rogues who, almost of one accord, ran up to Sancho and pulled him from his ass. Then one of them went in for the blanket from the host's bed and threw him on to it. But when they looked up they saw that the roof was rather too low for their purpose, and decided to go out into the back-yard, whose ceiling was the sky; and there, placing Sancho in the centre of the blanket, they began to toss him up and amuse themselves at his expense, as they do with dogs at Shrovetide.'[18]

The presence of Eros often made itself felt in the inns at night. In the story of *The Illustrious Kitchen-Maid*, two well-born youths disguised as lads of lesser station are attracted to the Posada del Sevillano by the fame of a beautiful kitchen-maid (who, like the boys, turns out to be of distinguished family). In the middle of the night, two Galician serving maids, no longer young but still susceptible to strong amorous impulses, knock softly on the boys' door and ask to be admitted, claiming they look like a couple of archduchesses. In no mood for the attention of such creatures, one of the lads exclaims: 'Arch-duchesses at this hour?... I don't believe in them; rather do I assume that you are witches or sly wenches. Begone, or else by — I swear that if I get up, with the buckles of my belt I'll leave your buttocks looking like poppies.' Before the disgruntled volunteer paramours sneak back to their own room, one of them whispers through the keyhole: 'Honey is not for the ass's mouth.'[19]

But not all travellers were as hard to please as the youths just mentioned. Readers of *Don Quixote* will remember the muleteer who makes his bed in the starry loft where the Knight is put to bed after he has been beaten up by the Yanguesan carriers. Unforgettable is Maritornes, the Asturian maid,

'broad-faced, flat-nosed, and with a head that seemed to have no back to it; she was blind of one eye and not too sound in the other. But she made up for her other shortcomings by her bodily allurements; she was not more than three feet high from head to toe, and her shoulders, which were rather on the heavy side, made her look down on the ground more than she liked.'[20]

Despite her looks and a breath 'that reeked of the stale salad of the night before', the muleteer looks forward to the fulfillment of her promise to come lie with him after the inn was asleep, for 'it is told to the credit of this good girl that she never made such promises without fulfilling them, even if she made them far away in the mountains and without any witness at all'.[21] The finale of this hilarious episode, after Don Quixote has intercepted Maritornes on her dark and groping way to the muleteer's bed, suggests that Cervantes'

142

rare powers of invention added something to what observation may have taught him about night life in the country inns.

Among the more conspicuous travellers of the time were the strolling entertainers of one kind or another. Although they offered their entertainment more often in the towns than in the country, they were not adverse to performing in the country inns when there were potential customers present. In *Don Quixote* Cervantes presents an example in the person of Master Peter with his fortune-telling ape and his puppet show. How the innkeeper reacted to such visits is clear: 'I would turn out the Duke of Alba himself to make room for Master Peter.... Bring the ape and the puppets, for there are people in the inn tonight who'll pay to see the show, and the ape's talents as well.'[22]

Reading aloud was still another form of occasional entertainment in the inns. Wherever there were a few books, someone could be found to read them. One of Cervantes' innkeepers, after mentioning two or three books of chivalry left at his inn, comments:

'For at harvest time a lot of the reapers come in here in the mid-day heat. There is always one of them who can read, and he takes up one of those books. Then as many as thirty of us sit round him, and we enjoy listening so much that it saves us countless grey hairs.'[23]

Cervantes exploited the custom of reading aloud by arranging for the Priest to read to the assembled guests his own story of *The Man Who Was Too Curious for His Own Good*.

125   An ambitious acrobatic performance outside the Real Alcázar, Madrid.

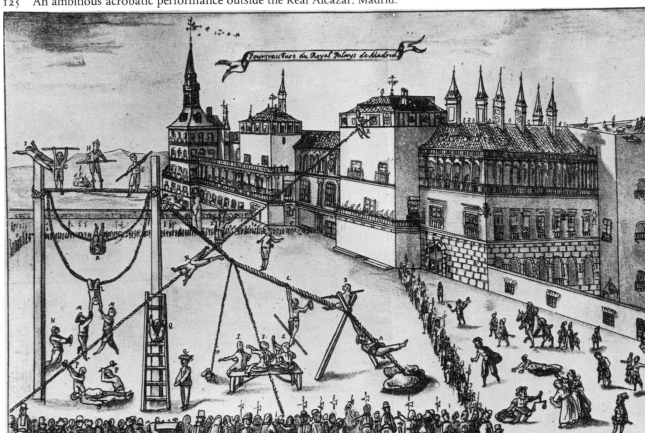

But, of course, the most dependable way of filling idle hours at the inns was with conversation. Over a period of time one could expect to talk with all sorts of exceptional people: enlightened ecclesiastics, such as the Canon of Toledo; licentiates in law, such as the Judge *en route* to the High Court of Mexico; soldiers returning from distant campaigns or from captivity in Algiers, such as the Captive Captain; members of the Holy Brotherhood in pursuit of criminals. Important items of news were exchanged and discussed: Alexander Farnese had captured the city of Antwerp; would he finally subdue the northern provinces of the Netherlands as he had the southern? The Turkish janissaries were said to be increasingly insubordinate; would Murad III be able to control them?

Without extensive exposure to the kinds of people, behavior and conversation suggested above, it is doubtful that even a man of Cervantes' inventive power could have populated the world of *Don Quixote* so convincingly with more than 650 characters. But beyond the plausible suggestions just advanced, it is possible to relate certain episodes in his great novel to verified historical incidences and conditions. This is not the place to study such matters exhaustively, but a couple of examples may prove interesting.

In the late fall of 1591, Cervantes' commission carried him to the charming Cordovan town of Montilla, famous for its exquisite wines. There, some twenty years earlier, three women known as the Camachas had been accused of sorcery by the mother of a girl seduced by a young nobleman. The Camachas were taken to Córdoba and tried by the Inquisition. The records of the trial have been lost, and one can only speculate about its outcome. But it created a great stir in its day, and the notoriety of the Camachas in that part of Andalusia lasted longer than their lives.[24] Here, from *The Colloquy of the Dogs*, is how Cervantes used what he heard in Montilla:

'You must know, my lad, that in this town there formerly lived the most famous witch in the world. She was called Camacha of Montilla and was so outstanding at her trade that the Erichthos, the Circes and the Medeas, of whom I am told the story-books are full, could not come up to her. She caused the clouds to congeal whenever she felt like doing so and with them covered the face of the sun, and when the whim seized her the most troub!ed sky would become serene once more. She would bring men back in an instant from far-off lands, and she had a marvelous cure for maidens who had been a bit careless in guarding their virginity. She took care of widows in such a way that they might be disrespectable and still be respected, she undid marriages and married off those whom she pleased. She had fresh roses in her garden in December, and in January reaped wheat [the translator mistakenly reads "sowed" for "reaped"]. As for growing watercress in a bowl, that wa~ the least of the things she did, and it was nothing at all for her, when so requested, to cause the living or the dead to appear in a mirror or upon the fingernail of a newborn child. She had a reputation for transforming men into animals, and for six years was said to have made use of a sacristan in the form of an ass.'[25]

Shortly before Cervantes went to Montilla, he had been in Baeza, Jaén and Úbeda. At the time of this visit to Úbeda, the great Spanish mystic and poet John of the Cross was living there, until, on 14 December 1591, he died and was buried in the town. Then, one night in the summer of 1593, while Miguel was in Seville, the remains of the venerable mystic were secretly exhumed and started on their way to a monastery in Segovia. According to a sixteenth-century life of St John of the Cross, that very night on the road north a man suddenly appeared beside the road and shouted: 'Where are you taking the body of the saint? Leave it where it was.'[26] As soon as Úbeda learned of the secret removal of the remains of their beloved friar, it instituted a suit against Segovia. The suit lasted for several years and was finally settled by dividing the remains between the two cities. In chapter 19 of Part One of *Don Quixote*, the mad knight stops a nocturnal funeral procession carrying a corpse from Baeza for burial in Segovia. It is of course impossible to prove that the fictitious adventure of the dead body was inspired by the historical translation of the remains of John of the Cross, but it seems altogether plausible, and in any case it may stand as an example of the kind of material that accrued to the literary account of a commissary of genius.

We have referred more than once to the irritations, complaints, and appeals of the villages, towns and cities to which the royal commissaries were sent to collect wheat and oil. Needless to say, the king and his councils were deluged with such complaints and appeals. In the light of so much dissatisfaction and of the less than satisfactory results achieved by the commissary system of supplying the Spanish navy, Philip decided in the spring of 1594 to abolish the system. The chief purveyor and all his commissaries found themselves abruptly unemployed. Miguel had been at the job for about seven years; he was now forty-six, and he still had no dependable livelihood. As he turned his face toward Madrid, he must have felt glad to be going home, glad to be relieved of his onerous duties, lucky to have escaped from them with honor, but preoccupied with the uncertainties of his future.

126   Sixteenth-century view of Granada, the city which, with the nearby Alpujarras Mountains, was the center of the Morisco culture until after the 1570 rebellion, when the Moriscos were forcibly expelled from the area.

GRANATA.

A. GRANADA.
B. ALVEISIN.
C. ALHAMBRE.
D. ANTIQVERVELA.
1. St. Hieronymo.
2. Hospital St. Juan.
3. Yglesia maior.
4. St. Christoual.
5. Castillo Acobir.
6. Castillo Maior.
7. St. Francesco.
8. Palacio Real nueuo.
9. Sancta Maria.
10. Sanct Genes.
11. Puerta serrada.
12. Sancta Helena.
13. Masmoros.
14. Los martires.
15. Gannos antigos.
16. Sierra neuada.
17. Sierra del Sol.

Occidens

Effigiabat Georgius Hoefnaglius

11 Final Years in Andalusia

Back in Madrid by the second half of June 1594, Cervantes still hoped to obtain a government job that would afford him a decent living. It is unlikely that his first choice would have been the commission granted him that summer, namely, that of collecting back taxes in the following cities and towns of the provinces of Granada and Málaga: Granada, Guadix, Baza, Motril, Salobreña, Almuñécar, Alhama, Loja, Vélez Málaga and Ronda. The amount to be collected was 2,459,989 maravedis. To visit all these towns and to negotiate with the proper officials for the payment of all this money, Miguel was allotted fifty days plus travel time from Madrid to Granada and back. His wages were set at 550 maravedis (16 reals) per day, which was about fifty per cent better than his last pay as commissary, and he was invested with the same kind of legal authority granted him in his previous assignments. Before he could actually be given the commission, however, he had to offer a surety of 1,500,000 maravedis, which was provided by a certain Francisco Suárez Gasco. That Miguel could find such backing speaks well for his reputation. Still, he and his wife were also required to sign an obligation committing their separate and joint possessions to the faithful discharge of his commission. Miguel received the royal letter of appointment on 23 August 1594, and must have set out at once, since by the end of the first week in September we find him already at work in the mountain towns of Guadix and Baza.

In some of the towns assigned to him, Cervantes had no trouble making his collections promptly; in others the officials stalled; in still others they claimed that the taxes demanded had already been paid. The delays occasioned by these last two categories obliged Cervantes to write to the king requesting more time and inquiring whether certain taxes had in fact already been paid. The king's answer granting him more time reached him in Málaga in early December. Before the end of the month, he had completed his mission with better than average results. Nevertheless, his small margin of failure, the carelessness or stupidity of the royal accountants, and the bankruptcy of a merchant in Seville combined to afflict Cervantes with a seemingly endless series of expenses and harassments which finally culminated in his imprisonment.[1]

Miguel was able to collect the full amount due in every town except Baza, Ronda and Vélez Málaga. The uncollected amounts of the first two

127 A Moorish woman of Granada.

147

towns were minor; in Vélez Málaga, however, he was able to collect only 136,000 maravedis out of 277,000 due. As the 136,000 maravedis were the last to come into his keeping before the return trip and as it appeared to him dangerous to carry them on his person, he deposited them and some money of his own in Seville with a well-known merchant named Simón Freire de Lima. Once back in Madrid, he waited with growing impatience for Freire to forward the money. After several weeks, he wrote to Freire, who in due time referred him to a certain Gabriel Rodríguez in Madrid. The latter either would not or could not pay. Another letter to Freire followed, and still more waiting, part of which Miguel may have spent in the familiar Castilian city of Toledo. At any rate, a recently discovered document shows that he was there on 18 May 1595.[2] It was probably some time after that date when the upsetting news arrived: Freire had gone bankrupt and disappeared with 60,000 ducats.

Miguel hurried to Seville to see if something could be done to salvage the king's money. He found that Freire's creditors had already attached his property. Back to Madrid he rode to report to the king and to the general accountant's office. At his request, the king issued an order to one of the judges in Seville to collect Cervantes' deposit provided it was not at the expense of creditors with claims prior to that of Cervantes. And so our dejected tax-collector rushed back to Seville with the king's order. It was now the middle of August 1595. The money was finally delivered to the king's agents in Madrid in January 1597! Nobody knows how much money and anguish Freire's bankruptcy cost Miguel, but it was surely an oppressive amount. By specific order of His Majesty, all the expenses incurred in the attempt to collect from Freire's estate were borne by Cervantes.[3] Sick of government service and tired of scuttling back and forth between Madrid and Seville, he decided to remain for a while in the latter city.

Decidedly, 1595 was a bad year for Miguel. It is true that he won first prize (three silver spoons) in a poetry contest sponsored by the Dominican monastery in Saragossa.[4] This may have encouraged him to renew his literary activity, but very little else was encouraging. His niece Constanza was deceived by a young nobleman with false promises of marriage.[5] Doña Catalina's uncle, Juan de Palacios, died in May. He was the priest who had married Miguel and Catalina and had in other ways been helpful in Esquivias during Miguel's long absences. He left Doña Catalina two small vineyards and some minor household goods.

What records there are suggest that Seville continued to be the headquarters of Cervantes' activities for most of the interval between the summer of 1595 and the summer of 1600. It is certain that he spent some portion of this time writing, but as he sold no books and had no government job it is not clear what he had to live on. Plausible conjecture points to some kind of business activity, and this is supported by meager evidence of periodic ups and downs in his personal finances otherwise difficult to account for and by a statement of his sister Magdalena in 1605 to the effect that he was both a writer and a businessman.[6]

128 Charles Howard,
First Earl of Nottingham
(Lord Howard of Effingham).

One of the ways of keeping up with Miguel and his activities during the final years of the century is through his reactions to public events. The English capture of Cádiz furnishes a good example. Ever since the defeat of the Armada, England and Spain had remained at war. Philip planned new invasions with particular emphasis on Ireland, while England attacked Spain's colonies and preyed on her shipping. Then in June 1596 an English squadron under Lord Howard of Effingham and the Earl of Essex sailed from Plymouth for the thriving port of Cádiz. Incredible as it must have seemed to the surviving veterans of Spain's mighty military and naval victories, the English were able not only to take and sack the city but also to remain there for more than two weeks. The Duke of Medina Sidonia, still bearing the title of Captain General of the Ocean Sea, was more active with his pen than with his sword during this period and kept well clear of Cádiz until the English were gone. The bold English invasion and the unbelievable conduct of the Spanish leaders were the subject of bitter conversation and even of poetic mockery in Seville that summer. Cervantes was one of the poets to satirize the event, and the sonnet he wrote was one of the best. It has been translated as follows:

> This July saw another Holy week,
>> When certain brotherhoods made quite a blaze,
>> Well-known as squads – in military phrase –
> Which made the mob and not the English shriek!
> So many feathers waved from peak to peak,
>> That in some fourteen, or some fifteen days,
>> Their Pigmies and Goliaths winged their ways,
> And all their pageant vanished like a freak.
> The Bull-calf bellowed; placed his squad in line;
>> The sky grew dark; a rumbling seized the ground,
>> Which threatened total ruin as it shook;
> And into Cádiz with a prudence fine,
>> Soon as the Earl had left it safe and sound,
>> In triumph marched Medina's mighty Duke![7]

149

(The next to the last line fails to capture the full irony of Cervantes' verse, which credits the Duke with 'no fear at all', now that the Earl of Essex was gone.)

If it is not possible to be sure of Miguel's whereabouts during the whole period under review, there is one seven-month stretch that can be fixed with considerable precision. In August 1597 the general accountant's office notified Francisco Suárez Gasco (Miguel's surety for the proper discharge of his tax-collecting mission) and Doña Catalina that Cervantes' accounts were 79,804 maravedis short. For all the good it did Cervantes, the accountant's records were faulty, their arithmetic demonstrably bad. Suárez Gasco didn't know this, of course, nor did he want to be obliged to put up any of his own money to rescue Miguel, so he requested the king to summon Miguel to Madrid to explain his accounts. This the king did, stipulating that Cervantes was to post bond that he would appear at court within twenty days, failing which he was to be arrested and sent under guard at his own expense to the royal prison in Madrid.[8] Incredibly, Judge Gaspar de Vallejo in Seville set Miguel's bond at 2,557,029 maravedis (he was accused of a deficit of only 79,804 maravedis)! Needless to say, Cervantes could not raise so exorbitant a bond, and so Gaspar de Vallejo had him sent, not to the royal prison in Madrid as instructed and where communication with the general accountant's office might have been possible, but to the royal prison in Seville. This was either in late September or early October, that is to say, close to the date of Miguel's fiftieth birthday. He wrote to the king requesting that he be released on some reasonable bond, so that he could obey the king's orders and render his accounts. On 1 December Philip sent a new provision to Judge Vallejo ordering him to release Cervantes on bail of 79,804 maravedis.[9] But for reasons which remain a mystery, Vallejo failed to do so.

Built in 1569, the royal prison of Seville was one of the newest, largest and most populous in all Spain. Contemporary documents describe it as a living hell of noise, confusion, violence and stench. The whole range of criminality was represented there, and it was widely believed that the warden and his staff were as corrupt as any of the involuntary inmates. Food, drink and special privileges were for sale, and living was tough for those unable to buy.[10] This is the place where fate offered Miguel yet another opportunity to learn 'patience in adversity', and the place he had in mind when he wrote this famous sentence in the Prologue to *Don Quixote*: 'And so, what could my sterile and ill-cultivated genius beget but the story of a lean, shrivelled, whimsical child, full of varied fancies that no one else ever imagined – much like one engendered in prison, where every discomfort has its seat and every dismal sound its habitation?'[11]

It cannot be proved that Cervantes began to write his novel in the Seville prison, but it seems likely. Somehow he had to liberate himself from the depressing circumstances of his incarceration. If they could confine his person to that dismal place, they had no power to confine his memory and his imagination. With more than ample time to take stock of his life, is it unlikely that he should call back his youthful dreams and the heroic deeds of

129 Landing a shoal of tunny fish in Cádiz harbour; as the home port of most of the treasure fleets from the New World, Cádiz achieved a high level of prosperity during this period.

his young manhood and contrast them in his mind with the disappointments and injustices of his mature years? Remembering the victories of Mühlberg and Tunis and Lepanto and knowing that Protestantism still flourished in Germany and untold Christian slaves still languished in Constantinople and North Africa, might he not begin to wonder whether outcomes bear any relation at all to intentions? Spain held to the illusion of being the most powerful nation on earth and yet her home port of Cádiz had been occupied for more than two weeks by insular upstarts. Spain could count on the fabulous treasure of the Indies, and yet she looked more and more like an asylum for beggars, *pícaros* and disabled veterans. Assuredly, things were seldom what they seemed. Could such thoughts and recollections as these move a writer to imagine a fictional world where it is difficult to discriminate between reality and illusion and to create a hero whose noble endeavors so often prove to be disheartening mistakes?

Towards the end of March 1598, royal accountants appeared in Seville to ask Cervantes for a sworn statement on the disposition of wheat and barley collected in 1591! Miguel responded that he would be glad to do so if they would let him out of jail so that he could consult his papers, most of which were in Málaga. He also mentioned that he had still to receive a sizable portion of the wages of that commission. After an exchange of letters between officials in Seville and the general accountant's office in Madrid, Miguel was finally released from jail, probably in late April. He had been

there about seven months. On 28 April 1598, he submitted his sworn statement on the handling of his commission in 1591. Apparently he was excused,
for the time being at least, from travelling to Madrid to explain the imagined
deficit in the accounts of his tax-collecting mission.[12]

During the late spring and summer, Miguel heard several items of news
that affected his life in one way or another. In November of the previous
year, Philip had ordered Spanish theaters to be closed as part of the national
mourning for the death of his daughter, the Duchess of Savoy. In May 1598
he was persuaded that it was in the interest of public morality to close them
permanently. This news cannot have pleased Cervantes nor encouraged him
to go back to writing for the theater. On 12 May 1598, Ana de Villafranca
died. The news of her death set him thinking about their daughter Isabel, for
whom proper provision would now have to be made. The gravest news of all
was that of King Philip's death on 13 September 1598. Philip the Prudent was
followed by his weak-willed son, who might well have been called Philip the
Improvident. The consequences of this change of rule would touch the lives
of all Spaniards.

At the end of Philip II's reign, Spain was still the most powerful country
in Europe – the only one, in fact, that could mobilize sufficient resources to
wage war at the same time against three such powers as England, France and
the Netherlands. But so much war had brought Spain to the brink of
economic disaster. If she had not yet fallen over the brink, it was largely
because Philip had been able to count on large supplies of gold and silver

130, 131 Treasure from
the 'new Spain'; these
pieces were recovered
from the wreck of a
Spanish galleon off
Bermuda. Left, a gold and
emerald pectoral cross,
c. 1594, and, right,
pieces of eight and
jewelry.

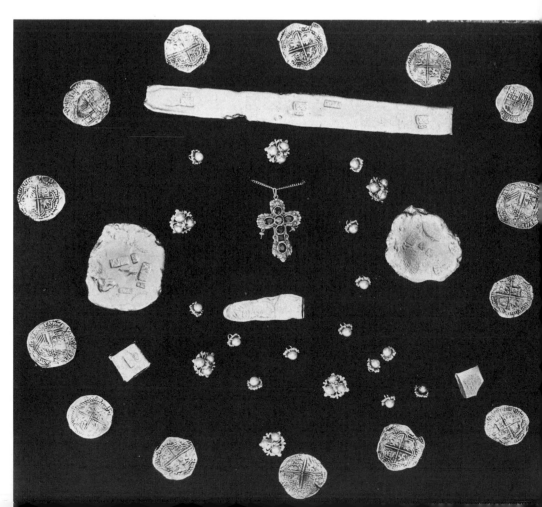

from his colonies in America. But even this wealth was not inexhaustible; furthermore, its effect was to promote inflation and neglect of home industry.

Spain desperately needed a new foreign policy – especially one that would extricate her from the intolerable burden of upholding Spanish authority in the Low Countries – and a sensible program of internal reform and development. Philip II failed to give these things to his country, and for this failure he has often been judged harshly by posterity. In his own time, however, he probably enjoyed the love and respect of the majority of his subjects. Even the mordant satirist Quevedo, who could see better than most the 'crumbled walls of his fatherland', summed up his reign with approval: 'He left peace in his kingdoms, fame for his arms, love among his vassals, fear among his enemies; because he lived in such a way as to prepare for his death and died in such a way as to do credit to his life.'[13]

Cervantes was also among the poets who wrote in praise of the dead king. A long poem of his was pinned to the catafalque which the town council of Seville commissioned to be built in the cathedral in honor to their departed monarch. This poem is of no great artistic value; it is of some interest, however, because several of its possibly ironic verses suggest that Cervantes' approval of Philip was less than whole-hearted[14] and because its presence on the catafalque may suggest something about Miguel's position in the literary world of Seville. In addition to this poem, he composed an amusing sonnet about the ostentatious catafalque, which became one of the most celebrated sonnets of its day. A contemporary manuscript tells us that a roguish poet (Cervantes) recited it in the cathedral on 29 December 1598. Although the translation falls short of doing justice to the original, it is still worth reproducing:

> I vow to God such grandeur stuns my brain!
>> I'd give a crown its wonders to detail;
>> For such a grand machine on such a scale
> Beggars description, makes invention vain.
> Now, by the living Christ, each piece, 'tis plain,
>> Is worth a million! Pity it should fail
>> To last an age! Hail, grand Sevilla, hail,
> In wit and wealth a second Rome again!
> I'd wager that the soul of the deceased,
>> On such a sight as this to gloat and gaze,
>> Hath left its joy eternal in the skies.
> A listening puppy answered: 'I at least,
>> Sir soldier, doubt not what your honour says,
>> Who dares to think the opposite – he lies!'
>>> On this, to my surprise,
>> The stripling stinted, fumbled with his blade,
> Looked sideways, vanished, and no more was said.[15]

Cervantes was still proud of this sonnet many years later, when he wrote in his *Journey to Parnassus*:

153

I penned the *Sonnet* with this opening strain
(To crown my writings with their chiefest grace),
I vow to God, such grandeur stuns my brain![16]

Less than a month after Miguel read his sonnet in the cathedral of Seville, Philip III journeyed to Valencia to participate in a double wedding: his own to the Archduchess Margaret of Austria and that of his sister Isabel Clara Eugenia to the Archduke Albert. The celebrations of the weddings in Valencia, Barcelona and Madrid, involving a seemingly endless succession of banquets, balls, tourneys, fireworks and bullfights, cost the astounding sum of 950,000 ducats and ushered in a reign of unparalleled extravagance precisely when Spain was sinking into an economic morass of poverty, inflation and over-taxation.

But if the king had an insatiable appetite for pleasure, he had none at all for work. He has been called the laziest king Spain ever had.[17] Being little interested in affairs of state, he allowed a favorite, the Duke of Lerma, to exercise most of the royal power and authority. Lerma, who was as greedy as the king was lazy, replaced many of the trusted advisors of Philip II with his own favorites and proceeded to use his privileged position to amass a huge personal fortune. The ostentatious beginnings of the new reign augured ill for the economic welfare of Spain, but they did provide the public with a brilliant and varied spectacle. One wonders how much of it Cervantes may have seen.

154

132, 133   The Archduke Albert of Austria
and his bride, the Infanta Isabel Clara Eugenia.

134-6   The new regime. Below, Philip III, painted
shortly after his accession, and, right, Margaret of
Austria, his queen. Below right, the Duke of Lerma,
Philip's favorite, who virtually ruled Spain through
a series of favorites of his own. 'The king has no
other will than that of the duke', commented the
Venetian ambassador.

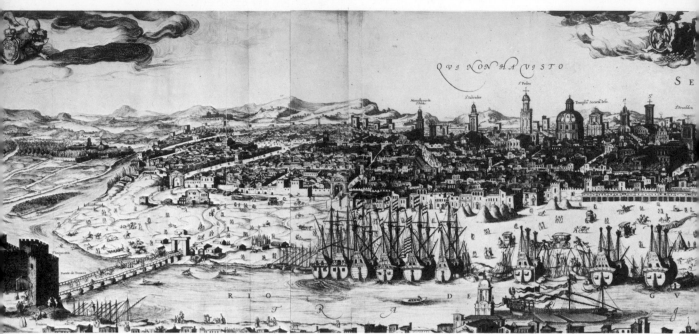

137 Panorama of Seville in 1617, seen from the other side of the Guadalquivir; Seville was

We know that he was in Seville in September 1598, since on that date he borrowed money for a new suit; we know he was there in early November, because there is record of his borrowing twelve ducats; we know he read his famous sonnet in Seville on 29 December 1598; and we know that on 10 February 1599 he collected in Seville a debt of ninety ducats owed him by a certain Juan de Cervantes.[18] After this last date there is no evidence of his presence in Seville for many months, and there are persuasive reasons for supposing that he went back to Esquivias and Madrid for a while. For one thing, an epidemic of bubonic plague had been raging in Seville, taking in 1599 some eight thousand lives;[19] for another, the establishment of the royal household in Madrid could be counted on to initiate changes worth watching; finally, there were family obligations to draw him north, particularly the obligation to provide for his recently 'orphaned' daughter.

If Miguel went to Madrid soon after he had collected the ninety ducats already mentioned, he would have been there at the time of the publication in March of one of the most famous and successful novels of the age, the picaresque *Guzmán de Alfarache* by Mateo Alemán. Alemán's life reveals a number of interesting similarities to that of Cervantes: he was born on 28 September 1547 (the day before the probable birthday of Cervantes); he was for part of his adult life a royal accountant obliged to travel extensively about Spain; and he was imprisoned (for debt) in the royal jail of Seville. In 1608 he managed, unlike Cervantes, to make his way to America. When he arrived in Veracruz on 18 August the local office of the Inquisition required for inspection a book he was carrying. It was *The Ingenious Gentleman Don Quixote de La Mancha*! Happily, the inquisitors decided he could keep it.[20]

156

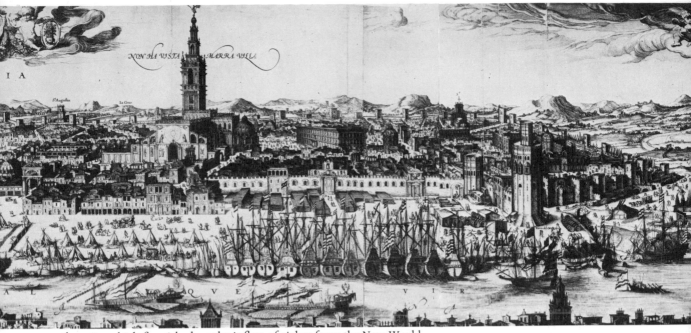

another city which flourished on the influx of riches from the New World.

Alemán's extraordinary novel is generally regarded by critics and historians of Spanish literature as the Spanish picaresque novel *par excellence*. It purports to be the autobiography of a wandering rogue who earns a precarious livelihood by serving many masters and by such thievery and fraud as circumstances seem to allow. Toward the end of the book, he tells how he was caught stealing and sentenced to row for a term in His Majesty's galleys. His sordid life has taught him that everything in this world is vanity, cruelty, deception and sin. Far from being the 'merry rascal' that the protagonist sometimes is in the picaresque novels of other nations, he is really an anti-hero who reduces all human values to the level of his own cynical philosophy.

Whether or not Cervantes was in Madrid when *Guzmán de Alfarache* was published, he inevitably read the new work at the earliest opportunity and with keen interest. His interest in the kind of life depicted by Alemán is amply attested, as we shall later see, by his inclusion of picaresque elements in a number of his own works, and by intimations that for a while at least he considered composing a full-fledged picaresque novel himself. One of the characters in *Don Quixote*, the liberated galley-slave Ginés de Pasamonte, claims to be writing his autobiography and opines that it is so good 'that Lazarillo de Tormes will have to look out, and so will everything in that style that has ever been written or ever will be'.[21] Cervantes was familiar not only with outstanding examples of fictional rogues, like Guzmán and Lazarillo, but also with whatever counterparts the real world had to offer. Yet he left us no finished life of Ginés de Pasamonte nor any other genuine picaresque novel. Inquiring minds have wondered why. The only useful avenue of

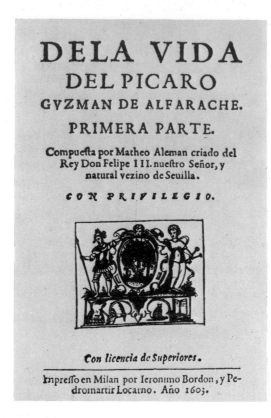

138　Title page of Mateo
Alemán's *Guzmán de Alfarache*
(edition of 1603).

investigation is to compare what he did write with the most representative example of the picaresque *genre*. It will be illuminating to return to this point when we consider Cervantes' exemplary novel, *Rinconete and Cortadillo*.

The best guess to be made about Cervantes' whereabouts during this final year of the sixteenth century is that from shortly before the publication of Alemán's sensational novel until shortly after the official return to court of the royal newly-weds on 24 October 1599 he alternated between Madrid and Esquivias. If this is true, he must certainly have had something to do with the activities of his daughter, about which records survive from the summer of 1599. On 9 August she appeared before legal authorities to have a guardian *ad litem* appointed to help her gain possession of her inheritance. In the document her name is inscribed as Isabel de Saavedra. Two days later she presented herself with her guardian before the same notary to make arrangements to live for two years, ostensibly as a servant, with Miguel's sister Magdalena.[22] This was the best he could do for his daughter until he was ready to disclose her existence to his wife.

Having seen the formal entrance of Philip III and his queen into Madrid and having sensed no probability of advancement at court for himself, Cervantes was doubtless ready in early November to return to Seville. That he had been away finds further possible confirmation in the fact that the next time his name crops up in a legal document in Seville it is accompanied by a new address.

During his final unemployed years in Andalusia, Miguel is generally believed to have done a considerable amount of writing. We have already noticed his occasional poems, at least two of which were much celebrated. He may also have continued to work on *Don Quixote*, and the chances are that he wrote two or more of his exemplary tales as well. Scholars have tried hard, but with meager success, to fix the date of composition of these stories. The best that can be done with certainty is to narrow the range of years within which one or another must have been written. Yet one cannot help generating convictions, however undocumented, about the writing of two or three of them. One of the tales that may very well have been written at this time is that of *Rinconete and Cortadillo*. A brief examination of it may help us to appreciate some aspects of Cervantes' character and to see how the story could have arisen out of the experience of his final years in Seville.

At the Molinillo Inn, on the road (so often travelled by Cervantes) from New Castile to Andalusia, two young ragamuffins meet and decide to continue their journey to Seville together. One is Rincón, a fledgling cardsharp; the other is Cortado, a neophyte pickpocket. In Seville they begin to ply their trade, only to learn that there is a kind of criminal guild or brotherhood to which they must report if they want to prosper and remain reasonably safe. The membership consists of ruffians, prostitutes, petty thieves, cardsharps, go-betweens, informers and other similar types. Their chief and mentor is Monipodio, at whose house they hold periodic meetings and find a kind of social club, protective society, and booking agency for commissioned crime. Cortado and Rincón are astounded at the demeanor of the denizens of the criminal *demi-monde* into which they have stumbled. As they wait silently in Monipodio's patio for him to appear, they observe the following scene:

'At that moment two youths, each about twenty years old, came in. They were dressed like students and were followed shortly afterward by two porters and a blind man; without saying a word, they all began strolling up and down the courtyard. It was not long before two old men entered, baize-clad and wearing spectacles, which gave them a grave and dignified appearance, as did the rosaries with tinkling beads that they carried in their hands. Behind them came an old woman in a full skirt. She was as silent as the others; she went into the room off the side [a kind of rough chapel], took some holy water, and very devoutly knelt before the image. She remained there for some little while; then, having first kissed the ground and lifted her arms and eyes heavenward three times in succession, she arose, tossed some coins into the basket, and came out to join the others in the patio.'[23]

In due time Monipodio enters the patio and 'all those who were waiting for him immediately dropped him a profound and sweeping curtsy, with the exception of the two ruffians, who merely lifted their hats in a don't-give-a-damn manner (as their kind are in the habit of saying) and then resumed their stroll along one side of the courtyard....'[24] Monipodio opens the meeting, whose first business becomes the examination, admission and instruction of Rincón and Cortado, whose names are changed to Rinconete and

Cortadillo. Then the assembly sits down to a session of eating and drinking together, interrupted by late arrivals and false alarms. Finally, Monipodio checks what his colleagues have been doing and have yet to do against a written list of annoyances, abuses, beatings and slashings that they have been commissioned to do by their clients.

The most striking characteristic of Monipodio's brotherhood is that it lives by accepted procedures, regulations and standards. The individual members take pride in their work and conduct their private lives without failing to worship God, the Virgin Mary and a variety of saints. The guide that leads Rincón and Cortado to Monipodio's house remarks to them in the beginning that 'everyone in this business may praise God, especially in view of the order that Monipodio keeps among his adopted sons'.[25] We have already shown an old woman at her devotions in our first quotation from this story. On leaving the meeting, she says to those who remain:

'Enjoy yourselves now while there is time, for when old age comes you will weep as I do for all the moments you lost in youth. Remember me to God in your prayers. I go to pray for myself and you, that He may free and preserve us in this dangerous trade of ours, and keep us out of the hands of the law.'[26]

The most startling example of this kind of religious attitude comes to light as one of the prostitutes tells about a cruel beating she has received at the hands of her ruffian lover:

'And why do you think he did it? Was it on account of anything I had done? Certainly not. He was gambling and losing, and he sent Cabrillas, his runner, to ask me for thirty reales, and I only sent him twenty-four – may all the hard work and trouble I had in earning them be counted in Heaven against my sins!'[27]

Cervantes is recognized as one of literature's great masters of irony, and nowhere does he use it more tellingly than in *Rinconete and Cortadillo*. Occasionally, the irony is direct, as when he calls Monipodio's brotherhood 'that virtuous company', but for the most part it is to be observed in the outrageous contrasts between the sordid acts the characters perform and the pious and self-respecting things they say. Rincón notices these contrasts, and

'marveled at the absolute assurance they all felt of going to Heaven when they died so long as they did not fail in their devotions, and this in spite of all the thefts, murders and other offenses of which they were guilty in the sight of God. He laughed also, as he thought of the old woman, Pipota, who, leaving the stolen hamper at home, went off to place her wax candles in front of the images; by doing so she was doubtless convinced that she would go to Heaven fully clothed and with her shoes on. He was no less astonished at the obedience and respect they all showed Monipodio, that coarse, unscrupulous barbarian.'[28]

The irony of these contrasts accounts for much of the humor in the story, and it accounts for something more subtle. Students of *Rinconete and Cortadillo*

160

have sensed in it a kind of innocence not obviously reconcilable with the low life portrayed. This sense of innocence springs from the sincerity of the characters and from the faithfulness with which they adhere to their code. If this fidelity is grotesque and laughable, it is also to some degree redeeming, especially when contrasted – and this is the supreme irony – with the faithlessness of the ministers of justice in Seville. Readers of the story are afforded an opportunity to observe the corruption of certain agents of the law, but should they fail to notice it, Cervantes allows them to share Rincón's conclusions: 'And, finally, he was astounded by the careless manner in which justice was administered in that famous city of Seville, with people so pernicious as those and possessed of such unusual instincts carrying on their pursuits almost openly.'[29]

It is no use trying to convey in a few pages the strangely light-hearted charm of this extraordinary story, but it may be enlightening to consider it briefly in relation to Cervantes' final Andalusian years. Cervantes' own experience of the careless justice of Seville makes it easy to understand the final irony of his story. That he could tell it with such gay good humor may say something about the resilience of his spirit as well as the character of his art. Both he and the author of *Guzmán de Alfarache* have been called realists. It is an excessively capacious label that will accommodate two such radically different visions of the same degrading environment and sordid characters. Consider what the true Spanish *pícaro*, Guzmán, has learned about such a world:

'It is beyond all hope. As we find it, so shall we leave it. Let no one hope for better times nor think the past was better. Everything has been, is, and ever will be the same. The first father was perfidious; the first mother, mendacious; the first son, thieving and fratricidal.'[30]

Nowhere in Cervantes' works can one find words of comparable bitterness and disillusionment.

140 'The sail hurled away both knight and horse along with it.' Illustration of Don Quixote's confrontation with the windmills by Gustave Doré.

12 Return to Castile

For thirteen of his middle years Cervantes had criss-crossed the provinces of Andalusia and made of the great city of Seville his operational headquarters, but now at the age of fifty-three he was back in Castile for the rest of his days. From midsummer 1600 until the summer of 1604, he seems to have spent most of his time in Toledo, Esquivias and Madrid. During these four years, it is only occasionally possible to state with certainty where he was on any given day, but one of the dates now reliably known helps to dispel the lingering notion of some scholars that Cervantes was locked up a second time in the royal jail of Seville. This is supposed to have occurred in 1601 or 1602, the later date being preferred by the best authorities.[1] But, aside from the fact that the belief in a second jailing in Seville has never been convincingly supported, it now turns out that Cervantes and Doña Juana de Gaitán were serving as godparents at a baptism in Esquivias on 27 January 1602,[2] and there is not a shred of evidence that he ever set foot in Seville after that date. It will be recalled that Juana de Gaitán was the widow of Miguel's long dead friend, the poet Pedro Laínez. Hers is a name to remember, for when three years later an unidentified assailant mortally wounded a dissolute nobleman in front of Cervantes' house in Valladolid, she occupied rooms in that same house.

Miguel's young brother-in-law, Fernando de Palacios, was in 1600 a novice in the Franciscan monastery of San Juan de los Reyes in Toledo. As part of the preparation for taking his final vows, he made a will on 19 August 1600 which named Miguel as one of his executors. It is possible to believe that Miguel and Catalina were present on that occasion and that they both remained in Toledo at least until 7 September 1600, which was when Fernando made his profession. Doña Catalina had inherited a house in Toledo, so it would be neither uncomfortable nor expensive for them to sojourn in that city whenever the occasion warranted. It may well be that Cervantes found it convenient to pursue his business interests there for a while and to resume the writing of *Don Quixote*.

The work of fiction engendered in prison – as its author suggested – was clearly not in 1597 projected as the monumental novel finally produced. More likely he first thought of it as a story of the dimensions of one of his *Exemplary Novels*. One of the clues supporting this view is that he did not narrate the early adventures in separate chapters. Some of the titles and divisions of the chapters that now constitute the first half of Part One are faulty and show signs of having been hastily done, perhaps at the time when the manuscript was being prepared for the printer.[3] Furthermore, the book we now label Part One (published in 1605) was divided into four parts, which suggests that when Cervantes was writing the second part of Part One he had no idea that he would ultimately write the Part Two that was published in 1615. One of the conclusions that may be safely drawn from these oddities of title, chapter and part is that the circumstances of the author's life obliged him to compose his masterpiece at irregular intervals.

It was in the four-year period now under consideration that he wrote most of the fifty-two chapters of Part One. Perhaps he wrote the first eight in jail in Seville. If so, he had already carried his hero through the celebrated attack on the windmill-giants and on to the stupendous battle with the Biscayan, which was interrupted as both combatants raised their swords aloft to risk victory or defeat on a single mighty stroke. At this critical point, Cervantes pretends that the documents on which Don Quixote's true history is based provide no further information about the battle. Chapter 9 begins with an account of how the author happened one day to be in Alcaná Street in Toledo when he met a lad who was trying to sell some Arabic manuscripts. Happily they turned out to be a history of Don Quixote written by the Arabic historian Cide Hamete Benengeli. Needless to say, Cervantes bought the history and caused it to be translated into Castilian, thus imitating a fiction much used in the romances of chivalry. But Cervantes put the device to artistic uses undreamed of by the authors he imitated.

It may very well be that Cervantes was truly in Toledo when he began chapter 9, but wherever he was the important thing to record is that he was now composing that great series of adventures that moved Don Quixote and Sancho gradually southward toward the heart of the Sierra Morena. These are the adventures of the two flocks of sheep, the dead body, the fulling mills and Mambrino's helmet. If to this short list we add the earlier encounter with the windmills, we will have a string of adventures well worth pausing to consider. Even in brief summary, they will help to evoke not only the flavor of the novel Cervantes was writing but also his vision of man's perpetual struggle to interpret the realities that constitute his personal world.

As Don Quixote and Sancho Panza are riding across the plain of Montiel, the knight calls to his squire's attention thirty or more giants with whom he proposes to fight. Sancho immediately recognizes the giants as windmills and warns his master not to attack them. But Don Quixote's head is too full of encounters between giants and knights to heed Sancho's warning. As readers of the novel will remember, he drives his lance into one of the sails of a windmill and is overthrown. This is one of abundant examples of Don Quixote's misinterpretations of reality. Sancho has no problem of interpretation. Only Don Quixote could make so ridiculous a mistake as to believe the windmills giants.

141 Map of the area around the Plaza Mayor, Madrid; the Calle de Atocha, leading to the >
old quarter where Cervantes and several other prominent literary figures made their homes, begins at bottom right.
Overleaf: 142 Exterior of Cervantes' house in Valladolid. Built as part of a crash building program in 1601, the house was the middle one of a group of five. Cervantes and his family occupied the second-floor apartment. 143, 144 The sitting-room (top) and kitchen of Cervantes' home in Valladolid, two of the five rooms which he shared with his wife, two sisters, his daughter and his niece.

Calle de las Fuentes

Calle de la Fuentas

Calle de S. Gines

D

Plaçuela de Selenque

CALLE MAI

El suela de Herradores

XXIII

Calle de la Sal

Calle del Abastecimi

Guadalajara

23

Calle de la Sal

Calle Nueua

L Cobertiza de Heria

Calle de

la Caua de S. Miguel

PLAÇA MAIOR

Calle de las Priscionis

30

45

M

PROVINÇIA

OLEDO

Calle Luperiab

Calle de la Lechuga

Plaçuela del C. de Barajas

Geronima

147, 148   A French view of Don Quixote attacked by the penitents and, right, a late nineteenth-century British portrayal of the Knight.

The adventure of the flocks of sheep begins when Don Quixote directs Sancho's attention to a large cloud of dust drifting their way. According to Don Quixote, the cloud conceals an advancing army recruited from many nations. This time Sancho is not quick to contradict his master. In fact, he supposes that two armies must be taking the field when he spies a similar cloud coming from the opposite direction. And he is fascinated by Don Quixote's fantastic account of the composition of the opposing armies and the motive of their quarrel. It is too late to stop his master's charge into the fray when, on closer inspection, Sancho perceives that the contending armies are really flocks of sheep. One difference between the two adventures just reviewed is that in the adventure of the windmills only Don Quixote could have misinterpreted the reality before him, while in the adventure of the sheep almost anyone might have misinterpreted it, although probably not for so long nor in the same way as Don Quixote does.

The adventure of the dead body takes place at night. As master and man pursue their dark and lonely way, they see approaching from afar a great number of mysterious lights. Watching closely, knight and squire at length make out that the lights are torches carried by some twenty white-surpliced figures on horseback, followed by a litter covered with mourning and by six other riders draped in black to the very hoofs of their mules. This eerie vision might puzzle anybody. Unable to interpret it, Don Quixote calls on the procession to halt and give an account of itself. Receiving an unsatisfactory answer, he lays about him with his lance and puts to rout all but one unlucky fellow whose mule has fallen on him and broken his leg. From the injured man Don Quixote discovers that the nocturnal cavalcade was a funeral procession taking a dead man to Segovia for burial. Once again he has

< 145   *Don Quixote and Sancho Panza,* by Honoré Daumier (1808-79).
< 146   *Don Quixote in his Study,* by Richard Parkes Bonington (1802-28).

misinterpreted reality, but here, more than in earlier adventures, circumstances were conducive to error. And sensible Sancho was able to lift no warning voice. It goes without saying that the white-surpliced figures also had a problem in interpreting Don Quixote: they took him for a demon from hell.

After this misadventure, squire and knight turn off the road and up a small mountain valley in search of water. They have not proceeded very far when they hear a roaring as of falling water. Continuing to advance, they soon hear the sound of measured blows and rattling chains. The fearsome din of falling water, heavy blows and rattling chains in a place so black and solitary might justify the wildest imaginings. Don Quixote and his squire have no means of interpreting it until the light of morning reveals the blows to be the rhythmic fall of fulling hammers operated by water power. Little by little, Cervantes makes his point: a man does not necessarily need to have his head full of chivalric chimeras to wander off the road of reason.

Shortly after Don Quixote and Sancho have left the site of the fulling mills, it begins to rain a little. As they ride along, the knight looks up and thinks he sees a mounted man with King Mambrino's golden helmet on his head. Actually it is a barber's basin worn by a travelling barber to protect his new hat from the rain. Without wasting words, Don Quixote charges the barber, who slides off his donkey, drops the basin and flees. So the knight wins a new helmet, and though it lacks a visor and fits him badly, for him it serves as Mambrino's enchanted helmet. From this point on the question of the helmet comes up over and over again. In chapter 45, the question of whether it is really a basin or a helmet provokes a violent fight among no less than twelve different guests of the inn where Don Quixote and Sancho are staying. It is the former who best expresses the variability of human judgment, when he remarks to his squire: 'So what seems to you to be a barber's basin appears to me to be Mambrino's helmet, and to another something else.'[4]

Cervantes greatly amused his contemporaries with his narration of adventures like those just reviewed. It would be interesting to know how many of them realized that he was up to more than simple amusement, that he was, in fact, saying something about man's difficult commerce with reality. It looks very much as though these adventures were contrived to reveal a gamut of misinterpretations of material reality leading from the spectacle of madness unable to discriminate fact from fiction to the realization that even the supposedly sane sometimes find such discrimination beyond their powers.[5]

Sometime in the fall of 1600 Miguel received the news that his brother Rodrigo had been killed in the battle of Nieuport in Flanders. It was now nearly thirty years since they had fallen into Algerian captivity together. One can imagine the memories evoked by the sad news. One thing Cervantes did not need to be reminded of was how poorly the Spanish state played the role of paymaster. Rodrigo had been eminently successful in winning the respect of his superiors but not in collecting his soldier's pay, which was always in arrears. From time to time, his heirs collected something, but as late as 1654 the government still owed his estate 36,000 maravedis.[6]

149   View of Valladolid.

On 10 January 1601, it was decreed that the royal court would move from Madrid to Valladolid. This Castilian city, situated on a high plain northwest of Madrid, had for centuries served a more important role in the life of the nation than Madrid; it had been the seat of parliaments and courts and had witnessed such notable events as the wedding of Ferdinand and Isabella, the death of Christopher Columbus and the birth of Philip II. The latter contributed to its decline when in 1560 he moved his court to Madrid. Still, in 1601 Valladolid remained a superior city, with its university and its many noble palaces, churches, convents and monasteries. What it did not have was enough housing to accommodate the numberless courtiers, pretenders, writers, actors, gamblers, prostitutes and others who found it necessary or expedient to follow the court. Naturally, the influx of people accelerated the building of houses as well as a rise in the cost of everything.

Among the writers attracted to the new capital was young Francisco de Quevedo.[7] Born of a noble family in Madrid in 1580, he had studied languages and philosophy at Alcalá de Henares and then came to the University of Valladolid in 1603 to study theology for three years. In due time he became an accomplished linguist, scholar, essayist, novelist and poet.

171

150-2 In poetry Cervantes' own efforts were surpassed by three contemporary writers who retain their places among the greatest men of letters Spain has ever produced. Left, Luis de Góngora (1561-1627), in whose hands the elaboration of poetic language (*culteranismo*) reached its peak. Near right, Francisco de Quevedo (1580-1645), writer of burlesques, novels and poems, many of them critical of Spanish society. Far right, Lope de Vega (1562-1635), who served in the Armada and created the three-act *comedia*; an astonishingly prolific writer, more than 400 of his plays survive, and he wrote in every literary *genre* known to his age.

Although not a handsome man – one of his legs was deformed and he wore heavy, dark-rimmed glasses – he moved in the high social circles of the court, where he was admired and feared for his mordant wit and deadly swordsmanship. About his ability with the sword stories abound. One day at a session of a literary academy, the leading fencing master of the day, Pacheco de Narváez, was expounding his views on scientific fencing (based on geometry) when Quevedo contradicted him. Quevedo insisted that they test their conflicting views with swords; in the ensuing test Quevedo's view prevailed.[8] In 1611 he killed in a duel a man whom he saw strike an unknown lady. Like Cervantes before him, he fled to Italy, where he stayed for a few months with his friend the Duke of Osuna, whose secretary and chief assistant he became during the years that Osuna was viceroy of Sicily and then of Naples. When he first appeared in Valladolid at the age of twenty-three he was already well known as a poet who had attracted attention by his polemical skirmishes with the Cordovan poet Luis de Góngora.

The three greatest poets of seventeenth-century Spain were undoubtedly Luis de Góngora, Lope de Vega and Francisco de Quevedo. The last two were literary enemies of the first, attacking him for the highly ornate and difficult poetry he created in such extensive poems as the *Soledades*. One may take from Lope a sample of the kind of versified darts these poets tossed at one another:

> Our poet *Soledad*, the able,
>   Hath writ a most romantic ditty,
>   In dreary length a very city,
> In sheer bewilderment a Babel.[9]

D. Fran. de Quevedo

Quevedo was apt to be much rougher, going so far as to insinuate unpleasant things about Góngora's person. But one need not feel sorry for Góngora. He was of good family; he had many admiring friends and followers; and he possessed the wit to give a good account of himself in these literary battles. In fact posterity would say that he won the war. Cervantes, who was personally acquainted with all three poets, apparently took no part in this particular war, although he did have his differences with Lope.

An indication that Valladolid was rapidly becoming the center of Spanish literary life is that Francisco de Robles, bookseller to Philip III, had opened a bookshop in that city. Son of the publisher of *La Galatea*, he was soon to be negotiating with Cervantes the publication of his masterpiece. Among the writers who had not yet moved to the new capital were the greatest of them all: Lope de Vega and Miguel de Cervantes, the latter being on the verge of moving there in the summer of 1604.

In addition to the easily imagined motives that drew Miguel to the new capital, there were economic motives of special importance to his sisters Andrea and Magdalena, who were to live with their brother in Valladolid. They earned their living by doing fine needlework for upper-class customers, many of whom had already followed the court to its new seat. It is not surprising, therefore, that in July 1604 Miguel journeyed to Valladolid to look for accommodations to rent. He found that a certain Juan de las Navas was about to complete five new double houses in the outskirts of the city, and he was able to rent what today would be called a second-floor apartment in the middle house. As soon as the deal was consummated, he hurried back to Esquivias to be present at the long-delayed division of his dead mother-in-

153 The El Greco family; middle-class women like these and the Cervantes sisters frequently kept themselves alive by doing fine needlework for the aristocracy.

law's property.[10] He and his women relatives had much to do to arrange for their move, but by late summer they were settled in their new home. For the first time in his married life, Miguel was able to collect his whole family under one roof. His household consisted of his wife, his two sisters, his daughter and his niece.

Cervantes' new house was on a street now called the Rastro de Valladolid. Directly in front of the house was a little bridge over the Esgueva river. The bridge is worth mentioning, because it was soon to be the scene of a duel of some consequence to Miguel and his family. Across the river stood the slaughterhouse; behind the new houses rose the Hospital of the Resurrection. This institution is of special interest to readers of Cervantes, because it furnished the setting for his delightful novella, *The Colloquy of the Dogs*. As can be imagined from its surroundings, Cervantes' new address was not an elegant one; but this should not be taken as proof that his financial condition had fallen even lower than usual. Rather was it an indication of the difficulty that everybody was having in finding a place to live in the over-crowded city. In the same house as Cervantes, there lived people well able to afford lodgings more centrally located if such had been available – people such as Juana de Gaitán and her husband, who had left Esquivias for the new capital at the same time as Miguel and his wife.

Not long before moving to Valladolid, Cervantes had completed the writing of Part One of *The Ingenious Gentleman Don Quixote de La Mancha*; the chances are that he had also sold it to Francisco de Robles and had used the proceeds (the sum involved is not known) to defray the costs of moving to his

174

154-6 The court's move to
Valladolid in 1601 is an example
of the absurd governmental
decisions which were a feature of
Philip III's reign: designed to save
money, the whole operation in
fact cost much more than staying
in Madrid would have done.
However that may be, the short-
lived blaze of glory surrounding
the city while Philip used it as
his capital was in many ways
Valladolid's swan song after
a long and distinguished career.
Left, courtyard in the
house of Philip II in Valladolid.
Above, façade of the
College of Santa Cruz, founded by
Cardinal Mendoza in 1483,
and a courtyard in the College.

new quarters. The royal privilege to publish was granted in Valladolid on 26 September 1604. Juan de la Cuesta's printing shop in Madrid had probably already begun to set the type. Now Cervantes had only to compose his Prologue and to find a suitable patron to whom to dedicate his book.

Few writers of the day published important works without patrons. It was a long-established custom, and an economic necessity for a writer who tried to live by his pen. As there were no royalties, all that he could expect to earn from a piece of writing was the modest sale price of his manuscript and whatever largesse his patron was moved to offer. On occasions the largesse might amount to much more than the sale price. Cervantes may have known that his friend Juan Rufo Gutiérrez had received five hundred ducats from Philip II when he dedicated his *Austriad* to that monarch.[11] Such a sum was more than four times what Blas de Robles had paid Cervantes for *La Galatea*. But how many patrons that generous might there be in Spain? Not many, if we may believe certain words put into Don Quixote's mouth by his creator: 'Not because they do not deserve the dedications, but because they do not like to accept them in case they may be under the obligation of making the authors the return to which they are entitled for their labour and courtesy.'[12] The patron to whom Cervantes finally decided to dedicate the first part of *Don Quixote* was Don Alonso Diego López de Zúñiga y Sotomayor, Duke of Béjar and Count of Belalcázar y Bañares. He does not seem to have been a man of any distinction beyond that conferred upon him by noble birth, wealth and social position. That other writers of renown had dedicated works to him may have made him look like a promising patron, but it appears that he proved disappointing. At any rate, Cervantes never dedicated another work to him.

Cervantes was fifty-seven years old when he sat down to pen the Prologue to his masterpiece. In it he pretends not to know what to say or how to dare to publish a book so devoid of the learned trappings used by other authors to adorn and lend authority to their publications. While he is deep in these disturbing thoughts, an intelligent friend comes to call and asks him why he is so pensive. Here is part of the answer:

'For how could you expect me not to be worried ... at what that ancient law-giver they call the public will say when it sees me now, after all these years I have been sleeping in the silence of oblivion, come out with all my years on my back, with a tale as dry as rush, barren of invention, devoid of style, poor in wit and lacking in all learning and instruction, without quotations in the margins or notes at the end of the book; whereas I see other works, never mind how fabulous or profane, so full of sentences from Aristotle, Plato and the whole herd of philosophers, as to impress their readers and get their authors a reputation for wide reading, erudition, and eloquence?'[13]

There is a good deal more of this mockery of the pretentious display of easy erudition. No doubt various targets of Cervantes' satire could be thought of, but none seems more plausible than Lope de Vega, who in 1604 had published a kind of adventure story called *El Peregrino en su Patria*, which was issued with exactly the sort of pedantic apparatus satirized by Cervantes.

157 Title page of
Lope de Vega's
*El Peregrino
en su Patria*, 1604.

Lope and Cervantes had known each other since the 1580s. Off and on for a period of nearly twenty years, Cervantes had praised Lope, beginning with the laudatory verses of 'Calliope's Song', published in *La Galatea* in 1585. A good example of Cervantes' generous praise is the sonnet he wrote for Lope's long poem on Sir Francis Drake, *La Dragontea* (1598). It plays on the name Vega, which as a common Spanish noun means a plain. Here is the way the sonnet has been translated:

> Within that part of Spain, the fairest known,
>   There lies a *Vega*, peaceful, ever green,
>   Whereon Apollo smiles with brow serene,
> And bathes it with the streams of Helicon.
> Jove, grand and mighty worker, there hath shown,
>   To make it bloom, his science vast and keen;
>   Cyllenius there disports with merry mien,
> Minerva claims it henceforth as her own;
> There have the Muses their Parnassus found,
>   Chaste Venus rears therein her teeming brood,
>   The blessed congregation of the Loves;
> And so with pleasure, and the whole year round,
>   New fruits it yieldeth for the general good,
>   Arms, angels, saints, and shepherds of the groves.[14]

For a while Lope reciprocated Cervantes' praise, although never with anything as full and cordial as the quoted sonnet. Despite the extraordinary success he had won in every literary *genre* known to his day, Lope was inclined to be both touchy and envious. What threw their friendship into full eclipse was probably their growing disagreement over the proper way to write for the theater, but Cervantes' fun at the expense of the hollow erudition of *El Peregrino en su Patria* probably cast the first shadow over their relations.

As to Cervantes' Prologue, his imaginary friend finds it simple to suggest ways of supplying the quotations and learned references needed by the author, and he brings his advice to a close with the following words:

'You have only to see that your sentences shall come out plain, in expressive, sober and well-ordered language, harmonious and gay, expressing your purpose to the best of your ability, and setting out your ideas without intricacies and obscurities. Be careful too that the reading of your story makes the melancholy laugh and the merry laugh louder; that the simpleton is not confused; that the intelligent admire your invention, the serious do not despise it, nor the prudent withhold their praise. In short, keep your aim steadily fixed on overthrowing the ill-based fabric of these books of chivalry, abhorred by so many yet praised by so many more; for if you achieve that, you will have achieved no small thing.'[15]

The world now knows how much more Cervantes achieved than the overthrowing of the vogue of the romances of chivalry, which were surely headed for oblivion without his help. His contemporaries could not have imagined the full stature and influence his great novel was to attain, but they could and did enjoy it enormously.

The title page of the first edition of *Don Quixote* gives 1605 as the publication date. It must have come out in the early days of the month of January, for it went on sale before the middle of the month. So great was the demand for the book that Robles put Juan de la Cuesta to work almost at once on a second edition, which was finished in May or June of the same year, though not before two pirated editions had been printed and were being sold in Lisbon. Probably one of the reasons for the hasty printing of a second authorized edition was the desire to anticipate the production of additional unauthorized ones; but there were other reasons as well, the principal one being the extraordinary demand for the new work. If its originality and its high value as sheer entertainment were enough to account for its immediate success, there were still other circumstances conducive to that kind of favorable reception.

Evidence exists that Don Quixote was well known in certain circles before his story made its way into print. For example, shortly after the appearance of Cervantes' novel, López de Úbeda published a novel called *La Pícara Justina*. This work contains a poem listing Don Quixote among other famous literary characters. This fact became significant when it was noticed that the royal privilege to print it bears the date of 22 August 1604, that is, some four months before *Don Quixote* was published. Then there is a record of a conversation that took place in 1604 in a bookshop in Alcalá de Henares, which reports a student's remark to the effect that a certain admirer of the romances of chivalry was another Don Quixote.[16] The evidence cited above has received more than one interpretation; but if it means that Don Quixote enjoyed a certain fame before his story was published, how could that fame have been acquired? The answer may well be that an early short version of his story had been read in manuscript by some of Miguel's literary friends and acquain-

158, 159 Title pages of, left, the first edition of *Don Quixote*, published in Madrid in 1605, and the pirated edition which appeared in Lisbon in the same year.

tances. This would account not only for the pre-publication fame of Don Quixote but also for the eager anticipation which contributed to the rapid exhaustion of the first edition. There is at least one other circumstance deserving of mention in this regard: three to four hundred (and possibly more) copies of the first edition were shipped to the Spanish colonies in America.[17]

Perhaps the spring of 1605 was an auspicious time for *Don Quixote* to be displayed in Francisco de Robles' bookshop in Valladolid. The city was becoming ever more crowded and ever more given to pleasure-seeking, and the occasions for celebrations and feasts grew more and more numerous. On 8 April 1605, the queen gave birth to the baby prince who would one day rule as Philip IV. On 26 May Lord Howard of Effingham, with a large retinue of English noblemen, arrived at the court to ratify with Spain a peace treaty that had been negotiated the year before in London. The new prince was baptized on 9 May. On 4 June Valladolid learned of the election of a new pope, Paul V. On 9 June the peace treaty with England was formally ratified. Lord Howard and his party departed for home on 18 June.

Hundreds of people must have swarmed to Valladolid to participate in the public celebration of such a concentration of notable events and to witness the processions, plays, fireworks, bullfights and jousts arranged to commemorate them. The public events that called forth these festivities inspired Góngora to write a clever but disapproving sonnet. His allusions to Lord Howard's retinue as 'six hundred heretics' and to the little prince Felipe Domenico Victor as the 'babe Dominican' are clear enough. What he meant by his reference to 'Don Quixote, Sancho, and his ass' will be told shortly, but first the sonnet:

> The queen brought forth. The Lutheran came here,
> Six hundred heretics and heresies
> To boot. In fifteen days a million flies
> To give them jewels, wine, and all good cheer.
> We gave a grand parade – a farce, I fear –
> And certain feasts, which were but flummeries,
> To please the English legate and his spies,
> Who swore on Calvin peace had brought him here.
> Then we baptized the babe Dominican,
> Born to become our Dominus in Spain.
> We gave a masque might for enchantment pass;
> Poor we became, Luther a wealthy man,
> And all these feats they bade be written plain
> By one Don Quixote, Sancho, and his ass.[18]

The last two verses tend to confirm the long-held belief that Cervantes was asked to chronicle the festivities held in honor of the birth of the new prince. Although the narrative he is supposed to have written is now lost, there is no good reason to doubt that he did write such a chronicle.[19] He was in Valladolid at the time; he was something of a celebrity because of the recent publication of *Don Quixote*; he later published (in *The Little Gypsy Girl*) a ballad he had composed in honor of the queen on the occasion of her attending mass two days after the baptism of her son. The ballad has the ring of something written by an eyewitness.

After slumbering in the literary oblivion of many years without major publication, Cervantes at last knew the high satisfaction of public acclaim for his new book; but as 'good seldom or never comes pure and unadulterated, accompanied or followed by no alarming evil',[20] something sinister occurred in the early summer which abruptly dissipated his feeling of euphoria.

On 27 June 1605, at about eleven o'clock at night, two men fought with swords on the little bridge in front of Cervantes' house. One of the two fell gravely wounded and was carried up to the apartment of a lady named Doña Luisa de Montoya, who lived in the same building as Cervantes. Magistrate Cristóbal de Villarroel was notified, and when he and his attendants reached Doña Luisa's rooms, they found a badly wounded man lying on an improvised bed on the floor. His name was Gaspar de Ezpeleta. He was being treated by a barber-surgeon, and his good friend, the Marquis of Falces, was at his bedside.

Ezpeleta was conscious and able to testify. He told the magistrate that after eating supper with the Marquis of Falces he had taken his sword and buckler and set out on foot in the direction of the slaughterhouse. At the corner of the Hospital of the Resurrection, a man had stopped him to ask where he was going. Ezpeleta answered to the effect that it was none of his business, whereupon the two drew their swords and began to fight; Ezpeleta fell wounded without ever having recognized his opponent, or so he said.

Villarroel commenced to take depositions from the residents of the building. It turned out that a number of them, attracted to the windows by the clash of swords below, had seen the final moments of the duel. The first to testify was Miguel. He declared that

'he knows by sight a gentleman of the Order of Saint James, who they say is named Gaspar, by which name he has heard him called tonight. Having gone to bed, at about eleven o'clock this witness heard noise and loud shouts in the street and that Don Luis de Garibay [another resident of the building] was calling him. This witness got up, and the aforesaid Don Luis asked this witness to help him carry a man upstairs, which this witness saw and recognized as the one he has declared. He was wounded, and soon a barber came followed by a second barber, and they treated a wound over his groin and they asked him who had wounded him and he refused to answer. And this is the truth sworn and signed by Miguel de Cervantes.'[21]

Miguel's sister Magdalena testified, among other things, that on the way home from prayers at the Church of Our Lady of San Llorente she and Doña Luisa and Don Esteban de Garibay had seen shortly before the fight a well-muffled man lurking near the Esgueva river, but neither she nor any of the other witnesses admitted to knowing who he was. What kind of an errand took Ezpeleta abroad that night is perhaps suggested by the later testimony of a servant girl who had been sent out for water. She said he had approached her, pinched her, and asked her to accompany him. She replied: 'Go to the devil. You must be a rogue.'[22]

The next day Villarroel returned to the room where Ezpeleta was resting to ask again who had fought with him. Ezpeleta confirmed his original testimony, adding that his unknown enemy had fought like an honorable man. Early on the morning of 29 June, Ezpeleta died without changing or adding anything significant to his earlier statements.

On the day Ezpeleta died nearly all the residents of the building where Cervantes lived were called to testify, many of them for the second time. All who had witnessed any of the events of the night of 27 June told essentially the same story, and no one could or would declare the identity of Ezpeleta's assailant. Seeking a motive for the crime, the judge tried without avail to establish some connection between Ezpeleta and Cervantes' daughter or sisters. No one was able to testify that the deceased had ever entered Cervantes' house. None of the testimony taken implicated Cervantes or the women of his household in the Ezpeleta affair, and yet the judge saw fit to arrest Miguel, his sister Andrea, his daughter Isabel, his niece Constanza and six other persons, all of whom were lodged for a day and a half in the royal jail of Valladolid.[23] Thus did Miguel follow, unhappily and through no fault of his own, in the footsteps of his father and grandfather, both of whom had served time in the same jail. In view of his innocence, he may well have reflected on Dame Fortune in much the same terms as Sancho Panza when he remarked: 'I've heard tell that Fortune, as they call her, is a drunken and capricious woman and, worse still, blind; and so she doesn't see what she's doing, and doesn't know whom she is casting down or raising up.'[24] A week or so after the prisoners were released, the authorities dropped the Ezpeleta case without further investigation.

If neither the experience Miguel and family had just endured nor the neighborhood in which they were living did anything to endear the city of Valladolid to them, these were not the only circumstances that set them to thinking about leaving it. For some time it had been rumored that the court would soon move back to Madrid. The municipal authorities of Madrid did. everything they could to induce the king to take that decision, and by January of 1606 they had his promise that it would be done. News of the removal of the court was officially announced on 24 January 1606, and the king and queen actually entered Madrid on 4 March. It was neither possible nor permissible for all the government agencies, the courtiers and all the other hangers-on at court to depart at once in pursuit of Their Majesties, but the exodus began in the spring and continued as fast as procurable transportation and housing would allow. This time the eclipse of Valladolid was final.

As far as the women of Miguel's family were concerned, the economic reason for settling in Valladolid had disappeared with the court, which is to say that the wealthy people for whom they made and repaired clothing were now back in Madrid. A number of friends and residents of their building had already moved out: Doña Juana de Gaitán, for example, had returned to her home in Esquivias. It is easy to understand why Cervantes and his family would be eager to go back to Madrid as soon as it could be arranged. There is no record of the exact date of their return, but a good guess might be the late summer of 1606.

During his two short years of residence in Valladolid, Miguel had become one of the most celebrated writers of the day. No doubt his recent success encouraged him to pursue his writing more vigorously than ever. Over these years he was certainly accumulating the stories eventually to be published under the title of *Exemplary Novels*. As previously noted, there is no reliable way of fixing the exact date of composition of these stories, but it is not illogical to suppose that two of the very best were written in Valladolid: *The Colloquy of the Dogs* and *Man of Glass*.

The Colloquy of the Dogs follows and is attached to another story, *The Deceitful Marriage*, and both must be examined to suggest how Cervantes was experimenting with forms designed to express his vision of man forever floundering in the thickets of illusion and deceit. One day as Lieutenant Campuzano, pale and emaciated, is leaving the Hospital of the Resurrection, he meets his friend Lawyer Peralta. Peralta inquires about his friend's obviously poor health, and invites him to have dinner with him so that he can bring him up to date on his recent activities. After dinner the lieutenant relates how he has met and married an adventuress, whom he believed to be rich and whom he courted with fake jewelry. Contrary to his intentions, he has played the role of the deceiver deceived, and has wound up without wife or jewelry and with a case of syphilis that landed him in the hospital for several weeks. One long and seemingly sleepless night there, thinking of past events and present misfortunes, he heard and almost saw the two watchdogs of the hospital lying on some old mats behind his bed and engaged in intelligible conversation. Astounded at this extraordinary occurrence, he resolved to write it all down on the following day.

After some discussion between Peralta and Campuzano as to what kind of dream or foolishness this can be, Campuzano hands the manuscript of his transcription to Peralta, who proceeds to read it while his friend takes a nap. The manuscript is, of course, *The Colloquy of the Dogs*, and the reader occupies the same relationship to it as Lawyer Peralta and is thus either as real or as fictitious as he.

The sub-title of *The Colloquy* runs like this: 'Dialogue that took place between Cipión and Berganza, dogs belonging to the Hospital of the Resurrection, which is in the city of Valladolid, outside the Puerta del Campo, the said dogs being commonly known as those of Mahudes.'[25] Both the dogs (whether talking or not) and Brother Alonso de Mahudes are historical,[26] and so it seems that Cervantes' imaginative tale began with his knowledge of these facts.

If the gift of speech lasts that long, the dogs agree that each may have one night to tell his story. Berganza is first, and he recounts the incidents connected with his progress from master to master until he has served a slaughterhouse butcher, a thieving shepherd, a rich merchant, a conniving constable (friendly to Monipodio and his crew), the drummer of a company of soldiers, some gypsies, a Morisco, a poet, a theatrical manager, and finally his master in the hospital. This broad experience of the social and moral world of the time teaches Berganza that it is full of wickedness and deceit; thus through the lieutenant's dream of the talking dogs his own vices and afflictions become generalized and characterize society at large. Superficially, Berganza's narrative of his service to many masters resembles a picaresque novel, but the difference is profound: Berganza does not share the *pícaro*'s cynical readiness to live dishonestly in a dishonest world. Even more than Rinconete and Cortadillo, the dog is moved by virtuous instincts. It is one of Cervantes' choicest ironies that his dogs cannot abide the cynical perversity of man.

As the title suggests, *The Colloquy of the Dogs* is more than a simple narrative. Cipión often interrupts Berganza to approve or disapprove of his way of telling his story and to comment with him on the innumerable topics that arise out of the events reported. Although what the dogs have to say is largely an indictment of human conduct the whole is presented in Cervantes' light and witty style. A fragment of their conversation will show both the wit and the fact that they share, not surprisingly, their creator's distaste for ostentatious learning:

BERGANZA. There are some whose native language is Spanish but who in their conversations let fly every so often with a concise bit of Latin, by way of giving their listeners to understand that they are great Latin scholars, whereas the truth is they can scarcely decline a noun or conjugate a verb.

CIPIÓN. In my opinion they are not as bad as some of those who really do know Latin and who, in speaking to a shoemaker or a tailor, pour it out like water.

BERGANZA. From that we may infer that he who speaks Latin in front of those who do not know it is as much to blame as he who pretends to know it when he does not.

CIPIÓN. There is another thing of which I would remind you, and that is that a knowledge of Latin does not keep a man from being an ass.

BERGANZA. There is no doubt of it, as is plainly to be seen when one recalls that in the time of the Romans Latin was spoken by everybody as his mother tongue, yet there must have been some blockhead among them who was a fool for all of that.[27]

Man of Glass is the tripartite story of a poor boy initially called Tomás Rodaja. The first part recounts his highly successful studies at the University of Salamanca; his travels through Italy, Flanders and part of France; his return to Salamanca to graduate with high honors in law; and the severe illness he suffers as a result of eating a poisoned quince given him by a lovesick woman. He recovers in time from the bodily illness but is left with the strange madness of believing himself made entirely of glass.

The second part deals with the two-year period of his madness, spent partly in Salamanca and partly in Valladolid. The fame of his bizarre madness and of his extraordinary learning causes crowds to follow him around and to ask him questions about all kinds and conditions of people. His answers are prompt, witty and satirical. During his years of madness he is known by the nickname of 'the Licentiate of Glass'.

The third part tells what happens to him when, finally cured of his mania, he assumes the name of Tomás Rueda and tries to earn his living as a lawyer. The society that found him an entertaining curiosity when he was insane cannot leave him alone to follow his profession in a normal way now that he has regained his sanity. Driven by their unwelcome attentions to abandon the court, he goes off to Flanders, where he wins honorable death and enduring fame as a soldier.

The writing of this story afforded Cervantes an opportunity to reflect again on the social reception of both insanity and learning, and it also sent him back in memory to the Italian cities he had known in his youth and still remembered so pleasantly. Among these pleasant memories was that of certain Italian wines. His writing about them in *Man of Glass* reveals a discriminating palate:

'It was then they came to know the smooth taste of Trebbiano, the full body of Montefiascone, the sharp tang of Asprino, the hearty flavor of those two Greek wines, Candia and Soma, the strength of Five Vineyards, the sweetness and charm of Lady Vernaccia, and the rude bite of Centola, all of which were such lordly vintages that the lowly Romancesco did not care to show its face among them.'[28]

Such passages as this – and there are others – confirm the notion that Cervantes was a great lover and drinker of good wine.

The more famous a man becomes, the more attention he can expect to receive, whether favorable or unfavorable. The animus that was developing between Cervantes and Lope de Vega found new expression in the last year of the former's sojourn in Valladolid. If the Prologue to *Don Quixote* irritated Lope, he would have discovered further cause for irritation on reading chapter 48, with its long and serious discussion of the contemporary theater, criticized on a number of grounds including its lack of verisimilitude, its failure to respect the three unities, and its venality. Although Lope is not named, one of his plays is, and there are other unmistakable allusions to him. As the following quotation shows, they are by no means entirely unfavorable nor couched in abusive language:

'But as plays have become a marketable commodity they say, and say truly, that the players would not buy them if they were not of the usual kind. And so the poet tries to adapt himself to the requirements of the manager who pays him for his work. The truth of that can be seen by the infinite number of plays written by one most fertile genius of these kingdoms with so much splendour and so much grace, with such well-turned verses, such choice language, such serious thought, and lastly, with so much eloquence and in so lofty a style, that the world is full of his fame; and yet, because he wishes to suit the taste of the actors, not all his pieces have achieved, as some have, the perfection which art requires.' [29]

Nevertheless, Lope was obviously annoyed. A manifestation of his annoyance was a letter he wrote to a friend in Valladolid, in which he said there was no poet so bad as Cervantes nor anyone so stupid as to praise *Don Quixote*. [30]

Another indication of the growing animosity between the two great writers was an exchange of uncomplimentary sonnets. [31] Cervantes' sonnet is witty and mocking, Lope's is vulgar and abusive. Cervantes never replied with the kind of insulting epithets used by Lope, but neither did he forget. Many years later in his *Appendix to the Parnassus*, he recalled the receipt of the sonnet:

'While I was living in Valladolid a letter was brought to my house for me, with a real for postage. A niece of mine received it and paid the postage, which she never ought to have paid. But she tendered as excuse, that she had often heard me say that money was well spent in doing three things: in giving alms, in feeing a good doctor, and in paying the postage of letters, whether from friends or enemies; for those of friends give goodly counsel, while those of enemies may afford some clue to their designs. I opened the missive, and there dropped from it a bad, pithless, graceless, pointless Sonnet in dispraise of the *Don Quixote*.' [32]

With his usual dignity and moderation, Cervantes says no more about the sonnet and nothing at all about its author.

13 Harvest

On 16 February 1608, Cervantes was called upon in Madrid to witness a legal document concerning a young man about to sail for the New World.[1] The young man was Gaspar de Gaete y Cervantes, and he belonged to the same branch of the Cervantes family as that cardinal who had been a friend of Cardinal Acquaviva, Miguel's one-time employer in Rome. That Miguel should be asked to serve as witness for young Gaspar suggests that the two branches of the family were still on good terms. It also provides the first documented date in Madrid after the return from Valladolid.

Miguel gave as his address the Plaza of Antón Martín, which is in that old section of the city lying on both sides of Atocha Street about halfway between the Plaza Mayor and the Plaza of the Emperor Charles V. This was the quarter favored by writers, including such notable ones as Lope de Vega and Francisco Quevedo; it was the quarter of the two famous theaters, El Corral de la Cruz and El Corral del Príncipe; and it was clearly Cervantes' favorite quarter, since he lived there until his death. Among the streets he is known to have lived in are the Duque de Alba, Magdalena, Huertas and León.[2]

Cervantes never lacked for painful problems to confront, and a new one was shaping up about the time of his return to Madrid. Towards the end of 1606, his daughter Isabel had married a certain Diego Sanz del Aguila, about whom next to nothing is known, and within a year Miguel had become grandfather to a baby girl. The new granddaughter was christened Isabel Sanz. The trouble was, though, that the baby's father was not Diego Sanz. When Diego died about six months later, Isabel moved into a house owned by Juan de Urbina, and it became clear who had fathered the child.

Urbina was a well-to-do, middle-aged businessman, whose position as secretary to the Duke of Savoy required him to travel a lot. At the time of his love affair with Isabel, his wife and children were in Italy. How Isabel had made his acquaintance remains a mystery, as does the true nature of their liaison. Was it an irresistible infatuation that led her into adultery or was it a deliberate attempt on her part to use a rich lover to escape what was beginning to look like the common fate of the Cervantes women? Isabel was probably familiar with at least the general outline of the unhappy love affairs of her father's sisters and niece. Clearly, it was not easy for girls without dowries to make good marriages. Being illegitimate as well as poor, Isabel may have considered her own prospects even dimmer than her aunts' had been. And she must have been weary of the shabby conditions of her life. If so, she may have been willing to settle for a rich lover.

Unwilling to accept his daughter's liaison and unhappy about the uncertain prospects of his new granddaughter, Cervantes intervened in the affair with vigor and dispatch. The first thing needed was a dowry for Isabel; the second, a new husband. The husband was found in the person of Luis de Molina. Agreements were reached with amazing speed. The marriage contract was signed on 28 August 1608 – only two months after Isabel had moved into Urbina's house – and the wedding ceremony was performed eleven days later. That the newly-weds were not tormented by the impatience of passion is suggested by the fact that they did not get around to living together for almost six months. Since there was no normal courtship between Luis and Isabel, one can only conclude that he was attracted by the truly handsome dowry which Urbina and Cervantes committed themselves to provide. Cervantes being as poor as ever, the commitment was effectively Urbina's alone. The rich dowry assigned to Cervantes' daughter was intended above all to ensure the proper care of her child. When the latter died (probably in 1610), Urbina thought he could escape some of the costly provisions of the marriage contract, but he was mistaken. Luis de Molina and his new wife were determined to hold him to the last penny of his legal commitments. To recount the litigation that ensued would cast no new light on Miguel's life. What this affair meant to him was the loss of his daughter. Apparently, she never forgave him for breaking up her affair with Urbina. Although she lived the rest of her life in easy circumstances, there is no evidence that she eased his financial straits or even visited him during the week of his final illness.[3]

During the years we have been reviewing, Cervantes must have been cheered from time to time by news of the continuing success of *Don Quixote*. The third Madrid edition brought the total number of editions up to seven, and more were soon to appear in Milan and Brussels.[4] But his fate always managed to balance whatever was cheerful with something less so. On 9 October 1609, his sister Andrea died of a fever at the age of sixty-five. As already mentioned, his granddaughter died soon thereafter, and his daughter remained alienated.

Over these years of disappearing family and continuing poverty, now aggravated by the beginnings of failing health, Miguel began to turn to the Church for comfort and support. The first of several formal steps in this direction was his joining in April 1609 of a society called the Brotherhood of the Slaves of the Most Holy Sacrament.[5] The purely religious importance of this act should not, however, be exaggerated. Soon to join the Brotherhood were the most famous writers in Madrid: Salas Barbadillo, Vicente Espinel, Francisco de Quevedo, Lope de Vega, Vélez de Guevara and others.[6] Miguel surely enjoyed the social aspect of his association with these gifted men. Still, there can be no doubt about the sincerity of his renewed interest in religion, which is amply confirmed by his faithful performance of the devotions required by the Brotherhood and by his subsequent religious affiliations. He was at an age, as he was soon to write, where 'one does not trifle with the life to come'.[7]

160-2 Foreign editions of *Don Quixote* were appearing all over Europe in the early years of seventeenth century. Left to right, title pages of a German edition, and of the first French and English editions.

To the fellowship of the religious fraternity he had just joined, Cervantes more than probably added that of one or more of the ephemeral literary academies that were springing up at that time. One of them, established in 1612, was attended by 'the greatest wits who in those days were at the Court'.[8]

The literary academies were usually sponsored by aristocrats who dabbled in poetry and liked to surround themselves with men of letters. At their meetings, poetry was read and a variety of literary, moral and scientific questions discussed. It appears that the discussions could be quite heated. Mention has already been made of the 'scientific' discussion that led to a duel between Quevedo and Pacheco de Narváez. Another piece of evidence comes from a letter by Lope de Vega to his patron, the Duke of Sessa: 'The academies are furious: at the past session two licentiates threw their caps at each other; I read some verses with Cervantes' glasses, which looked like a couple of badly fried eggs.'[9] If Lope was able to borrow Cervantes' cracked glasses, it looks as though their relations had improved; at any rate they seem to have attended the same academy.[10]

The last decade of Cervantes' life belongs almost wholly to literature. During this period he completed five books, four of which were published during his lifetime and one shortly after his death. As we shall soon see, the dedications and prologues to these books express something of the informal and intimate quality of personal letters. Revealing Cervantes' personality more clearly than anything yet presented, they testify to a courage still undaunted by the relentless poverty of his lot.

Throughout these productive years, Cervantes always had more than one book in the works at any given time. We have already had occasion to refer to several of the tales he was soon to publish under the title of *Exemplary*

Novels. From time to time, he wrote one of these. It is possible to follow in a vague and not wholly dependable way the writing of Part Two of *Don Quixote*, whose composition engaged his attention off and on over a period of at least seven years. For example, in chapter 3 the knight's new friend, Sansón Carrasco, informs him of a report that a new edition of Part One is being printed in Antwerp. In fact no Antwerp edition was printed in these years, but in 1607 a new edition was being printed in Brussels. If it is plausible to suppose that Cervantes might have mistaken the one Flemish city for the other, then we can assume that he was composing chapter 3 in 1607. In chapter 54 there is an episode connected with the expulsion from Spain of the Moriscos. Since the edict ordering their expulsion from Old and New Castile, La Mancha and Extremadura was issued on 28 December 1609, [11] it is logical to conclude that chapter 54 cannot have been written before that date.

Cervantes' creation of an episode related to the expulsion of the Moriscos offers much interest beyond what it suggests about the rate of composition of the second part of *Don Quixote*. It provides another example of a tendency to reflect recent public events and an opportunity to compare his attitudes with those of some of his contemporaries. The threat of an expanding Islam had been a constant Spanish concern throughout most of the sixteenth century, but by 1609 this was no longer true. The Ottoman Empire was in decline, and Spain, at peace for once with England, France and the Netherlands, could concentrate much of her fighting strength in the Mediterranean. There was no longer a serious danger of effective military collusion between the Moriscos and the Barbary States. And yet the Spanish were still deeply preoccupied by the presence of the Moriscos. Why?

163 The expulsion of the Moriscos in 1609; the Duke of Lerma's savage solution to this perennial problem brought bankruptcy to many parts of Spain.

For a partial answer (but quite similar, as far as it goes, to that given by modern historians), we may turn to some things Berganza believed he had learned during the month or so he spent with a Morisco:

'It is only by a miracle if you find among them one who really believes in the holy law of Christianity. Their only concern is to hoard and accumulate money, and in order to do so they work hard and eat practically nothing.... They are Spain's strongbox, its moths, its magpies, its weasels: everything that they get hold of they devour or hide away.... There is no such thing as chastity among them. Neither the men nor the women enter convents or monasteries, but they all marry and multiply, and their sober mode of life increases their generative powers.'[12]

Berganza's views were widely held in 1609, and most Spaniards favored the expulsion of the Moriscos. Those who opposed wholesale expulsion were mostly rural landholders who didn't want to lose their tenant farmers. But there was little or no tolerance of Islam. Juan de Rivera, the Archbishop of Valencia, not only favored expulsion but also recommended the confiscation of Morisco property and enslavement of the Moriscos for work in galleys and mines or for sale abroad.[13]

Against this background, it is instructive to consider some remarks directed to Sancho Panza by his Morisco friend and neighbor, Ricote. He speaks of the justification of the edict of expulsion and of Morisco reaction to it:

'Not that we were all guilty, for some of us were steadfast and true Christians. But we were so few that we could not make head against those who were not; and it is no good thing to nourish a snake in your bosom and have enemies within your own house. In fact it was with good reason that all of us were punished with exile; a mild and merciful penalty in the opinion of some, though to us it was the most terrible that could be inflicted. Wherever we are we weep for Spain; for after all, we were born here and this is our native country. Nowhere do we find the reception our misery requires. In Barbary and in all those parts of Africa where we hoped to be received, entertained and welcomed we were worst treated and abused. We did not know our good fortune till we had lost it, and so ardently do almost all of us long to return to Spain that most of those – and there are plenty – who know the language, as I do, return and leave their wives and children over there unprotected; such is our love for Spain. For now I know by experience the truth of the saying, that the love of one's country is sweet.'[14]

To judge by these remarks, Cervantes shared contemporary apprehensions about the Moriscos and hence considered their expulsion necessary; but, unlike the Archbishop of Valencia, he was able to see them as sorrowing men and women driven from their ancestral homes.

From childhood Cervantes had been attracted to the theater. In the 1580s, as we have seen, he had tried his hand at writing plays, with some success. In 1607 the two Madrid theaters began to function again, and it was only natural that Miguel should be tempted to try once more. In the period 1607-08, he may have written the following plays: *The Bagnios of Algiers*, *The Gallant Spaniard*, *The Grand Sultana*, and *Pedro de Urdemalas*.[15] How persistently the memories of his Algerian captivity returned to our author! He had used them in one of his earlier plays, *The Manners of Algiers*, and again in *The Captive Captain*, whose story occupies chapters 39-41 of *Don Quixote*. But these exotic themes had lost their novelty, and the theater-going public had developed tastes better satisfied by other playwrights. Nevertheless, Cervantes continued for a while to seek recognition in the theater. In the *Appendix to the Parnassus*, he admits to having on hand six plays and six dramatic interludes. He had written two more plays and two more interludes by 1615, when he published his *Eight Comedies and Eight Interludes*. In the Prologue to this collection, reflecting sadly on his final effort to win success in the theater, he wrote:

'Some years ago I returned to my former idleness, and thinking that the times when I was praised might still persist, I set myself to composing comedies again; but I found no birds in last year's nest; I mean I found no impresario to ask me for them although they knew I had them, and so I shut them up in a trunk and sentenced them to perpetual silence.'[16]

Cervantes realized, as he remarked in this same Prologue, that Lope de Vega had made off with the crown of the theatrical monarchy.

If Miguel failed to win the kind of recognition he had hoped for as a writer of full-length plays, posterity has ranked him first among the Spanish writers of one-act farces. To classify his interludes (*entremeses*) as farces is accurate in so far as it is characteristic both of farces and of Cervantes' interludes to deal in slapstick fashion with low comedy episodes, but it is not accurate in so far as it may suggest that plot depends almost entirely on situation rather than character. The *dramatis personae* of the interludes not only reveal their creator's genius for characterization, but, in certain cases, their characters have at least as much to do with what happens as the contrived situations in which they are placed.

Because the interludes belong to the period of Cervantes' supreme creativity, it is of special interest to inquire what kind of world he chose to create in them. In settings usually small-town or underworld, he animated a motley crew consisting of bullies, peasants, pimps, whores, aldermen, clerks, judges, gypsies, impostors, sacristans, serving girls, soldiers, students, confiding husbands, jealous husbands, nagging wives and unfaithful wives. If the predominance of low-life types is appropriate to the farce, it is also compatible with the literary interest already expressed in such works as *Rinconete and Cortadillo*. It is true that in the interludes Cervantes has dealt with certain sordid and *risqué* subjects more freely than in his other works. About this the intriguing question might be, did the traditional impudence of the farce pull Cervantes along in its wake or did he take advantage of it to express his values and views with an openness he would have hesitated to employ in his other works?

A few words about three of the interludes may help to characterize them all. The last one in the collection duplicates almost exactly the situation of the exemplary novel called *The Jealous Man from Extremadura*, to which we will soon turn our attention. The *Jealous Old Man* is noteworthy because it reflects Cervantes' hearty disapproval of men in their sixties or seventies marrying girls in their 'teens and because it illustrates the greater freedom he permitted himself in the interlude as contrasted with the exemplary novel. With the help of an experienced woman, the fifteen-year-old wife of the jealous old man manages to introduce into her bedroom a young lover. Confident that her old husband will think she is only teasing him because he trusts in his multiple locks, she describes to him from behind her locked door her first experience of the delights of young love.

Another interlude worth recalling is one that has been translated under the title, *Trampagos, The Pimp Who Lost His Moll*. The Spanish title includes the word 'widower', and this is important because it helps to suggest how Trampagos apes in his squalid loves the sentimental norms of conventional society. Here, as in *Rinconete and Cortadillo*, Cervantes contemplates with irony and fascination the attempts of those who inhabit the disordered underworld to impose some kind of order upon it. After a brief spell of exaggerated lament for his deceased whore, Trampagos chooses a new one and what started as mourning turns into celebration.

If there is one aspect of human nature that Cervantes dwells on more than another in his interludes, it is man's capacity to live by wish-fulfilling illusions. An obvious example of this theme is found in the interlude called *The Marvelous Pageant*. It picks up the old theme of the magic cloth (as in *The Emperor's New Clothes*) that can be seen only by people of legitimate birth. In Cervantes' version the magic cloth is replaced by a spectacle of varied wonders, and to the category of people unable to see the spectacle is added that of persons with Jewish blood. In the society of Cervantes' day, it was as important to be an 'old Christian', that is, free from the taint of Moslem and Jewish ancestry, as it was to be of legitimate birth. That Cervantes should mock in this interlude and elsewhere the ridiculous lengths to which people would go to be thought 'old Christians' is more evidence of his ability to view human beings for what they were rather than for what they might be labeled by contemporary prejudice.

On 27 January 1611 Miguel's sister Magdalena died in his house on León Street. Her burial certificate states that she was so poor that responsibility for her interment was assumed by the Franciscan Tertiaries, to whose Order she had been affiliated for a number of years.[17] Cervantes would have liked to be able to bury this sister, who had sacrificed so much to accumulate the ransom that finally redeemed him from Algerian captivity; but he was poor too, and not only poor but in debt to his publisher for advances against the sale of the manuscript of *Don Quixote*, Part Two. Since the completion of this manuscript was not in sight and since he was unable to sell his new plays, it is understandable that he should turn his attention to a literary project susceptible of early completion. Such a project was the collection of tales to

164   *The Ship of the Church*, part of an allegorical painting of the Catholic Church in its progress over the 'sea of this age'.

be called the *Exemplary Novels*. Twelve of them would make a fair volume. By the time of Magdalena's death, he probably had at least half that number already written. His task was to revise them and compose five or six more. The job was done by early summer of 1612, when his publisher, Francisco de Robles, sent the manuscript off for official approbation. [18]

The *Exemplary Novels* were not actually published until the summer of 1613. Cervantes signed his dedication to the Count of Lemos on 14 July 1613. One of the most intelligent, cultivated and influential grandees of Spain, the count was a new patron, to whom Miguel would have reason to be grateful during what little was left of his life. Soon after the dedication came the writing of the famous Prologue. Like many another artist, Cervantes left us a self-portrait. It is exhibited in the Prologue and looks like this:

'This man you see here with the aquiline countenance, the chestnut hair, the smooth, untroubled brow, the bright eyes, the hooked yet well-proportioned nose, the silvery beard that less than a score of years ago was golden, the big mustache, the small mouth, the teeth that are scarcely worth mentioning (there are but half a dozen of them altogether, in bad condition and very badly placed, no two of them corresponding to another pair), the body of medium height, neither tall nor short, the high complexion that is fair rather than dark, the slightly stooping shoulders, and the somewhat heavy build – this, I may tell you, is the author of *La Galatea* and *Don Quixote de la Mancha*; he it was who composed the *Journey to Parnassus*, in imitation of Cesare Caporali of Perusa, as well as other works that are straying about in these parts – without the owner's name, likely as not.

He is commonly called Miguel de Cervantes Saavedra. He was a soldier for many years and a captive for five and a half [actually, five], an experience that taught him patience in adversity. In the naval battle of Lepanto he lost [the use of] his left hand as the result of a harquebus shot, a wound which, however unsightly it may appear, he looks upon as beautiful, for the reason that it was received on the most memorable and sublime occasion that past ages have known or those to come may hope to know; for he was fighting beneath the victorious banner of the son of that thunderbolt of war, Charles V of blessed memory.' [19]

How the heroic memories of his youth lived on!

In this same Prologue, Cervantes affirmed the ancient tenet, repeatedly expressed in his writings, that literature should both delight and instruct. He develops the notion that man cannot always be about his business. There is a time for rest and recreation. His intention in publishing his stories was 'to set up in the public square of our country a billiard table where everyone may come to amuse himself without harm to body and soul; for pleasing pastimes are profitable rather than harmful.' [20] Solace to the tired spirit is part of the profit, but there is more: 'I have given these stories the title of Exemplary; and if you look closely there is not one of them that does not afford a useful example.' [21] His final remark about the wholesome quality of his novels is this: 'If I believed that the reading of these *Novels* would in any way arouse

165 The Count of Lemos, Cervantes' patron.　166 Cardinal Fernando Niño de Guevara.

an evil thought or desire, I would sooner cut off the hand that wrote them than see them published.'[22]

Cervantes' insistence on the exemplary character of his novels seems to have been accepted by the four 'literary experts' who wrote formal approbations of the *Exemplary Novels*. For example, Father Juan Bautista Capataz opined 'that true eutrapelia resides in these novels, because with their novelty they entertain, with their examples they teach one to flee vice and follow virtue, and the author accomplishes his purpose, with which he brings honor to our Castilian tongue....'[23] Cervantes' claim to have written truly 'exemplary' stories has given some readers a good deal to think about, even to the point of prompting one of the great Cervantine scholars to call him a skillful hypocrite.[24] The main reason for accusing him of hypocrisy is that he protests his moral intentions while depicting immorality. The story called *The Jealous Man from Extremadura* is most often used to support this argument. It may be enlightening to look into it briefly.

The story concerns a jealous old man, a beautiful young girl, a handsome gallant and a house converted into a fortress. The old man marries the girl and keeps her in luxury behind three locked doors, where no man but himself is ever permitted to enter. The ingenious gallant finds a way to penetrate the fortress, however, and he and the girl wind up in bed. The old man forgives his young wife and dies, recognizing that the spiritual poison that kills him is of his own making.

By happy chance, an early manuscript version of this story has been preserved. In the early years of the seventeenth century, an ecclesiastic by the name of Porras de la Cámara compiled some recreational readings for Archbishop Niño de Guevara of Seville. Among the stories included in the

195

manuscript is *The Jealous Man from Extremadura*. This version of the story ends with the seduction of the young bride; but in the version finally published the bride claims to have resisted her would-be seducer even though he manages to get her into bed. Cervantes' alleged hypocrisy can now be described more explicitly. To present a true case of adultery would not be in keeping with the announced exemplariness of his novels, and so he is obliged to end his story implausibly without adultery.[25] But nowhere in his Prologue does Cervantes suggest that the exemplariness of his novels consists of keeping them free of conduct regarded as immoral; and, as a matter of fact, he deals with immoral love in two other stories in this same collection. In his other published works, too, genuine cases of adultery are presented.[26] What Cervantes does do is to assure his readers that these matters will be treated with a certain restraint and that they will afford useful examples. That of *The Jealous Man from Extremadura* is clear and explicit: virtue cannot be secured by high walls and locked doors. The refrain in the duenna's song expresses it very well: 'If I guard not myself, Ill wilt thou guard me'.[27]

Cervantes was pleased to think that with his new book he had extended the frontiers of Spanish literature:

'I believe I am the first to have written novels in the Castilian tongue, since the many that are printed in Spanish have all been translated from foreign languages, whereas these are my own, neither imitated nor stolen. My mind conceived them, my pen brought them forth, and they have grown in the arms of the printing press.'[28]

What he meant by 'novels' is the kind of short story written by Italian authors like Boccaccio, and he was indeed the first to write them in the Castilian tongue.

Cervantes must have been pleased by the reception of his new book, starting with the approbation written by the novelist Salas Barbadillo, who said, among other things, that he found in the stories 'nothing offensive to the Christian religion nor prejudicial to good customs; rather does the author of this work confirm the just esteem in which his clear wit, unique in invention and copious in language, is held both in and out of Spain....'[29] Salas Barbadillo was one of Cervantes' friends, but his good opinion of the new book was evidently shared by many readers, since it ran through at least six editions during the remaining three years of the author's life. Even Lope de Vega eventually got around to admitting that in his novels 'Cervantes was not lacking in humor and style'. Quevedo too thought well of the novels, to judge by a satirical piece, written long after Cervantes' death, in which he advises Pérez de Montalbán 'to leave novels to Cervantes and plays to Lope'.[30]

In the final paragraph of his Prologue, Cervantes promised his readers that they would soon have the continuation of 'Don Quixote's exploits and Sancho Panza's drolleries', followed by *Weeks in the Garden* (now lost and perhaps never written), and the *Labors of Persiles*. But the reader will remember that in his self-portrait he had mentioned, as though it already existed, another work called the *Journey to Parnassus*. This book is an indispensable

196

document for the study of Cervantes' life. Some of its autobiographical material has already been referred to, but much more remains to be examined.

The *Journey to Parnassus* is a narrative poem in eight chapters describing a journey by land and by sea to Mount Parnassus, where a great battle takes place between the good poets and the bad. To understand how and when Cervantes came to write it, we must return to the Count of Lemos. We have already noted that the *Exemplary Novels* were dedicated to him; we shall shortly see that the second part of *Don Quixote* and the *Persiles* were also so dedicated. The *Journey to Parnassus*, however, was not, which suggests that relations between its author and the count may have been under a temporary cloud. If so, the reason for it can be discovered in the following circumstances.

In 1610 the count was appointed to the exalted position of viceroy of Naples, previously held by his father. Naming the well-known poet, Lupercio Leonardo de Argensola, as his secretary, he entrusted to Lupercio and his brother Bartolomé the task of recruiting poets to grace his court. Both because he had no job and because Naples represented for him a fondly remembered part of his past, Miguel was eager to go. He believed that the Argensolas had promised him a place in the viceregal court, but time drifted by and no invitation came. This disappointing experience is clearly reflected in his poem. As the ship carrying the good poets comes within sight of Naples, Mercury tries to send Miguel ashore to recruit the Argensolas for the coming fray. Miguel refuses on the grounds that he would make a poor ambassador to men whose good will he seems to have lost. Here is how he expresses to Mercury his disappointment at their failure to remember him and their promises:

> Had one of all the promises ta'en root
> They gave on parting, never God me aid
> If in thy galley I had e'er set foot;
> I hoped for much when much protest they made,
> But it may be, that strange affairs and new
> Have caused them to forget the thing they said![31]

Cervantes began to compose his account of the struggle for Parnassus while it still remained in doubt which poets would win places in the viceroy's court and which would not. The probable symbolism of the battle for Parnassus is thus not hard to see. Cervantes had finished his poem by the summer of 1613 when he mentioned it in the Prologue to his *Exemplary Novels*. It was published in the early fall of 1614, and was accompanied by an interesting prose *Appendix* dated 22 July of the same year.

In his new work, Cervantes passed in review virtually all of the Spanish poets, good and bad, of his time. Much of what he has to say about these poets has a conventional ring, and many of the poets are now happily forgotten; but such is not the case of the great triad of Lope, Quevedo and Góngora. Furthermore, there is a point to be made about the relations of each of them with Cervantes. To the end of his life, and despite their recurring disagreements, Miguel continued to rate Lope at the top of the scale:

> Another cloud rained down that poet grand,
>> Lope de Vega, whom in prose or verse
>> None can surpass, nor one beside him stand. [32]

However just this encomium may be, it betrays no trace of personal warmth. The praise bestowed on Quevedo is quite different; it is more particularized and it contains a jesting allusion to his lameness:

> He is Apollo's son, son of the Muse
>> Calliope; we cannot, it is clear,
>> Go hence without him, and I do not chuse;
> He is the scourge of all the poets drear,
>> And from Parnassus, at the point of wit,
>> Will chase the miscreants we expect and fear!
> 'My Lord,' I said, 'his pace is most unfit,
>> He'll be a century upon the route!' [33]

This mixture of high praise and banter indicates how relaxed and friendly were the relations between the two great writers. The references to Góngora are the most remarkable of the three. So far as is known, Góngora never publicly recognized Cervantes' literary achievements, and yet Cervantes praises him three times in the *Journey to Parnassus*. More extraordinary than the mere fact of this triple eulogy is that one of the three passages refers to the *Fable of Polyphemus and Galatea*, a long poem in the brilliant but obscure style which came to be called Gongorism and which came under such heavy attack by Lope, Quevedo and others. Here are the pertinent verses:

> Ye Polyphemian stanzas, leave your scar,
>> And with the sharp edge, on the poet's face
>> Who will not take you as his guiding star!
> Your matchless splendour, fraught with hidden grace,
>> Proclaim you as the standard at all cost,
>> To which all other elegance gives place! [34]

One of Cervantes' major biographers considers these verses to be the first critical reference to the *Fable of Polyphemus and Galatea*. [35] If Cervantes was indeed the first publicly to affirm the value of the difficult new style of poetry, it was not to repay a debt of flattery but to express an independent judgment.

Perhaps the most fascinating autobiographical elements in the *Journey to Parnassus* are those that seem to bear directly on some of the key questions raised about Cervantes' own career as a writer. The editor of a recent collection of essays about Cervantes and his works speaks of him as 'persistently failing at the popular literary *genres* of the time', [36] and it is fairly common to see him referred to as alienated from the society of his day, embittered by the overwhelming popularity of Lope and resentful of the neglect in which he lived out his twilight years.[37] What one finally thinks about these questions will help to determine what one thinks about Cervantes as a man.

Was he truly a failure at the popular literary *genres* of the day? Before attempting a rational answer to such a question, one would have to make certain arbitrary decisions about the criteria by which success is to be judged and about the degree of success required to merit the name.

In his writing career, Cervantes enjoyed three bookstore successes, but at the time in 1613 when he was finishing the *Journey to Parnassus* only one had yet materialized, that of *Don Quixote*, Part One. It was surely gratifying, but for him it was not a financial success, since his earnings bore no relation to its sales. Was it a success of prestige? Well, it brought him considerable renown, but then novels at their best ranked below good poetry.

In the traditional hierarchy of literary *genres* the epic stood first. It was partly in defense of his own narrative art that Cervantes prompted one of his most cultivated characters to assert that 'the epic may be written in prose as well as in verse'.[38] In the Spanish theater of the 1580s, Cervantes claims to have met with more than modest success, but we have just noted in the Prologue to his *Eight Comedies and Eight Interludes* his confession that the impresarios were aware that he had new plays but did not ask him for them. As for poetry, two of his sonnets became as celebrated as any of the age, but had he written enough superior poetry to be considered a successful poet? Maybe a more interesting question to ask would be this: did Cervantes regard himself as a successful writer? And to this question his *Journey to Parnassus* provides a satisfactory answer.

Miguel sets forth upon his journey to Mount Parnassus unburdened by excessive optimism; experience has taught him to expect little from Dame Fortune:

> For in the load I bear upon my back,
> > Which Fortune there has placed with heavy hand,
> > I read the hopes which all fruition lack. [39]

One of the heavy burdens on his back was his unrelenting poverty. It appears, wrapped in the cloak of wit, in his farewell to Madrid:

> A wheaten-loaf, with eight small scraps of cheese,
> > Was all the stock my wallet did contain,
> > Good for the road, and carried with great ease;
> 'Farewell,' quoth I, 'my humble home and plain!' [40]

Reaching at last the heights of Mount Parnassus, he finds all the seats occupied by the assembled poets. Stung by the slight that leaves him without a seat, he turns to Apollo to protest and to review the credentials that qualify him for a seat among the deserving poets:

I cut and fashioned by my wit the dress,
    With which fair *Galatea* sought the light,
    And left the region of forgetfulness;
I'm he whose *La Confusa*, handsome quite,
    Made in the theatres a grand display,
    If common fame hath told the matter right;
I've *Comedies* composed whose style of play
    To reason so conformed, that on the stage
    They showed fair mingling of the grave and gay;
I've given in *Don Quixote*, to assuage
    The melancholy and the moping breast,
    Pastime for every mood, in every age;
I've in my *Novels* opened, for the rest,
    A way whereby the language of Castile
    May season fiction with becoming zest;
I'm he who soareth in creative skill
    'Bove many men; who lacks a goodly share
    Of this, his fame at last will fare but ill;
From tender years I've loved, with passion rare,
    The winsome art of Poesy the gay,
    In this to please thee hath been all my care;
My humble pen hath never winged its way
    Athwart the field satiric, that low plain
    Which leads to foul rewards, and quick decay;
I penned the *Sonnet* with this opening strain,
    (To crown my writings with their chiefest grace),
    I vow to God, such grandeur stuns my brain!
I've of *Romances* penned a countless race –
    The one of Jealousy I prize the best –
    The rest, I trow, are in a parlous case;
And so I'm very wroth, and much distressed
    To see me here on foot, alone to gaze,
    No tree to give me but a little rest....[41]

The man who wrote these verses hardly considered himself a failure. On the whole, he was very proud of his literary achievements; this doesn't mean, of course, that he was ignorant of his limitations. It has been noted in a previous chapter that to his cherished *Galatea* he accorded only half-praise at best. Despite his lifelong devotion to 'the winsome art of Poesy', he knew that the ultimate grace of poetry had been denied him:

I, who do toil and strain my being whole
    To shew, what Heaven's grace will not allow,
    The semblance of a poet's gracious soul....[42]

But he also understood that he had blazed new trails in prose fiction, and he was free to admit he desired the recognition due him:

> I never sat content beneath the spell
> > Of prim mock-modesty; without pretence
> > I courted praise for that which I did well![43]

Apollo responds to Cervantes' claim to a seat on Mount Parnassus by inviting him to fold his cape and sit on it:

> 'My lord, it hath escaped you quite, I fear,
> > That I possess no cloak!' was my reply.
> > 'No less,' quoth he, 'I'm glad to see thee here,
> For virtue is the cloak which poverty
> > Wraps round her form, to clothe withal her shame,
> > And so the shafts of envy pass her by!'
> I bowed my head before the court of Fame,
> > And stood on foot; good seat hath none by right,
> > If wealth or favour do not urge the claim.[44]

From all these self-revealing verses, it is surely safe to conclude that Cervantes was anything but pleased at the discrepancy he perceived between the magnitude of his literary accomplishments and the measure of recognition they had brought him. He was disappointed, yes, as he had been disappointed not to win a military commission, not to escape from his Algerian captivity, not to be granted a post in America, not to be invited to joint the Count of Lemos' court in Naples, and so many other things besides. But perhaps words like 'alienated' and 'embittered' cannot accurately describe a spirit as vigorous and resilient as his. The *Journey to Parnassus* does reveal some disappointments and frustrations; it also reveals a man who could make them the butt of his jests.

At the end of the *Appendix to the Parnassus*, there appears a friendly letter from Apollo to Miguel. In it Apollo shows himself solicitous about his friend's health: 'Let your worship take heed to your health, and look to yourself....'[45] And well he might be solicitous, for Cervantes' health was no longer good.

Of the 74 chapters that constitute Part Two of *Don Quixote*, Cervantes was writing chapter 59 when it came to his attention that a spurious Part Two was beginning to circulate in Madrid. This was in the fall of 1614. The author of the new work called himself Alonso Fernández de Avellaneda and claimed to be from the Castilian town of Tordesillas. I say 'called himself', because to this day his true identity remains a mystery. That he should dare to write a sequel to *Don Quixote* need not have been surprising nor even particularly irritating. The literature of Spain's Golden Age contains many similar examples – except that most of them were not accompanied by prefaces heaping abuse on the original authors. Avellaneda, however, who may have been a playwright and most certainly was a partisan of Lope de Vega, did launch in his preface a scurrilous attack on Cervantes. Among the things he makes derisive reference to are Miguel's advanced age, his crippled hand, his poverty, his having been in jail and his envy of Lope's success. Needless to say, Miguel was stung by this attack and reacted to it several times as he

167 Title page of
Alonzo Fernández
de Avellaneda's
spurious sequel to
Don Quixote,
published in
Tarragona in 1614.

168 Doré's
sketch of Don
Quixote attacking
Avellaneda's
spurious Part Two.

was writing the last fifteen chapters and Prologue of his own Part Two. An amusing example of his response occurs in chapter 70, where Altisidora describes a vision that came to her in her death-like coma. She claims to have seen at the gates of Hell approximately a dozen devils with flaming rackets batting books about which served as balls because they were filled with wind and fluff. When the devils discover that one of the books is Avellaneda's, they toss it immediately into the fiery abyss.

The happy consequence of Avellaneda's attack was that it stimulated Cervantes to complete his own Part Two in something like three months. Given the precarious state of his health, he might not have completed it at all without the provocation of the apocryphal version. The way he felt about his achievement and his rival is eloquently expressed in his final paragraph:

'For me alone Don Quixote was born and I for him. His was the power of action, mine of writing. Only we two are at one, despite that fictitious Tordesillescan scribe who has dared, and may dare again, to pen the deeds of my valorous knight with his coarse and ill-trimmed ostrich feather. This is no weight for his shoulders, no task for his frozen intellect; and should you chance to make his acquaintance, you may tell him to leave Don Quixote's weary and mouldering bones to rest in the grave, nor seek, against all the canons of death, to carry him off to Old Castile, or to bring him out of the tomb, where he most certainly lies, stretched at full length and powerless to make a third journey, or to embark on any new expedition. For the two on which he rode out are enough to make a mockery of all the countless forays undertaken by all the countless knights errant, such has been the delight and approval they have won from all to whose notice they have come, both here and abroad. Thus you will comply with your Christian profession by offering good counsel to one who wishes you ill, and I shall be proud and satisfied to have been the first author to enjoy the pleasure of witnessing the full effect of

169 Cervantes on a winged horse triumphs over the Spanish literary world. An illustration by Gustave Doré to the Preface of Part Two of *Don Quixote*.

his own writing. For my sole object has been to arouse men's contempt for all fabulous and absurd stories of knight errantry, whose credit this tale of my genuine Don Quixote has already shaken, and which will, without a doubt, soon tumble to the ground. Farewell.'[46]

Cervantes seems to have been aware that in attempting to discredit the absurd romances of chivalry he had written the greatest of them all.

The words just quoted were probably written no later than the first days of February 1615, since the first official approbation was dated 27 February of that year. The author of the approbation was the licentiate Francisco Márquez Torres, one of the chaplains of the Archbishop of Toledo. Seldom has a censor composed an approbation so laudatory as the one signed by Márquez Torres. He begins by stating that he has found in Cervantes' book nothing indecent or contrary to Christian principles; he proceeds to commend the smooth and unaffected Castilian language employed therein; he goes on to praise the author for correcting vices within the prudent laws of Christian reprehension; finally, he describes – and illustrates with an anecdote – the high regard in which Cervantes and his books are held in foreign lands:

'For even as they would wish to behold a miracle, so do the men of other lands desire to lay eyes upon the author of those books that, by reason of their circumspection and propriety as well as their urbanity and other pleasing qualities, have met with general applause in Spain, France, Italy, Germany and Flanders.'[47]

The anecdote is of a visit paid by the Archbishop of Toledo to the French ambassador in Spain. In the ambassador's retinue were a number of French gentlemen 'as courteous as they were intelligent and fond of good literature',[48] who inquired about the most worthwhile books then current in

Spain. Hearing the name of Miguel de Cervantes mentioned, they spoke enthusiastically of him and of the high regard in which his works were held in France. Learning that he was an old soldier and an impoverished gentleman, one of them asked: 'How comes it Spain does not see to it that such a man is maintained in luxury out of the public treasury?'[49] Whereupon one of the other French gentlemen remarked: 'If it is necessity that obliges him to write, then God grant he never be possessed of abundance, in order that, while poor himself, he may continue to enrich all the world.'[50]

As he took up his pen to write the Prologue to Part Two of his masterpiece, Cervantes imagined his readers eager to learn what abuse he might be tempted to heap upon Avellaneda's head: 'You would like me to call him ass, fool and bully; but I have not even thought of doing so. Let his sin be his punishment – with his bread let him eat it, and there let it rest.'[51] But he doesn't really let it rest there: 'What I cannot help resenting is that he upbraids me for being old and crippled, as if it were in my power to stop the passage of time, or as if the loss of my hand had taken place in some tavern, and not on the greatest occasion which any age, past, present, or future, ever saw or can ever hope to see.'[52] As for his envy of Lope de Vega, he denies it flatly: 'And if it was on behalf of a certain person that he wrote what he did, he is absolutely mistaken; for I revere that man's genius, and admire his works and his virtuous and unceasing activity.'[53]

There is no doubt about his admiration for Lope's genius, but his reference to Lope's virtuous industry is tinged with irony. Lope's *amours* were as well-known and unceasing as his writing of comedies. In the rest of the Prologue, Cervantes invites the reader to see Avellaneda as resembling two madmen about whom he tells amusing anecdotes, and he pays tribute to the benefactors who sustain his final years. 'Long live the great Count of Lemos, whose Christian charity and famous generosity keep me on my feet despite all the blows of my scant fortune. And long live the supreme beneficence of his Eminence of Toledo, Don Bernardo de Sandoval y Rojas....'[54] His final words promise the prompt completion of *Persiles* and of *La Galatea*.

In his dedication to the Count of Lemos (signed on the last day of October 1615) Cervantes tells of a letter from the emperor of China inviting him to be rector of a new college for the teaching of Castilian with *The History of Don Quixote* as its principal text. In his refusal, Cervantes mentions that he is in ill health and short of money. Despite these unhappy circumstances, his enthusiasm for his literary projects remains undiminished. Of his *Persiles* he affirms that it is 'a book which I shall finish within four months, *Deo volente*, and which is sure to be either the worst or the best written of books of entertainment in our tongue – but I must say that I repent of having said the worst. For, according to the opinions of my friends, it will attain the highest possible excellence.'[55] Regrettably, few, if any, contemporary readers would agree with his optimistic estimate of the worth of his last work.

By mid-November 1615, Part Two of *The Ingenious Gentleman Don Quixote de la Mancha* was on sale. The price for which Cervantes sold the manuscript to Francisco de Robles has not been discovered, but, judging by what he had received before, it was anything but munificent – perhaps no more than enough to cover the advances already spent. With or without much material gain, it was a triumphant achievement. In chapter 3, Don Quixote is proud and pleased to hear Sansón Carrasco's news about the popular acclaim with which Part One of his 'true history' has been received:

'Little children leaf through it, young people read it, adults appreciate it, and the aged sing its praises. In short, it is so thumbed and read and so well known to persons of every walk in life that no sooner do folks see some skinny nag than they at once cry, "There goes Rocinante". Those that like it best of all are the pages; for there is no lord's antechamber where a *Don Quixote* is not to be found. If one lays it down, another will pick it up; one will pounce upon it, and another will beg for it. It affords the pleasantest and least harmful reading of any book that has been published up to now.'[56]

The reception accorded to Part Two was equally enthusiastic. If authors seldom surpass their acknowledged masterpieces when attempting worthy sequels, Cervantes stands apart in this respect as in so many others. To modern taste, at least, the continuation is better than the original.

In Part One – especially in the early chapters – knight and squire are to some degree confined by the roles that parody conceived for them. In Part Two whatever was typical has become fully idiosyncratic. By the high magic of his art, Cervantes has made Don Quixote and Sancho Panza so real that their lives seem independent of the very book that opened their door to immortality. If the magnitude of this accomplishment in the creation of autonomous lives was not fully recognized by Cervantes' contemporaries, they were able to appreciate his novel as the supreme comic work of the day. An anecdote, probably apocryphal, may serve to suggest the extent to which this was so. According to it, Philip III was on the balcony of his palace in Madrid one day when he chanced to see a student reading a book on the bank of the Manzanares river. As the king watched, he noticed that the student interrupted his reading from time to time to slap his forehead and exhibit other signs of extraordinary pleasure and mirth. Philip quickly guessed the cause: 'Either that student is out of his mind or he is reading *Don Quixote*.'[57]

Cervantes' final months became a race between death and the completion of his *Labors of Persiles and Sigismunda*, the fantastic romance of adventure written in imitation of the fourth-century Greek author Heliodorus. As has already been noted, Miguel held high hopes for his *Persiles* and worked on it as diligently as his illness would allow. On the last day of October 1615, he had promised the Count of Lemos that with God's help he would finish it within four months. He was almost able to keep his promise. All the writing (except the dedication and Prologue) was finished by early March 1616. But then his malady took a turn for the worse, and he had to postpone the completion of the final pages.

That Miguel knew his days were numbered is confirmed in many ways. Back in July 1613, on the occasion of a brief visit to Alcalá de Henares, he

170 J. Vanderbank's painting of
Don Quixote holding forth about
the age of gold to the goatherds,
who 'devoutly listened, but
edified little, the discourse not
being suited to their capacities'.

took the habit of the Venerable Order of Franciscan Tertiaries. [58] Taking the
habit was an intermediate step in joining this lay order. Now, on 2 April 1616
in his home on León Street, he took the final step of profession in the
Order. [59] His wife and two sisters had long since done the same.

What disease was now sweeping Miguel so swiftly to his grave? In one of
the last pages he ever wrote, he refers to it as dropsy. Some present-day
writers think that it was diabetes. Whatever it was, it kept him to his bed
with increasing frequency. Early in April his doctor recommended a sojourn
in Esquivias. [60] It was hoped that country air and good food and wine would
reinvigorate him. They did not; in fact, the effort demanded by the trip
seems to have aggravated his condition. By the middle of April he was back
in Madrid. On the 18th he had failed enough to ask for extreme unction. On
Tuesday the 19th he mustered sufficient strength to pick up his pen and
compose his last dedication to the Count of Lemos. Both touching and serene,
it deserves our attention:

Those old verses, so famous in their day, that began 'With my foot already
in the stirrup', are more appropriate to this epistle of mine than I should
wish, because I can begin with almost the same words:

> With my foot already in the stirrup,
> And the anguish of death upon me,
> I write thee, great Lord, this epistle.

Yesterday they gave me extreme unction, and today I write this. Time is short, anguish grows, hopes diminish, and yet I carry my life on the desire I have to live, and I should not like to bring it to an end until I kiss your feet again. It might be that the satisfaction of seeing Your Excellency well in Spain would restore me to life. But if it is decreed that I am to lose it, let Heaven's will be done. I want Your Excellency to know, at least, of this desire of mine, and that you had in me a servant so willing that he wanted his will to serve to live beyond his death. I am happy, withal, at the prospect of your arrival, I rejoice to see you honored, and I am doubly glad at the realization of my hopes, extended through the fame of Your Excellency's kindnesses.

There still remain in my spirit some relics and signs of *Weeks in the Garden* and *The Famous Bernardo*. If by some luck of mine – it would be more miracle than luck – Heaven should prolong my life, you shall see them and also the end of *La Galatea*, which I know Your Excellency has taken a liking to. With these words and my continuing good wishes, may God in His power preserve Your Excellency. At Madrid, the 19th of April 1616.

Your Excellency's Servant

Miguel de Cervantes[61]

On this same Tuesday, or at the latest, on Wednesday, Miguel penned his final Prologue. In it he describes an encounter with a student on the way back from his recent visit to Esquivias. The student shows himself extremely pleased to meet, as he says, 'the famous one, the merry author, the jubilation of the Muses'.[62] As they ride along, the conversation turns to Cervantes' health. Calling the malady 'dropsy', the student advises Cervantes to curb his drinking. To which the latter replies: 'Many have told me ... but I find it as difficult not to drink my fill as though I had been born for that purpose alone. My life is coming to an end, and by the tempo of my pulse beats, I judge that their career and mine will be over on Sunday at the latest.'[63] The Prologue then describes the parting of the new friends and closes with an all-embracing farewell: 'Farewell to the Graces, farewell to wit, farewell to cheerful friends, for I am dying in the desire to see you soon contented in the other life.'[64]

Preparing the death of Don Quixote, Cervantes had begun the final chapter of his story with these words: 'As all human things, especially the lives of men, are transitory, being ever on the decline from their beginnings till they reach their final end, and as Don Quixote had no privilege from Heaven exempting him from the common fate....'[65] The serenity of these words fits their author's own death. It came on Friday, 22 April 1616, in his home on León Street.[66] The last sacraments were administered by the licentiate Francisco Martínez, who owned the house where Cervantes lived. What people were with him at the end is unknown, but we can be confident of two: his wife Catalina and his niece Constanza.

On Saturday, 23 April 1616, dressed in the brown habit of St Francis, he was buried in the nearby convent of Trinitarian nuns. No stone or cross was set to mark his grave.

Notes

CHAPTER 1

1 1 An excellent short account of Charles V and his reign may be found in *The New Cambridge Modern History*, II (Cambridge 1958), 301-33.
2 Quoted in English by Salvador de Madariaga in *Spain* (New York 1943), 43-4.
3 Karl Brandi, *The Emperor Charles V* (London 1939), 131.
4 Brandi, op. cit., 306.
5 *Idearum español* (Granada 1897; reprinted Buenos Aires 1940), 72.
6 Claudio Sánchez-Albornoz, *España: Un Enigma Histórico*, II (Buenos Aires 1956), 516-17.

CHAPTER 2

1 See L. Astrana Marín, *Vida ejemplar y heroica de Miguel de Cervantes Saavedra*, I (Madrid 1948), ch. 1. (Hereafter referred to as Astrana Marín).
2 This story is documented in Astrana Marín I, ch. 5.
3 Documented by F. Ródriguez Marín, *Nuevos documentos cervantinos* (Madrid 1914), 90, 134, 142, 146, 148; interpreted in Astrana Marín I, 166-8.
4 Rodríguez Marín, op. cit., 142.
5 ibid., 90-1.
6 Much new information about the Cortinas family (but not about Leonor herself) is offered by Astrana Marín II (Madrid 1949), ch. 18.
7 Spain accepted the reformed calendar of Pope Gregory XIII as soon as it was published (in October 1582). On the other hand, England did not accept it until 1751, which means that dates of importance to this biography are given in different ways by Spanish and English historians. To illustrate, it is often said that Shakespeare and Cervantes died on the same date (23 April 1616). By the reformed calendar Shakespeare died on 3 May 1616.

8 The complete list is recorded in Rodríguez Marín, op. cit., 69-70.
9 The document which provides this information is important, because it establishes the approximate beginning of Miguel's boyhood residence in Córdoba (Astrana Marín I, 286).

CHAPTER 3

1 This description is derived from Cervantes' self-portrait in the prologue to his *Exemplary Novels*.
2 *Three Exemplary Novels*, tr. Samuel Putnam (New York 1950), 151. Joaquín Castalduero argues against an autobiographical interpretation of this passage in his *Sentido y Forma de las Novelas Ejemplares* (Buenos Aires 1943), 207.
3 See Astrana Marín I, 359-61.
4 The evidence is the will of Rodrigo's mother, given in full in Astrana Marín I, 366-8.
5 ibid., 370-1.
6 ibid., 444-5.
7 *Three Exemplary Novels*, ed. cit., 151.
8 ibid., 152.
9 *Obras completas* (Madrid 1965), 179.
10 Astrana Marín I, 460-3.
11 The entire document was published by Cristóbal Pérez Pastor in *Documentos cervantinos* II (Madrid 1902), 1-4. See also Astrana Marín II, 69.

CHAPTER 4

1 P. Luis Fernández y Fernández de Retana, *España en tiempo de Felipe II*, I (Madrid 1966), 623-30.
2 ibid., 743-77.
3 Both the sonnet and the words by López de Hoyos may be found in Cervantes' *Obras completas*, ed. cit., 42.
4 For a brief account of the Morisco problem and the war of Granada, see John Lynch, *Spain under the Hapsburgs*, I (New York 1964), 205-18.

5 See Astrana Marín II, 173-6.
6 The order is reproduced in full in Astrana Marín II, 185-6.
7 *The Adventures of Don Quixote*, tr. J.M. Cohen (Baltimore 1963), 928. (Hereafter referred to as Cohen.)
8 *Obras completas*, ed. cit., 1961.
9 ibid., 1681.
10 ibid.
11 ibid., 878.
12 See Cervantes' *Journey to Parnassus*, tr. James Y. Gibson (London 1883), lxii-lxiii. (Hereafter referred to as Gibson.)
13 *Three Exemplary Novels*, ed. cit., 85-6.
14 Pérez Pastor adduces reasons for believing that López de Hoyos was instrumental in getting Miguel recommended to Acquaviva. See *Documentos cervantinos* II, ed. cit., 357-61. But more recent archival research suggests that Gaspar de Cervantes y Gaeté was responsible. See Amalia Billi di Sandorno, 'El Cardenal Gaspar de Cervantes y Gaete, Ignorado Protector de Miguel de Cervantes Saavedra', *Anales cervantinos*, II (Madrid 1952), 335-58.
15 *Three Exemplary Novels*, ed. cit., 145.
16 This may be the place to indicate that Américo Castro (among others) has concluded that Cervantes must have been a 'new Christian', that is, the descendant of converted Jews. I do not find his arguments convincing, but the interested reader may judge for himself by reading 'Cervantes y el Quijote a Nueva Luz', in *Cervantes y los casticismos españoles* (Madrid 1966), 3-183.
17 Cohen, 628.
18 In his story *The Liberal Lover* Cervantes has Ricardo lament the fall of Nicosia. See *Obras completas*, ed. cit., 808.
19 Cohen, 343.

CHAPTER 5

1 Gibson, 245.
2 Cohen, 347.
3 The basic facts about Lepanto are taken largely from Lynch, op. cit., 224-30.
4 Cohen, 354.
5 These words recalled by an eyewitness are quoted in M. Fernández de Navarrete, *Vida de Miguel de Cervantes Saavedra* (Madrid 1819), 318. (Hereafter referred to as Fernández de Navarrete.)
6 Cohen, 344.
7 L. Cabrera de Córdoba, *Felipe II, Rey de España*, II (Madrid 1876), 113.

8 Gibson, 319.
9 See Astrana Marín II, 336.
10 Cohen, 348.
11 See Charles Petrie, *Don John of Austria* (New York 1967), 186.
12 Astrana Marín II, 347.
13 Cohen, 349-50.
14 Astrana Marín II, 422.
15 Gibson, 247-9.

CHAPTER 6

1 The date traditionally given for Cervantes' departure from Naples is 20 September 1575. Professor Juan Bautista Avalle-Arce, however, corrected this date and several other circumstances connected with the capture of Cervantes. See 'La Captura de Cervantes', *Boletín de la Real Academia Española*, 1968, 237-80.
2 Gibson, 321.
3 See Fernández de Navarrete, 313-14.
4 ibid., 317-18.
5 Astrana Marín II, 475. Astrana Marín does not indicate the source for this sum. It may be a misprint for 500.
6 Diego de Haedo, *Topografía e historia general de Argel*, I (Madrid 1927), 77. See also Petrie, op. cit., 74-7.
7 See Haedo, op. cit., 195.
8 Haedo, op. cit., II (Madrid 1929), 101-3.
9 Quoted by Fernández de Navarrete, 321, from an indispensable document known as the *Información de Argel*, described at the end of this chapter (pp. 93-4).
10 In the early sixteenth century, the ducat was the standard Spanish gold coin (23.75 carats fine). Although replaced by the escudo after 1537, the ducat continued to be used as a unit of account, being worth about 94% of an escudo.
11 Cohen, 354.
12 ibid., 355-6.
13 Gibson, 325. Professor Joaquín Casalduero considers the *Epistle to Mateo Vázquez* to be a nineteenth-century forgery. He may be correct, although the evidence presented is very slight. See his *Sentido y Forma del Teatro de Cervantes* (Madrid 1966), 225, note 2. In any case, the verses cited also appear in Cervantes' play, *El Trato de Argel*. See *Obras completas*, ed. cit., 117-18.
14 Fernández de Navarrete, 323.
15 Haedo, op. cit., II, 164-5.
16 ibid.
17 Fernández de Navarrete, 330.

18 *Obras completas*, ed. cit., 295.
19 Details of the fourth attempt at escape are presented in Astrana Marín III, 39-64.
20 Cohen, 837.
21 Fernández de Navarrete, 336.
22 ibid., 337.
23 ibid., 338.
24 ibid., 340-1.

CHAPTER 7

1 G. Mattingly, *The Armada* (New York 1959), 74.
2 Gibson, 307.
3 For a brief account of the Spanish acquisition of Portugal, see R. Trevor Davies, *The Golden Century of Spain* (New York 1964), 185-92.
4 Astrana Marín III, 142.
5 *Obras completas*, ed. cit., 1628.
6 The letter to Antonio de Eraso was not discovered until 1954. It is reproduced in Astrana Marín VI (Madrid 1956), 511-12.
7 *Obras completas*, ed. cit., 693.

CHAPTER 8

1 See Astrana Marín III, 212-13. In Book IV of *La Galatea* it is recorded that Lauso (Cervantes) spent a few years in courtly exercises before serving as a soldier (*Obras completas*, ed. cit., 692).
2 *Obras completas*, ed. cit., 712.
3 Gibson, 107.
4 Cohen, 86.
5 *Three Exemplary Novels*, ed. cit., 139-40.
6 For an up-to-date discussion of Cervantes and the pastoral *genre*, see J. B. Avalle-Arce, *La novela pastoril española* (Madrid 1959), 197-231.
7 Cohen, 62.
8 Astrana Marín III, 277-9.
9 For a detailed account of the Spanish stage in the sixteenth and seventeenth centuries, see Hugo A. Rennert, *The Spanish Stage* (New York 1909), particularly 26-46.
10 Cohen, 535.
11 *Obras completas*, ed. cit., 180.
12 Gibson, 275.
13 Probably written in 1583, but see Astrana Marín III, 328, note 1.
14 The real was the standard silver coin. An escudo was worth 11.76 reals. *La Galatea*, therefore, earned for Cervantes about 114 escudos, a little more than he had earned for his brief mission to North Africa.
15 See Astrana Marín III, ch. 41, and V (Madrid 1953), 45-7.

16 Cohen, 590.
17 For the entire will, see Astrana Marín VI (Madrid 1956), 397-400.
18 See Astrana Marín VII (Madrid 1958), 521.
19 Rodrigo's will is published in Pérez Pastor, *Documentos cervantinos*, I (Madrid 1897), 83-6.
20 *Three Exemplary Novels*, ed. cit., 121.

CHAPTER 9

1 The maravedi was the basic small denomination. During most of Cervantes' adult life, it took 400 maravedis to equal an escudo. So the money borrowed in Seville could be expressed as 510 escudos, that is, a little more than the ransom money required to free him from slavery in Algiers.
2 See Astrana Marín III, 503-5.
3 See ibid., 557-9.
4 *Obras completas*, ed. cit., 1649.
5 Mattingly, op. cit., 71.
6 See Astrana Marín IV, 7.
7 Cohen, 438.
8 ibid., 34.
9 There is no documentary proof that Friar Alonso believed the romances of chivalry were true, but see Astrana Marín IV, 17-27 and F. Rodríguez Marín, *Nueva edición crítica de 'El Ingenioso Hidalgo Don Quijote de la Mancha'*, VII (Madrid 1928), apéndice xl.
10 See Astrana Marín IV, 29.
11 I do not mean to suggest that the location of Esquivias is consistent with the geography of Don Quixote's comings and goings. I do mean that it was in Esquivias that Cervantes absorbed the atmosphere and some of the names that would enter into the creation of the anonymous village where Don Quixote and Sancho Panza made their home.
12 See Astrana Marín IV, 63-7.

CHAPTER 10

1 See Mattingly, op. cit., chs. 7 and 9.
2 See Astrana Marín IV, 63.
3 ibid., 134.
4 For prices of common commodities, see Astrana Marín VII (Madrid 1958), 773-4.
5 Cohen, 147-8.
6 This brief account of the engagements fought between the Armada and the English is condensed from Mattingly, op. cit., chs. 22-31.
7 *Three Exemplary Novels*, ed. cit., 213.
8 Quoted by F. Rodríguez Marín, *Nuevos do-*

cumentos cervantinos, ed. cit., 246.

9   ibid., 248.

10 See Astrana Marín IV, 375-87.

11 ibid., 203.

12 ibid., 455-6 for the Spanish original.

13 See ibid., 233 for an interesting example.

14 ibid., 534-5.

15 Astrana Marín V, 32-3.

16 ibid., 39-42.

17 ibid., 29-31.

18 Cohen, 130-1.

19 *Obras completas*, ed. cit., 935.

20 Cohen, 118.

21 ibid., 120.

22 ibid., 633.

23 ibid., 277.

24 See Astrana Marín IV, 516-30.

25 *Three Exemplary Novels*, ed. cit., 182.

26 Recorded by Fernández de Navarrete, 79.

CHAPTER 11

1   For a full account of this mission, see Astrana Marín V, ch. 59.

2   See Jaime Sánchez Romeralo, 'Miguel de Cervantes y Su Cuñado Francisco de Palacios', *Actas del Segundo Congreso Internacional de Hispanistas* (Nijmegen 1967), 563-72.

3   Astrana Marín V, 154.

4   ibid., 157.

5   ibid., 158-9.

6   See Astrana Marín VI, 95.

7   Gibson, 376.

8   See Astrana Marín V, 220-1.

9   ibid., 238-9.

10 ibid., 230-8.

11 Cohen, 25. Professor G. Stagg thinks Cervantes began to write *Don Quixote* in Castro del Río, but his imprisonment there was too short to render that plausible. Still, see 'Castro del Río, ¿Cuna del Quijote?', *Clavileño*, 1955, 1-11.

12 Some biographers think Miguel was released in December 1597. For documentation of the version I have accepted, see Astrana Marín V, 287-97.

13 Francisco de Quevedo Villegas, 'Grandes Anales de Quince Días', in *Biblioteca de Autores Españoles*, XXIII (Madrid 1923), 216. My quotation is taken from a brief portrait of Philip II penned by Quevedo long after the king's death. The portrait is very favorable, though not one hundred per cent so. Astrana Marín (V, 313) takes it as favorable, but two other distinguished scholars, quoting only the briefest of fragments, use the portrait to criticize Philip harshly. See A. Castro, *The Structure of Spanish History* (Princeton 1954), 298; C. Sánchez-Albornoz, *España: Un Enigma Histórico*, II (Buenos Aires 1956), 522.

14 A. Castro thinks Cervantes detested Philip. See, for example, his *Cervantes y los casticismos españoles*, ed. cit., 130, 150 (note 71).

15 Gibson, 375.

16 ibid., 107.

17 Lynch, op. cit., II (Oxford 1969), 15.

18 Astrana Marín V, 308, 309, 339-40.

19 A. Domínguez Ortiz, *La sociedad española en el siglo XVII* (Madrid 1963), 69.

20 See Germán Bleiberg, 'Nuevos Datos Biográficos de Mateo Alemán', *Actas del Segundo Congreso Internacional de Hispanistas*, 25-6.

21 Cohen, 176.

22 See Astrana Marín V, 348-9.

23 *Three Exemplary Novels*, ed. cit., 30.

24 ibid., 32.

25 ibid., 27.

26 ibid., 45.

27 ibid., 49.

28 ibid., 68.

29 ibid. In a manuscript version of this story, one finds several sentences that do not appear in the version Cervantes published. One of them speaks of abominating 'a life so detestable and which is so prevalent in a city that should be the mirror of truth and justice in the world, as it is of grandeur'. See Astrana Marín V, 337.

30 Mateo Alemán, *Guzmán de Alfarache* (5 vols. Madrid 1926-36), II, 167-8.

CHAPTER 12

1   See the critical edition of *Rinconete y Cortadillo* by F. Rodríguez Marín (Madrid 1920), 156.

2   See Astrana Marín V, 460-1.

3   Professor R.S. Willis, in his interesting *The Phantom Chapters of the Quijote* (New York 1953), argues that the chapter divisions are an authentic part of the original composition. But the more I think about it the more I doubt that this it true, particularly of the early chapters.

4   Cohen, 204.

5   For a fuller discussion of Don Quixote's adventures, see my *The World of Don Quixote* (Cambridge, Mass., 1967), 17-35.

6   See Astrana Marín V, 435.

7   Among other famous writers drawn to Valladolid one might mention Salas Barbadillo,

Vélez de Guevara, Bartolomé Leonardo de Argensola and Vicente Espinel. See N. Alonso Cortés, *Cervantes en Valladolid* (Valladolid 1918), 49.

8   See Astrana Marín VI, 282-3.
9   Gibson, 343.
10 See Astrana Marín V, 537.
11 See Astrana Marín III, 445.
12 Cohen, 625.
13 ibid., 26.
14 Gibson, 357.
15 Cohen, 30.
16 See J. Oliver Asín, 'El Quijote de 1604', *Boletín de la Real Academia Española*, 1948, 89-126. Oliver Asín uses this incident to argue for an edition of *Don Quixote* in 1604. If there was such an edition it is odd that no copy has ever been found. It might be mentioned in passing that many scholars have referred to a letter of Lope de Vega dated 4 August 1604 and containing a reference to *Don Quixote*, but it seems that the date is wrong. See Astrana Marín VI, 141-6.
17 For an interesting account of Don Quixote's first invasion of America see Irving A. Leonard, *Books of the Brave* (Cambridge, Mass., 1949), 270-312.
18 Gibson, 344.
19 See Fernández de Navarrete, 456; Astrana Marín VI, 37.
20 Cohen, 375-6.
21 See Pérez Pastor, *Documentos cervantinos*, II, ed. cit., 461-2.
22 N. Alonso Cortés, op. cit., 88.
23 Astrana Marín provides a detailed account of this affair, reproducing much of the original testimony (VI, ch. 73). He presents evidence to show that the judge knew that Ezpeleta was having a love affair with a married woman but preferred not to embarrass friends by pursuing that line of inquiry. The entire record of the criminal process is given in Pérez Pastor, op. cit., II, 455-537.
24 Cohen, 896.
25 *Three Exemplary Novels*, ed. cit., 125.
26 Astrana Marín V, 569.
27 *Three Exemplary Novels*, ed. cit., 156.
28 ibid., 82.
29 Cohen, 430.
30 For the text of the letter, see Astrana Marín VI, 141-2.
31 ibid., 114, 116.
32 Gibson, 277-9.

CHAPTER 13

1   See José López Navío, 'Un documento inédito sobre Cervantes', *Anales cervantinos*, IX (Madrid 1961-62), 247-52.
2   See Fernández de Navarrete, 475-6; Astrana Marín VI, 328.
3   A detailed account of Isabel's two marriages and her affair with Urbina is given in Astrana Marín VI, chs. 76 and 78.
4   How many copies this amounted to cannot be told, although it can be said that a single printing of 1,500 copies was fairly common. In chapter 3 of Part Two Sansón Carrasco remarks to Don Quixote that he believes that there are more than 12,000 copies in print. Later (chapter 16), Don Quixote himself claims there are 30,000 copies of his book.
5   See Fernández de Navarrete, 479.
6   See Astrana Marín VI, 323.
7   *Three Exemplary Novels*, ed. cit., 5.
8   Fernández de Navarrete, 124.
9   Astrana Marín VII, 16.
10 For what little more is known about the literary academies see Astrana Marín VI, 280-1, 317-18, 546-55; VII, 19; Fernández de Navarrete, 123-4, 482-5.
11 Trevor Davies, *The Golden Century of Spain*, ed. cit., 250.
12 *Three Exemplary Novels*, ed. cit., 202-3; cf. Lynch, op. cit., II, 42-51.
13 See Lynch, op. cit., II, 44.
14 Cohen, 819.
15 Astrana Marín (VI, 237) has suggested a chronology of the composition of the plays of Cervantes' second period.
16 *Obras completas*, ed. cit., 180.
17 See Astrana Marín VI, 435.
18 See Astrana Marín VII, 51.
19 *Three Exemplary Novels*, ed. cit., 3-4.
20 ibid., 5.
21 ibid.
22 ibid.
23 *Novelas ejemplares*, ed. Rodolfo Schevill and Adolfo Bonilla (Madrid 1922), 10.
24 A. Castro, *El Pensamiento de Cervantes* (Madrid 1925), 244.
25 See Castro, op. cit., 136. Over the years Castro has continued to reflect on these matters. For his latest thinking on this story see *Hacia Cervantes* (3rd ed. Madrid 1967), 420-50.
26 For example, that of Camila in *The Man Who Was Too Curious For His Own Good* and that of Lorenza in *The Jealous Old Man*.

27 *Obras completas*, ed. cit., 914.
28 *Three Exemplary Novels*, ed. cit., 6.
29 *Novelas ejemplares*, ed. cit., 13.
30 For the last two references plus a brief indication of the early seventeenth-century critical response to the *Exemplary Novels* see Dana B. Drake, *Cervantes: A Critical Biography*, I (Blacksburg, Virginia, 1968), 5-6, 114, 136.
31 Gibson, 83.
32 ibid., 63.
33 ibid., 57.
34 ibid., 223.
35 See Astrana Marín VII, 144-5.
36 *Cervantes: A Collection of Critical Essays*, ed. Lowry Nelson, Jr (Englewood Cliffs, N.J., 1969), 2.
37 See Otis H. Green, 'El Licenciado Vidriera: Its Relation to the *Viaje del Parnaso* and the *Examen de Ingenios* of Huarte', in Alessandro S. Crisafulli, ed., *Linguistic and Literary Studies in Honor of Helmut A. Hatzfeld* (Washington D.C. 1964), 214-15; also Castro, *Cervantes y los casticismos españoles*, ed. cit., 26-7, 96, *et passim*.
38 Cohen, 426.
39 Gibson, 11.
40 ibid., 17.
41 ibid., 105-7.
42 ibid., 11.
43 ibid., 129.
44 ibid., 111.
45 ibid., 287.
46 Cohen, 940.
47 *Don Quijote*, Part II, tr. Samuel Putnam (New York 1949), 502. It is clear that Márquez Torres was one of Cervantes' friends. For some interesting comments on his approbation see Elias L. Rivers, 'On the Prefatory Pages of *Don Quijote*, Part Two', *Modern Language Notes*, 1960, 214-21.
48 Putnam, op. cit., 502.
49 ibid.
50 ibid.
51 Cohen, 467.
52 ibid.
53 ibid., 468.
54 ibid., 469.
55 ibid., 465-6.
56 Putnam, op. cit., 531.
57 Fernández de Navarrete, 168.
58 ibid., 579, note 341.
59 See Astrana Marín VII, 118.
60 ibid.
61 *Obras completas*, ed. cit., 1527-8.
62 ibid., 1528.
63 ibid.
64 ibid., 1529.
65 Cohen, 934.
66 The traditional date is 23 April 1616, but I have accepted Astrana Marín's argument for 22 April; see Astrana Marín VII, 458-9, 463.

Bibliography

Over the quarter of a century that I have been teaching courses on Cervantes and his works, I have tried to read most of the books and articles written on the subject. I wish I could readily determine and acknowledge the specific contributions made by the authors of these studies to this new biography of Cervantes, but it hardly seems practical. All I can do is to record in the notes and bibliography the sources I have cited. No name appears so frequently as that of Luis Astrana Marín. Perhaps this calls for a few words of explanation.

Between 1948 and 1958, Astrana Marín published his truly monumental *Vida ejemplar y heroica de Miguel de Cervantes Saavedra* in seven large, copiously illustrated tomes. It is both irritating and absolutely indispensable: irritating, because it is so pointlessly prolix in certain parts and because it is weighted with more than a scholar's quota of personal bias; indispensable, because it is such an incredibly rich mine of documentation. The author has done a heroic job of archival investigation. He claims to have published a thousand heretofore unpublished documents. I am prepared to believe it without counting them. He has also used, sometimes corrected, and often re-published the archival discoveries of such landmark investigators as Cristóbal Pérez Pastor, Narciso Alonso Cortés and Francisco Rodríguez Marín. I have had all of these constantly before me. If I have sometimes cited only Astrana Marín, it is because he usually cites the other sources and thus provides the interested reader with the quickest path to the combined bibliography.

Astrana Marín writes as though he had definitively resolved more mysteries about Cervantes' life than most scholars are as yet willing to give him credit for. This is particularly true of the first twenty years of Cervantes' life, about which solid information is still exceedingly meager. Because this is unquestionably so, Astrana Marín has had to construct his version of these years on what little is undeniably known plus a mountain of circumstantial evidence and a fair amount of frequently plausible conjecture. Rather than leave these years almost blank, I have accepted the conjecture whenever I could find no persuasive reasons for rejecting it.

One other aspect of the bibliography used in this volume requires a word of explanation. I have quoted much from Cervantes' own writings. Where standard translations have been available I have quoted from them. For *Don Quixote* J.M. Cohen's contemporary translation (1950) has been my mainstay, although I have occasionally preferred Samuel Putnam's rendering of a particular passage. I have also freely used Putnam's translation of *Three Exemplary Novels* (1950). I have quoted much from James Y. Gibson's skillful, if somewhat quaint, verse translation of the *Journey to Parnassus* (1883). Where I cite Cervantes' *Obras completas* the translations are mine. Needless to say, none of the translations sound quite like Cervantes, but there is no remedy for that.

ALEMÁN, MATEO, *Guzmán de Alfarache*. Ed. Samuel Gili Gaya. ('Clásicos castellanos': 73, 83, 90, 93, 114), Madrid, 1926-36.

ALONSO CORTÉS, NARCISO, *Cervantes en Valladolid*. Valladolid, 1918.

ASTRANA MARÍN, LUIS, *Vida ejemplar y heroica de Miguel de Cervantes Saavedra*. 7 vols, Madrid, 1948-58.

AVALLE-ARCE, JUAN BAUTISTA, 'La Captura de Cervantes', *Boletín de la Real Academia Española*, 1968, 237-80.

La novela pastoril española. Madrid, 1959.

BILLI DE SANDORNO, AMALIA, 'El Cardenal Gaspar de Cervantes y Gaete, Ignorado Protector de Miguel de Cervantes Saavedra', *Anales cervantinos*, II (Madrid, 1952), 335-58.

BLEIBERG, GERMÁN, 'Nuevos Datos Biográficos de Mateo Alemán', *Actas del Segundo Congreso Internacional de Hispanistas* (Nijmegen, 1967), 25-50.

BRANDI, KARL, *The Emperor Charles V*. London, 1939.

CABRERA DE CÓRDOBA, LUIS, *Felipe II, Rey de España*, II. Madrid, 1876.

CASALDUERO, JOAQUÍN, *Sentido y Forma del Teatro de Cervantes*. Madrid, 1966.

CASTRO, AMÉRICO, *Cervantes y los casticismos españoles*. Madrid, 1966.

Hacia Cervantes, 3rd ed. Madrid, 1967.

El Pensamiento de Cervantes. Madrid, 1925.

The Structure of Spanish History. Princeton, 1954.

CERVANTES, MIGUEL DE, *The Adventures of Don Quixote*. Translated by J. M. Cohen. Baltimore, 1963.

El Ingenioso Hidalgo Don Quijote de la Mancha. Ed. F. Rodríguez Marín. 10 vols, Madrid, 1947-49.

The Ingenious Gentleman Don Quixote de la Mancha. Translated by Samuel Putnam. 2 vols, New York, 1949.

Journey to Parnassus. Translated by James Y. Gibson. London, 1883.

Novelas ejemplares. Ed. R. Schevill and A. Bonilla. 3 vols, Madrid, 1922-25.

Obras completas. Ed. Angel Valbuena Prat. Madrid, 1965.

Rinconete y Cortadillo. Ed. F. Rodríguez Marín. Madrid, 1920.

Three Exemplary Novels. Translated by Samuel Putnam. New York, 1950.

DAVIES, REGINALD TREVOR, *The Golden Century of Spain*. New York, 1964.

DOMÍNGUEZ ORTIZ, ANTONIO, *La sociedad española en el siglo XVII*. Madrid, 1963.

DRAKE, DANA B., *Cervantes: A Critical Bibliography*, I. Virginia Polytechnic Institute, Blacksburg, 1968.

FERNÁNDEZ DE NAVARRETE, MARTÍN, *Vida de Miguel de Cervantes Saavedra*. Madrid, 1819.

FERNÁNDEZ Y FERNÁNDEZ DE RETANA, P. LUIS, *España en tiempo de Felipe II*, I (t. 19 of *Historia de España* directed by R. Menéndez Pidal). Madrid, 1966.

GANIVET, ANGEL, *Idearium español y El porvenir de España*. Buenos Aires, 1940.

GREEN, OTIS H., '*El Licenciado Vidriera*: Its Relation to the *Viaje del Parnaso* and the *Examen de Ingenios* of Huarte', in *Linguistic and Literary Studies in Honor of Helmut. A. Hatzfeld*, ed. Alessandro S. Crisafulli (Washington, 1964), 213-20.

GUILLÉN, CLAUDIO, 'Luis Sánchez, Ginés de Pasamonte y los Inventores de Género Picaresco', in *Homenaje a Rodríguez Moñino*, I (Madrid, 1966), 221-31.

HAEDO, DIEGO DE, *Topografía e historia general de Argel*, I. Madrid, 1927.

KOENIGSBERGER, H., 'The Empire of Charles V in Europe', in *The New Cambridge Modern History*, II (Cambridge, 1958), 301-33.

LEONARD, IRVING A., *Books of the Brave*. Cambridge, Mass., 1949.

LYNCH, JOHN, *Spain under the Hapsburgs*. 2 vols. New York, 1964-69.

MADARIAGA, SALVADOR DE, *Spain*. New York, 1943.

MATTINGLY, GARRETT, *The Armada*. New York, 1959.

NELSON, LOWRY, JR (ed.), *Cervantes: A Collection of Critical Essays*. Englewood Cliffs, 1969.

OLIVER ASÍN, JAIME, 'El Quijote de 1604', *Boletín de la Real Academia Española*, 1948, 89-126.

PÉREZ PASTOR, CRISTÓBAL, *Documentos cervantinos*. 2 vols, Madrid, 1897-1902.

PETRIE, CHARLES, *Don John of Austria*. New York, 1967.

PREDMORE, RICHARD L., *The World of Don Quixote*. Cambridge, Mass., 1967.

QUEVEDO VILLEGAS, FRANCISCO DE, 'Grandes Anales de Quince Días. Adición', in *Biblioteca de Autores Españoles*, XXIII, Madrid, 1923.

RENNERT, HUGO A., *The Spanish Stage*. New York, 1909.

RIVERS, ELIAS L., 'On the Prefatory Pages of *Don Quijote*, Part Two', *Modern Language Notes*, 1960, 214-21.

RODRÍGUEZ MARÍN, FRANCISCO, *Estudios cervantinos*. Madrid, 1947.

Nuevos documentos cervantinos. Madrid, 1914.

SÁNCHEZ-ALBORNOZ, CLAUDIO, *España: Un Enigma Histórico*. 2 vols, Buenos Aires, 1956.

SÁNCHEZ ROMERALO, JAIME, 'Miguel de Cervantes y Su Cuñado Francisco de Palacios', in *Actas del Segundo Congreso Internacional de Hispanistas* (Nijmegen, 1967), 563-72.

STAGG, GEOFFREY, 'Castro del Río, ¿Cuna del Quijote?', *Clavileño*, 1955, 1-11.

WILLIS, RAYMOND S., *The Phantom Chapters of the Quijote*. New York, 1953.

List of illustrations

27 Font from the Church of Santa María la Mayor, Alcalá de Henares, now in the Church of Santa María, Alcázar de San Juan. Photo Mas

28 View of Córdoba, 1567; drawing by A. van den Wyngaerde from *Views in Spain*, 1567-70. Victoria and Albert Museum, London

29 Plaza del Potro, Córdoba. Photo Mas

30 A bandit; woodcut from Pere Giberga's *Cobles*, Barcelona, 1545(?); from M. Aguilo y Fuster, *Canconer de los obretes en nostra langua materna*, 1877

31 Moorish leather shield with the arms of the house of Fernández de Córdoba; early sixteenth century. Real Armería, Madrid. Photo Mas

32 Sixteenth-century house in Cabra. Photo Mas

33 View of Seville; engraving by Georg Hoefnagel, 1593. Albertina, Vienna

34 The silver mine at Potosí, Bolivia; illustration from a sea chart, 1584. The Hispanic Society of America, New York

35 *The Virgin of the Navigators*; center of an altarpiece by Alejo Fernández, 1531-36. Archivo de Indias, Seville. Photo Mas

36 Lope de Rueda; woodcut from his *Las primeras dos elegantes y graciosas Comedias del excellente Poeta*, Valencia, 1567

37 *Charles V on horseback at the battle of Mühlberg* by Titian, 1548. Prado, Madrid. Photo Giraudon

38 The capture of Tunis, 1535; manuscript illumination by Giulio Clovio from *The Victories of the Emperor Charles V*, mid-sixteenth century. British Museum, London

39 Portrait of a Turk on horseback, probably Suleiman the Magnificent, by Hans Eworth, 1549. Collection Earl of Yarborough. Photo Sid Burton

40 Portrait of Henry VIII by Hans Holbein, 1936. Thyssen Bornemisza Collection, Lugano

41 Portrait of Francis I attributed to Jean Clouet, first half of the sixteenth century. Louvre, Paris. Photo Garanger-Giraudon

42 Characters from *Eufemia* and *Armelina* by Lope de Rueda; from his *Las primeras dos elegantes y graciosas Comedias del excellente Poeta*, Valencia, 1567

43 Map of Spain in the sixteenth century; drawn by Shalom Schotten

44 St Teresa of Ávila by Fray Juan de la Miseria, 1576. Convento de Carmelitas Descalzas de Santa Teresa, Seville. Photo Mas

45 View of Madrid; pen and wash drawing by A. van den Wyngaerde from *Villes d'Espagne*, mid-sixteenth century. Österreichische Nationalbibliothek, Vienna

46 Portrait of Philip II (1527-98) by El Greco. Casa del Greco, Toledo

47 Portrait of Elizabeth de Valois (1545-68) by A. Sánchez Coello. Kunsthistorisches Museum, Vienna

48 Portrait of Isabel Clara Eugenia and Catalina Micaela, daughters of Philip II, by A. Sánchez Coello, 1571. Prado, Madrid. Photo Mas

49 Cervantes' earliest known poetic composition, c. 1576; autograph manuscript. Bibliothèque Nationale, Paris

50 Philip II, three of his wives and Don Carlos; tomb of Philip II by Pompeo Leoni, 1600. Escorial, Madrid. Photo Mas

51 Portrait of Don Carlos as a child by Antonis Mor, mid sixteenth century. Staatliche Gemäldegalerie, Kassel. Photo Marburg

52 Portrait of A. Vesalius; engraving from his *De humani corporis fabrica*, 1543

53 Don Juan of Austria (1545-78) as a young man; anonymous miniature. Rijksmuseum, Amsterdam

54 Portrait of Alessandro Farnese by A. Sánchez Coello, c. 1560. National Gallery of Ireland, Dublin

55 Portrait of Anne of Austria by A. Sánchez Coello, 1571. Kunsthistorisches Museum, Vienna

56 Execution of Counts Egmont and Horne, 1568; contemporary engraving. British Museum, London

57 Baptism of Moors; wood relief by Felipe de Borgoña on the high altar of the Royal Chapel of Granada cathedral, 1520-22. Photo Mas

Index

Page numbers in italics refer to illustrations